Critical Response to Literatures in English

Critical Response to Literatures in English

Reena Mitra

ATLANTIC®
PUBLISHERS & DISTRIBUTORS

Published by
ATLANTIC®
PUBLISHERS & DISTRIBUTORS
B-2, Vishal Enclave, Opp. Rajouri Garden,
New Delhi-110027
Phones : 25413460, 25429987, 25466842

Sales Office
7/22, Ansari Road, Darya Ganj,
New Delhi-110002
Phones : 23273880, 23275880, 23280451
Fax : 91-11-23285873
web : www.atlanticbooks.com
e-mail : info@atlanticbooks.com

ISBN 81-269-0585-9

Printed in India
at Nice Printing Press, Delhi

To
My husband and children

Preface

This book offers mainly a collection of papers presented by me at various national seminars and conferences spanning the last decade or so. Some of these papers have already been published in books on particular authors undertaken for analysis or in the proceedings of the respective seminars or conferences but it gives me a singular sense of achievement and joy to see them published all together for they bring back to my mind the academic path traversed by me in the past. The number of essays on Indian writing in English far exceeds those on other literatures in the language for this has been my area of interest from as early as my postgraduation days in Lucknow University in 1970. I was initiated into the then nascent Indian English literature by my teacher, Dr. A.K. Srivastava, who had proposed that for my M.A. dissertation. I work on a thematic study of the fiction of Bhabani Bhattacharya, whose novel, *Shadow from Ladakh*, had acquired the distinction of winning the Sahitya Akademi Award for 1967. I complied, and thus began my association with Indian writing in English, more specifically fiction.

It is somewhat of a paradox that despite the intensified academic interest shown by scholars in Indian English in the 1960s and 70s, there was no perceptible corresponding spurt in the study of Indian English literature and it attracted little critical attention. Persistence, however, was rewarded and recognition finally came, though belated. Initially, we were looking for the validation of anything written in English to

England and subsequently America, where such validation and recognition was slow and unforthcoming. It is to the credit of the linguists of our country that by establishing the separate identity of Indian English, they gave us the linguistic self-respect followed by the final literary acceptance enabling us to evaluate and judge our literature by our own ample criteria. Today, the myth that for a people whose mother tongue is not English there is no room for creative work in the language stands exploded. As established by Bhabani Bhattacharya, the mother tongue may not necessarily be the most appropriate medium of creative expression and, in certain cases, a foreign language may better be able to contain the creative urge. Indian writers, who have chosen English as their medium of utterance, have proved time and again that the choice of a foreign idiom for creative ends does not in any way hamper the realization of their creative endeavours. So have the native writers of other countries like Africa and Australia given convincing evidence of the fact that their country belongs to them by what C.D. Narasimhaiah calls "right of vision" and writing in English only facilitates their expression of their national sensibilities.

The characteristic differences between the writers of two countries stem from the difference in cultures and the terms of discourse are undoubtedly generated by the needs of the culture to which one belongs rather than the imperatives set by a supposedly superior nation with a political and civilizational lead. Till about half a century ago, academic interest in literary texts was governed by global aesthetic norms prescribed by the powers that be in the European literary world. All relevant critical discourse till the mid-twentieth century was believed to be emanating from the imperial centre of power alone. After that things changed. With the moribund empire receding to the background not by choice but by circumstantial pressure, the erstwhile marginalized literature found an identity and a voice. The "lingo of lesser breeds" and the "derelict dialects" of Standard English that came to prevail metamorphosed the world of literary discourse into one that thwarted homogenization effectuated by conformity to the one global mode and empowered literature born of what Home Bhabha in *The Location of Culture* (1994) calls "the affective experience of social marginality."

The challenge for all non-British writers writing in English is the question of adapting an alien language to conform to the native spirit and introducing verbal images that are reminiscent of aboriginal strengths and realities. One cannot, however, in one's obsession with the various literatures in English emerging today in a big way as pronouncements of their respective national aspirations and perceptions, ignore the primacy of English literature in rendering valuable imaginative experience in the language much before many other literatures found an audible voice.

I do hope that the present selection of essays will be of value to students and teachers of the various literatures in English as most of the texts undertaken for analysis in them are prescribed for study in postgraduate classes in most universities of the country, and in some universities, they are a part of the syllabus for the undergraduates as well.

It now remains for me to record my appreciation of the unfailing support and encouragement that I received from my husband in the completion of this work. My children, too, were always there for me whenever I needed a boost to steer my energies towards concluding this endeavour.

REENA MITRA

Kanpur
September, 2005

Contents

1

Mulk Raj Anand and The Human Predicament

Mulk Raj Anand was one of "the founding fathers"[1] of Indian English fiction for whom the art of fiction was as important as the communication it sought to convey. This was a form which soon established itself as best suited to the Indian sensibility and as one to which Indian writers have made amazing contributions. In her essay, 'Mulk Raj Anand and the Thirties Movement in England'[2] Gillian Packham perceptively notes that Anand became an essentially 'thirties' man in thought and sensibility and was markedly influenced by Marxism. Anand, however, regarded himself more as a rational humanist than as a Marxist. Confining himself to Indian social ground, he makes a case in an indignant reformist way for those subjected to inhumanities perpetrated by grinding poverty, discriminating caste and class assertions and injustices meted out to women, orphans, urban labourers and the so-called "untouchables." It is the predicament of such characters that Anand seeks to depict in his novels. Anna Rutherford[3] categorizes Anand's characters in his novels into three classes, namely the victims, the oppressors who oppose change and progress, and the good. It is the "victims" who are generally the protagonists in his novels and in fighting for them, despite his perceptible propagandist inclinations, he often proves to be a writer of considerable power.

A novel approach to the works of Anand is that of Dieter Riemenschneider, who, in his essay, 'The Function of Labour in

Mulk Raj Anand's Novels'[4] explores the socio-literary implications of human labour and observes that analyzing the problem of human labour as presented in literary works may provide an important insight into the ideological as well as the aesthetic aspects of such works. Labour, according to the author, is the eternal and natural condition of the human predicament and is unassociated with any specific form of life. It is a free activity of man because its objectives are determined by man himself. Thus, as Riemenschneider puts it, "labour means self-realization of man, an act of real freedom,"[5] but labour, as it is always performed in society, is necessarily a social activity as well. In literature, when man is considered as a member of a particular species, what defines him fully by presenting his essential nature is the totality of his social activities and relations. In Anand's novels the problem of labour is aesthetically presented through character and event. All the main characters in his major works are "forced to sell their labour in order to survive."[6] By portraying these characters, not only does Anand demonstrate his interest in their individual lives but also conveys the economic and social changes taking place in India under colonial rule and depicts the gradual transformation of a feudal society into a capitalistic one.

Anand's pre-Independence novels deal with the problems of industrial labour and with several aspects of social reform, including the pathetic conditions of the untouchables who were cruelly discriminated against. The realism in his works touches the heart but his humanistic persuasions are so overpowering that they often colour his narratives to an extent that corrodes the principal artistic values in his fiction. And yet, we cannot but appreciate Anand as a writer with a mission, a mission which seeks to uphold the centrality of human beings in any community of men for he regards all mankind as one, with no viable and justifiable barriers to vindicate the ever-widening gulf between man and man—between the rich and the poor, between the "haves" and the "have nots." His purpose is undoubtedly a sympathetic consideration of the plight of the "have-nots" and a focused series of efforts to improve the lot of the deprived. He displays a tenacious dramatic power which, in conformity with social and psychological realism demonstrates moral issues through the counter pointing of good and evil. He believes that evil forces have to be identified and contained—eradicated if possible—and obscurantism has to be resolutely uprooted if the individual has to grow and progress. His denunciation of violence arising from caste/class politics could be related to the entire humanity in the context of the World War in which his character, Lalu Singh, appearing in more than one novel, goes to fight in Europe. He was convinced that the writer's spirit could not be subdued and crushed by the Imperialistic policies of the British. He said, in 1973:

> I meant much more than writing a novel of the war. I meant to condemn civilization the way it was drifting towards violence and bloodshed and world pain [...].[7]

Anand presents an indictment of the British rule which apparently upheld the ideals of liberty and equality but perpetrated unmistakable racial discrimination.

Mulk Raj Anand, with other contemporary writers of his time like Raja Rao and R.K. Narayan, wished to fashion a language for a genuine social purpose, a language which would communicate nuances and shades of meaning involved in every meaningful experience. The creative process, Anand believes, behind most of Indian English writing is a natural expression of a bilingual or trilingual talent seeking communion beyond communication, almost as compellingly and vehemently as a writer using his mother-tongue, for, in both cases, what is important is the sincerity and the imaginative intensity that is brought to bear upon the work to transform the raw material into art and to enable us, in Shelley's phrase, "to connect."

One of the prime reasons for writing, Anand asserts, is "to make contacts with other human beings."[8] According to him, one often feels an "inexplicable urge"[9] to convey to others what one feels intensely and this compulsion in turn leads one to dramatize oneself in writing, the communication leading to a kind of solidarity with other people by virtue of the truth of life and the truth of human relations given expression through "felt experience."[10]

Anand has made an extensive and intensive study of human life in all its perversions of violence, hatred, avarice and envy and in all its consonances of peace, love and truth that transcend the "dailiness" of a mechanical human existence. His observations on the human predicament have, however, narrowed down on a realistic portrayal of life in the India of his times. He was determined to present a picture of India which would demolish the Westerner's image of India as a land of mystery and allurement. As a young Marxist he identified caste and class inequalities as factors stalling progress in Indian society. He looked upon Brahmin arrogance rather than British high-handedness as the plague infesting the Indians and expressed his concern about the outmoded and anachronous religious and social practices which were prevalent even in the second quarter of the twentieth century and were largely responsible for many of the inhumanities perpetrated against women and the underprivileged. He observantly remarked:

> When one looked at the lot of the less privileged populations, for instance in a country like India, one noticed how they had been deliberately kept at a level of subhumanity.[11]

To take up the cudgels on behalf of the deprived, Anand has chosen the medium of English, which, he avers, is not really an alien language, and, with all our past of exposure to the British rule we are quite at home with English as a medium for an expression of our urges. Only, Anand strongly believes with Raja Rao that "We cannot write like the English. We should not. We can write only as Indians."[12]

Thus, the choice of a foreign medium—English—for creative expression does not make Mulk Raj Anand any less Indian in thought and spirit than one would expect a man so deeply immersed in eradicating the social evils that came to prevail in his times to be. Mulk Raj Anand has "an inalienable faith in man,"[13] G.S. Balarama Gupta rightly observes, for Anand is a humanist all the way and his prime concern is the human predicament in all its dimensions. As a novelist Anand displays an unflagging interest in restoring the basic human rights to the underprivileged and the dispossessed in the Indian society. An exposure of the economic exploitation of the deprived and a castigation of the existing caste and class distinctions in India has been a major preoccupation of the writer.

Recent detractors of Anand like Meenakshi Mukherjee[14] bring him to account for certain experimental aspects of language like the literal translation of Hindi and Punjabi idioms into English, the interpolation of Hindi words into English sentences and the changing of the spelling of English words to suggest uneducated speech but a consideration of these lapses can willingly be relegated to the background if one is able to comprehend and assess the magnitude of his sincerity and commitment to the extirpation of unjust social discrimination in the community of men. Anand persistently focuses on the trials and tribulations of the "have-nots" and seeks to diminish their anguish. No social injustice ever escapes Anand's observant eye. Religion and social distinctions, he believes, often become reactionary forces, instruments of oppression and obstacles to the development of independent thought. It is in this connection that K.R.S. Iyengar refers to Mulk Raj Anand as one of the few novelists who have shown "anything like stamina and stern consistency of purpose."[15]

The India of the "thirties" was characterized by a national upsurge that had stirred the entire country on an unprecedented scale and Mulk Raj Anand was a major contributor in bringing about this consciousness among the people of the times. M.K. Naik has aptly referred to him as "the novelist of the social man"[16] for his novels compelled the contemporary society into self-awareness and introspection and aroused the conscience of humanity.

Anand retrieved the Indo-Anglian novel from the domains of history and romance and writing prolifically, led it to take cognizance of the prevailing conditions and the hard realities of the pre-Independence social scene. His first three novels, namely, *Untouchable* (1935), *Coolie* (1936) and *Two Leaves and a Bud* (1937) form a natural trilogy for all three have a victimized, oppressed and outcast proletarian protagonist whose lot represents the fate of India enslaved by the British and the lot of the hapless workers indentured to the capitalist system. In these novels, Anand, determined to demolish the rose-tinted edifice of India that prevailed and offered a realistic picture of the country as she actually is, seen in Marxian terms as "a cockpit of the class-struggle and a sordid one at that."[17] India to Anand, meant repressive privations, the millstone of the caste-system round the neck of the poorest, adherence to outmoded mores and customs and ceaseless subjection to foreign rule.

Untouchable and *Coolie* are both eye-openers with regard to the maltreatment of the depressed classes in the 1930s. In *Untouchable*, Bakha, a toilet-cleaner, is depicted as a great admirer of the British, wearing clothes cast-off by them and enjoying life to the full, totally oblivious of the "class-feeling" that prevailed among men. It is only when, at the age of eighteen, he happens to touch a Brahmin and the latter flinches from the contact in anger and hatred that he is made aware of his status in the society as "unclean" because of the nature of his work. From then onwards Bakha is conscious of the curse of the untouchable that he has inherited from his father. It is this awakening to painful knowledge that is depicted with great sensitivity by Anand. A temple priest's attempt at molesting Bakha's sister, Sohini, is an alarming exposure of the hypocrisy of the Brahmins who clearly lived in double standards. The priest who avoided even the shadow of an untouchable surrendered to his sensual and sexual urge with absolutely no qualms of conscience.

Anand offers three solutions to Bakha to step out of the agony of self-abasement and ceaseless frustration. A Salvation Army colonel offers conversion to Christianity as a resolution of the problem but without much success. Later, Bakha is drawn to Mahatma Gandhi, who inspires as well as distresses him when he refers to the untouchables as God's own people—the 'Harijans.' A third solution, which Anand is inclined to underline as the final one, is the one offered by the poet, Iqbal, in the novel, when the latter waxes eloquent on the advantages of the scientific materialistic progress which may, he believes, bring social justice and relief to Bakha and the like. Resolutions to deep-seated problems are, however, not so easy to come by.

Anand's commitment to the philosophy of humanism informs every line of his creative ventures. *Untouchable*, a sensitive record of the events of a single day in the life of a teenaged sweeper in a small town in the Punjab is neatly assessed by Edgel Rickword as "essentially a tragic poem of the individual caught in the net of the age-old caste-system,"[18] the caste stratification being an unfortunate characteristic of the decadent Indian society of the times.

Coolie, the novel that established Anand as a novelist depicting the social realism of the 1930s, does not concentrate on caste-consciousness as does *Untouchable*. Picaresque in nature, it is the story of Munoo, the landless peasant, the young innocent boy of fourteen who is compelled to leave his home in the idyllic hills of North-West India in the late 1920s in search of a livelihood in the plains, a livelihood that would enable him to sustain himself amidst all hardships.

Munoo becomes, by turns, a servant, a labourer and a rickshawpuller, each phase of his life bringing more humiliation than the previous one. The young lad subjected to the corruption rampant in the society and to the pressures of an egocentric world is razed to the ground never to rise again. This effectively demonstrates the helplessness and powerlessness of an underdog in the face of the grinding machinery of economic and religious oppression. Anand's protagonist in this novel was modelled on his own childhood playmate, Munoo, who was consigned to endless labour in a pickle-factory and who accepted his lot in life with total resignation.

Munoo is treated as "the scum of the earth" and is called so when be happens to be standing in front of a Sikh's shop. He is looked upon as a leper whose very touch would defile others. Added to this are the deprecations heaped on him by the cart-driver. *Coolie* is a saga of unrelieved pain and suffering with glimpses of hope so evanescent that one almost fails to register them. It depicts the travails and tribulations of a wretched and forlorn coolie in a class-conscious society where the awareness of this so-called superiority of some in terms of class—economic, cultural and political—has a largely deleterious effect on social cohesion. The sanctity of human relationships is flagrantly violated. The only irrefutable truth that emerges from the mayhem of divisiveness is the ever-widening gulf between the rich and the poor, the latter gradually sliding into perpetual misery and ultimate obliteration.

Munoo's tale can conveniently be divided into three phases. In the first he is an awkward and gauche servant in an Indian household of social climbers who have no reservations in prostrating before the British but whose efforts at rising in social esteem are foiled by the clumsy and inept behaviour of Munoo. Anand's object of satire, here, is the British 'sahib' who is blissfully ignorant of India and the ways of Indians.

In the second phase of his life, Munoo visits a Punjabi town called Daulatpur to work in a pickle-factory there. His lovable nature endears him to the factory owner, Prabha, and his wife, Parbati. Prabha's generosity, however, soon leads him into financial straits and subjects him to violence at the hands of corrupt policemen. Anand's purpose in this series of incidents in the novel is to expose the treachery of men in various capacities—employers, exploiters, policemen and financiers.

Munoo next goes to Bombay where Anand demonstrates the prevalence of a different kind of capitalism from that of the Daulatpur pickle-factory. Working in a cotton mill owned by a Britisher, Munoo experiences a total loss of identity for he is only one of the herd callously driven to the wall. In his depiction of the harsh life of the workers Anand unmistakably feels strongly and sympathetically for this class. Besides this display of affiliations, his introduction of the communal riots is meant to underscore the communication that capitalists and British imperialists both use communal differences to divide and rule.

In the last phase of his life, Munoo finds himself in an extremely ironic situation. He is taken under the patronage of Mrs. Mainwaring, a rich Eurasian woman in Simla. The mixed traits characterizing Mrs. Mainwaring are neurosis, the maternal instinct and nymphomania. The now handsome and young Munoo becomes the lady's rickshaw puller and lover. This apparently comfortable existence becomes for Munoo his cross for it leads to his ultimate depravity and finally, his inevitable end through the consumption that he has contracted. Before he dies, he listens to the outbursts of his friend, Mohan the communist, who holds the capitalist system responsible for Munoo's fate. It is through Mohan that the writer wishes to declare the "thesis" of his novel which focuses on the evils of a devouring socio-economic system. Munoo, however, has been a victim not only of systems and conventions but of human selfishness and religious fanaticism as well. On the aesthetic side, Munoo's gradual emergence from innocence to experience and knowledge is a triumph of compelling psychological portrayal.

'*Two Leaves and a Bud*' (1937) the third of the supposed trio of Anand's novels referred to at the very outset is an imaginative account of British oppression in a tea-plantation in Assam. This is another of Anand's novels of indignation and protest in which he dissects and analyzes human motives from an ironical slant. Gangu, the coolie, (an older and maturer version of Munoo in *Coolie*) is ensnared to join work in a tea-estate in Assam owned by the British. The novel, on the pattern of *Untouchable* and *Coolie*, is, again, a tale of woe—a tale of Gangu's ever-increasing exploitation coming to a grinding halt with his murder by an English overseer, believably, on the verge of insanity. Anand's purpose is again the indictment of the systems of capitalism and imperialism for their total demolition of the identity of the poor Indian who is vulnerable to assault and exploitation either by the more privileged Indians or by the insular British who isolate themselves from the Indians but never lose an opportunity to seduce their wives and daughters.

Two Leaves and a Bud, has unmistakable echoes of Forster's *A Passage to India*. The callous and unfeeling British represented by Croft-Cooke, the manager, and Reggie Hunt, a drunkard and a womanizer, are in flagrant disagreement with the humanist. Dr. De La Havre and his beloved, Barbara, both of whom are clearly for the Indians and condemn the latter's exploitation by the British imperialists and capitalists. Anand's irony, however, is not as trenchant at that of Forster for it is diluted to some extent by the tender moving pathos of depiction.

Two Leaves and a Bud dramatizes, like *Untouchable* and *Coolie*, moral issues by the counterpointing of good and evil.

Gangu, the protagonist, accompanied by his wife, Sajani, his daughter, Leila, and his son, Budhoo, moves from his native village in the Punjab to distant Assam to take up a job in Macpherson Tea Estate owned by an Englishman. Initially excited at the prospect of starting life afresh in the plantation, Gangu soon comes to realize that his days at the tea estate have been nothing but a series of deprivations—his wife dies, there is an attempt at raping his daughter, Leila, and ultimately, he himself is shot dead by Reggie Hunt. The final moment of disillusionment comes with impact of the communication that Hunt is exonerated of the charge of murder by a British jury.

Much as the novel moves us to compassion and anger, there is no gainsaying the fact that had Anand's "purpose" not intruded so vehemently and persistently upon the aesthetic and imaginative aspect of this work of fiction, *Two Leaves and a Bud* would have been a novel with a far greater psychological subtlety and a more piercing irony. *Untouchable* and *Coolie* tend to offer a cogent balance of Anand's propagandist protest and his persuasive sympathetic realism and are relatively more convincing as literary exercises. However, one can, perhaps, relax the stricture against *Two Leaves and a Bud* by suggesting that the novel is intended to be "more an extended moral allegory than an exercise in creating believable human beings."[19]

Mulk Raj Anand was the most important writer that activated the new wave of realism in the nineteen twenties and the nineteen thirties. All Anand's novels, especially the early—and the best—ones are motivated attempts to expose the agony and misery of the lower castes and classes of India. The novel, a form befitting the aspirations and objectives of a social realist like Anand, remains today—and largely owing to his generous contribution—the dominant genre for Indo-Anglian writers.

References

1. William Walsh, *Indian Literature in English* (London: Longman, 1990) p. 62; the other two "founding fathers" referred to by Walsh are R.K. Narayan and Raja Rao.
2. Gillian Packham, "Mulk Raj Anand and the Thirties Movement in England," *Perspectives on Mulk Raj Anand* ed. K.K. Sharma (Ghaziabad: Vimal Prakashan, 1978) p. 52.

3. Referred to in *Commonwealth Literature* ed. James Vinson (London, 1979) p. 22.
4. Dieter Riemenschneider, 'The Function of Labour in Mulk Raj Anand's Novels,' *Essays in Criticism on Indian Literature in English* ed. M.S. Nagarajan et. al. (New Delhi: S. Chand and Co. Ltd., 1991) p. 67.
5. *Ibid.*, p. 68.
6. *Ibid.*, p. 70.
7. Gita Bamezai, *Mulk Raj Anand, The Journalist* (New Delhi: Kanishka Publishers, 2000).
8. Mulk Raj Anand, "Why I Write? " *Indo-English Literature* ed. K.K. Sharma (Ghaziabad: Vimal Prakashan, 1977), p. 11.
9. *Ibid.*, p. 10.
10. *Ibid.*, p. 14.
11. Cited in G.N. Agnihotri, *Indian Life and the Problems in the Novels of Mulk Raj Anand, Raja Rao and R.K. Narayan* (Meerut: Shalabh Book House, 1984) p. 39.
12. Cited in *Studies in Australian and Indian Literature* (Proceedings of a Seminar). ed. C.D. Narasimhaiah and S. Nagarajan (New Delhi: Indian Council for Cultural Relations, Azad Bhawan, 1971) p. 228.
13. G.S. Balarama Gupta, "Towards a Closer Understanding of Anand," *Indo-English Literature* ed. K.K. Sharma (Ghaziabad: Vimal Prakashan, 1977), p. 115.
14. Meenakshi Mukherjee's charges against Mulk Raj Anand have been enumerated in Saros Cowasjee's article "Mulk Raj Anand and His Critics," *The Banasthali Patrika* ed. Rameshwar Gupta, Special Number on Indo-English Literature, January, 1969, Number 12.
15. K.R.S. Iyengar, *Indian Writing in English* (New Delhi: Sterling Publishers Pvt. Ltd., 1962).
16. M.K. Naik, *The Ironic Vision.* (New Delhi: Sterling Publications, 1962), p. 1.
17. H.M. Williams, *Indo-Anglian Literature* (1800-1970: A Survey), (New Delhi: Orient Longman, 1976) p. 37.
18. Edgel Rickword, *Mulk Raj Anand* (London: Malcom Courby, 1962) p. 16.
19. Munir Khan, ed., *Indian English Writing* (New Delhi: S.G. Publications, 1994) p. 214.

2

Indian English Fiction: The Theme of India's Partition

We, in India, seem increasingly to be living in an age of nostalgia. The pace of technological advancement effecting swift changes in society necessitates on the rebound, misty-eyed visions of the past. Regurgitation of the trauma of the Partition seems to be a continuing trend in Indian English fiction. One wonders what the reason for this spate of "Partition" novels is—is it a cathartic exercise or is it a necessary exorcising of the ghosts that refuse to be ignored? Or, is it just a clearing and defining of perspectives sought with the passage of time by circumventing the possibility of the picture "breaking up into dots?"[1] Or, again, is it the writer's unmistakable nostalgic "urge to reclaim"[2] the past as experiential reality that filters through to us in the work? With the battle lines fast being re-drawn, with the communal tensions rising in a crescendo, the exercise of writing novels of the Partition is being cheered and welcomed.

With history today "more novelistic than the novel,"[3] and the novel more historical and non-fictional in content and spirit, the elastic confines of the novel give the writer relative freedom to weed out pure facts or even to twist facts, as long as the final view of history conforms to the general tenor of the times and the larger scheme of events as they took place.

Focusing on a particular period in history, creative artists often experiment with the reality of the times to create a timeless reality of their own. They endeavour to recreate the ethos of the specific period chosen and to capture its prevailing mood. History, and specifically the partition of India, undertaken by the Indian English fiction writer and explored as literary capital, refers always to the particular in which there is an attempt to present history as sensory detail, as visual image, as time which reverberates in our own time. The comments of two major practitioners and critics of the novel form are largely relevant here: one by Truman Capote, who, when be first published *In Cold Blood* referred to it as "a narrative form that employed all the techniques of fictional art but was nevertheless immaculately factual;"[4] and, another by Michael Wood, who asserts that "fiction is the only shape we can give to facts."[5] Clearly then, there is no knowable reality, only personal observation.

India is a land of the past. People in India turn to the past for inspiration, self-evaluation or self-congratulation. In the West that looks more to the future, it is chiefly the sophisticated intellectuals or creative writers who experience the need to turn to the past, its historical or mythical structures or paradigms, to interpret their present existential problems or dilemmas or to search for meanings at a time when the meaninglessness of life threatens traditional certainties. In India, on the contrary, even the common man is able to place his present in the context of the past, see the continuity of history and accept its consequences as part of the grand design of Fate. In other words, our general attitude to history or myth makes them not just something that once happened—in real life or in imagination—but something that forms an inalienable part of the present and makes us conscious, to quote T.S. Eliot's words, "not only of the pastness of the past but of its presence [...]."[6]

The significance of history and mythology in Indian life cannot be denied for they influence greatly our ways of life, our objectives and our ideals. Creative writers, too, have taken cognisance of this fact, and, it is not surprising that several writers of Indian English fiction have turned to historical events for the purpose of their fictional art, history providing them the necessary inspiration as well as richness and depth.

The politico-historical dimension that characterized Indian English fiction from the very beginning was, however, initially determined not solely by the importance of history in Indian life but also by the times in which the Indian English novel was born. A close correspondence has been traced by literary historians between the growth of the freedom movement and the development of the Indian novel in English. Two of the earliest works of Indian English fiction, namely, K.C. Dutt's *A Journal of Forty-Eight Hours of the Year 1945* (1835) and S.C. Dutt's *Republic of Orissa: Annals from the Pages of the Twentieth Century* (1845) have both strong political and historical overtones.

An abiding interest in the Indian political history of the pre- and post-Independence days manifests itself in a large number of Indian English novels. As is natural, however, the imagination of different novelists was stirred by different aspects and phases of the Indian struggle for freedom, the attainment of Independence and the concurrent partition of the country. These tumultuous years in the history of the nation constituted a reality that was irresistible. Some writers who were moved by the turbulent events depicted them in their works which, though predominantly historical in content, are often categorized as political novels because the political events of the period dominated the scene and covered a major part of the historical record of the times so that the political movements and the historical developments of the period became synchronous. In the ultimate analysis, however, what is important is not their being labelled political or historical novels but the different perspectives that they communicate.

Several Indian English writers of fiction have considered the partition of India and its aftermath as potential literary material for novelistic representation. They have drawn upon this theme according to their own proclivities and individual geniuses. One of the earliest writers to deal with the terrible tragedy caused by the Partition was Khushwant Singh. His *Train to Pakistan*, a realistic rendition of the inhumanities perpetrated and the tremendous losses caused by large scale rioting and killing, was published in 1956. Three years later appeared Balachandra

Rajan's *The Dark Dancer* (1958), which uses the freedom movement and, later, the Partition, as a meaningful backdrop to the action in the novel. Rajan shows how Gandhiji's concept of non-violence tacitly provides the heroine her source of strength while the riots at the time of the Partition enable her to demonstrate the triumph of her ideology. Attia Hosain's *Sunlight on a Broken Column* (1961) is the only novel on the Partition written in English by a Muslim living in India. It focuses on the impact of the great event on the lives of the Muslims in India. Manohar Malgonkar in *A Bend in the Ganges* (1964) employs a wider canvas than in his earlier novel, *Distant Drum* (1960), in which he had given the theme only limited treatment. In his later novel, he presents, at considerable length, the whole struggle for Independence and its after effects, though his depiction of the violence and bloodshed consequent upon the Partition is confined to the last three chapters of the book. Then came Chaman Nahal's *Azadi* (1975), which realizes the trauma of the Partition in terms of the displacement, communal discord and indignities that had to be endured by the people driven to find a new home and a new identity. More recent is Salman Rushdie's *Midnight's Children* (1981), which makes of India's Independence only a starting point for a deeply personal and fantastic account of the political and historical growth of the nation till the time of the Emergency which was declared in 1977. As *India Today* observes, the novel is "in fictional terms one of the most ferocious indictments of India's evolution since Independence."[7]

The novels enumerated above, spanning a period of about a quarter of a century, afford us an understanding of the most important event of our near past from varying perspectives which were influenced by each writer's distance from the event as well as his perception of its import.

Apart from these novels there are many others that also have for their theme or concern, some phase of Indian history. There is for instance, such an early novel as Raja Rao's *Kanthapura* (1938). This novel traces the impact of the Gandhian ideology of non-violence and non-cooperation on the obscure village of Kanthapura in the South of India. Then, there is Mulk

Raj Anand's *The Sword and the Sickle* (1942), which is set in the second decade of the twentieth century and deals with the rise of Gandhi bringing in a period of intense activity in the national freedom struggle. Another novel which deserves mention is K.A. Abbas' *Inquilab* (1955) which gives a detailed portrayal of the Indian political scene of the first quarter of the twentieth century though the effect is that of a piling up of events rather than that of a coherent representation. *Shadow from Ladakh* (1966) is a more recent work by Bhabani Bhattacharya. Set against the Chinese aggression of 1965, it presents a conflict between Gandhism and industrialism.

It is evident, then, that history, especially the recent political history of India, has been a continuous concern or source of inspiration for the Indian English writer of fiction. The theme of the Partition has been remarkably seminal. Indeed, it continues to appear in the works of contemporary writers who seem to find still uncharted or unexplored possibilities in it. Thus we have, as a testimony of the unmitigated aesthetic appeal of the theme, Bapsi Sidhwa's *Ice-Candy Man* and Gurcharan Das's *A Fine Family* published as recently as 1988 and 1990 respectively. The former novel has a significantly fresh approach to the violence unleashed by the Partition in that it sees this turbulent world through the innocent eyes of an eight year old Parsi girl Lenny, who is polio-stricken and can only sit back and experience the agonies of perception. Lenny, who is baffled and perplexed by the adult world of shifting loyalties, changing attitudes and widening gulfs, has at the centre of her world, her relationship with her loving Ayah, her ardent cousin-suitor and her Godmother with her companion, Slave Sister. The novel traces the child's slow awakening to sexuality and experiences of adolescent urges that enable her to interpret the duplicities and deceptions of a savage adult world. The latter novel, having a much vaster scope, traces three generations of a Punjabi family from 1942 till the second tenure of Indira Gandhi as Prime Minister. The novel does not end in bloodshed and despair as most novels on the Partition do and its characters do not, as they do in Rushdie's *Midnight's Children*, shape history. They are simple men and women who are compelled by circumstances to take up certain stances in life. They are contented middle class people with middle class aspirations and dreams but they possess true grit and emerge out of each crisis with honour and dignity as the family moves from the Kacheri Bazaar bungalow in Lyallpur to Chota Simla first and then to Bombay. It is the story of Lala Dewan Chand, popularly known as Bauji, a prosperous lawyer and a man of substance, who witnesses the world around him collapse as his nephew is lost to the freedom movement, his daughter, Tara, unwillingly submits to an arranged marital alliance and he is compelled to leave Lyallpur as his close Muslim friends espouse the cause of Pakistan.

One is struck by the fact that the further we move from the momentous event, the stronger and more persistent does its pull become; the deeper it recedes into the past, the more poignantly it surfaces in the fictional creations of our time.

The novelists writing about the recent Indian past can all, in some way, and to some extent, be categorized as writers of historical fiction. The term "historical fiction" may seem paradoxical,[8] for history is a verifiable record of the past and the word "fiction" means "a feigned or false story."[9] Apparently the two are irreconcilable but a reconciliation is effected when we consider the historical novelist not as a chronicler of facts but as one who accomplishes a vision of history more comprehensive than recorded history. He is a "maker" in the sense that Aristotle's poet is, for to give us a feel of the times which he represents, he creates a whole community of individuals who give us a better insight into the age than do the real figures of recorded history. Besides, he visualizes and establishes connections between events which historical records never wholly reveal to us. As Gore Vidal aptly observes, "For the novelist it is the imagining of connections that brings life to what was."[10]

Place and time are of great significance in historical fiction. In the words of Eudora Welty, "Fiction is properly at work on the here and now, or the past made here and now; [...].[11] The latter part of the observation refers to the historical novel which realizes the past in terms of the present, that is, the present of the characters in the novel which is co-extensive with the historical past and makes us conscious of the ethos of the times. Thus place lends a recognizable identity to its inhabitants and richness to the aesthetic experience.

A historical novel has none of the "non-resolution of meanings"[12] that is characteristic of a modern novel. Its meaning and structure are provided to it by the experience furnished by a specific period in history—the experience itself as derived from the work is the meaning, for it provides an insight into the age portrayed, through a careful choice of word, character and action.

In a work of historical fiction we may have historical symbols in the form of characters and actions that are presented in such a way as to illuminate the attitudes and the ways of living of the inhabitants of a given place and a given time.[13] But the historical symbols with their reverberating meanings, must expand into symbols of the human situation so that the narrative refers, not only to an aspect of man's past but also to a vista of humanity at large, caught in the embroils of destiny. The articulation of meaning in fiction through symbolic and mythical explorations of truth is the novelist's creative response to the problems of existence as he sees them.

It would be useful at this point to briefly state our assumptions regarding the responsibilities of the author in transforming history into art. A historical novel like a non-fictional text has, what Eric Heyne terms "factual status"[14] but it may, in spite of certain inaccuracies of fact, present an account of the past that is essentially authentic, for inaccuracy is not necessarily fatal to historical fiction. If the implications of an event are successfully conveyed and made to fit into the author's overall intentions in the work, it would not be easy to assail the truth conveyed by the work. A historical novelist presents an aesthetically acceptable version of the "unwashed mass of facts"[15] that prevailed in a particular period of time by meaningfully organizing the raw data of experience. Thus, instead of merely reflecting fragmentary reality, he creates a coherent vision of it.

The aesthetic latitude allowed to the historical novelist does not, however, permit him to distort history for he is, as R.K. Dhawan observes, "as much a historian as a novelist."[16] Chaman Nahal, emphasizing the need for factual accuracy in a historical novel writes:

> [...] Herein lies the additional burden that a historical novel places on the artist. The novelist is allowed to do careful research into the period he has chosen for presentation and every detail of that period has to be accurate.[17]

History clearly imposes limitations on the novelist who has to strike a balance between the facts of history and the flights of imagination.

Augustus M. Kolich speaks of "the thin line between fact and fiction"[18] that is "rapidly disappearing"[19] in the contemporary novel. The novel today is certainly more concerned with historical and non-fictional material, and history, as Norman Mailer puts it and as cited earlier, has become "more novelistic than the novel"[20]. Treatment and "invention"[21] of history within a novel connote a certain merging of the forms of history and fiction. History as explored by the novelist, refers always to a particular and specific past time which is evoked and which reverberates in the present. In the *Executioner's Song*, Norman Mailer depicts the history of a specific time and culture as built on the particulars of a single life that is fictionalized. He creates a historical framework and conveys to us "how things really were"[22] at that time.

A historical novelist, to be able to present a convincing picture of the past, must be equipped with a knowledge of human nature and the ability to identify himself with the people of the times, thinking and feeling as they must have thought and felt.

The Indian English novelists have explored almost the entire range of the historical novel. Regarding the scope of this type of novel, Watson observes:

> At its most historical it can tell of protagonists, events and settings that are all recorded in history; [...]. Or it can set

> imaginary events in real settings, and with allusions, or something more, to real historical personages [...]. Or it can, at its novelistic extreme, use history only as a backdrop and exclude historical characters[...].[23] The Indian English novelists make available to us the many gradations of this type.

Khushwant Singh in *Train to Pakistan*, Balachandra Rajan in *The Dark Dancer*, Attia Hosain in *Sunlight on a Broken Column,* Malgonkar in a *Bend in the Ganges*, Chaman Nahal in *Azadi,* Salman Rushdie in *Midnight's Children*, Bapsi Sidhwa in *Ice Candy Man* and Gurcharan Das in *A Fine Family*, all represent the variety of ways in which history and fiction may interact in a novel. It would be a rewarding exercise in critical analysis (a) to reveal the characteristic ways in which each of the selected novelists recreates history through fiction by integrating historical material with fictional narrative and (b) to explore the nature and extent of their differences. It is important to understand not only the significance of their choice of historical events for their works, but also the inner springs which gave direction to and determined the form of their novels.

In each of the above mentioned novels the human emotions portrayed, though essentially personal, have been subjected to and conditioned by the pressures of the times. The novelists here, unlike historians, do not concentrate on a general marshalling of events; rather, they try to relate the particular lot of the individual to the general fate of the nation. It is each writer's distinctive way of presenting the interplay of the particular and the general that sets him apart from the others. Each in his own way apprehends the social and psychological upheaval caused by the mechanics of history and shows what history does to character and what character makes of history.

Each of the novelists here, presents a retrospective view of an important period of recent Indian history in terms of the impact of the historical events on the different sections of Indian society. The variety in their depictions springs from the difference in their points of view and from the specific selection by each of them of some facts for special emphasis, bringing to bear upon this selection his interests, beliefs and values which clearly determine what he takes to be important. In other words, each of our novelists has produced a narrative of the past from his or her present point of view.

The partition of the country is an event that figures in each of the novels referred to. All the authors mentioned here, except Rushdie, have themselves undergone the agony of the Partition and their novels are the result of their aesthetic response to their compulsion to write about this harrowing experience. Rushdie alone, born in June 1947, was too young then to personally experience the aftermath of the Partition and his recreation of life in India, from the day of Independence till the time that he was mature enough to register events, is a product of his creative imagination and his reading.

The novels on which we focus our attention are individual attempts at a reconstruction of the past and at a partial objectification of an experience that has left an indelible mark on the minds of their authors. In none of these, however, can the protagonist be identified with the author himself except in *Midnight's Children* in which we may fruitfully try to trace some degree of similarity between the protagonist and the author. This may well be justified by the parallel between some of the problems and events in the lives of both. In *Sunlight on a Broken Column*, too, there is some measure of resemblance between the novelist and the central character in the work but there is no consistent analogy that may be drawn between the two.

The time gap between the writing of a novel and the period of the past that is portrayed is a major factor determining the extent of objectivity in the depiction. The farther away a novelist is in point of time from the events he is reconstructing in his work, the less obfuscated is his picture and the more impartial his presentation. As Rushdie's narrator in *Midnight's Children* observes, "Reality is a question of perspective,"[24] and when we are very close to what happens, perspective is impossible,"[25] the picture breaks up into dots, and "only subjective judgements are possible."[26]

Of all the novelists included here Khushwant Singh is the closest in point of time to the event of the Partition, which, as we have already observed, happens to be an occurrence of common focus, Rushdie and Das being the only two to spread their canvas much wider. Singh's anger and repulsion at the violence and the inhumanities that he witnessed during the Partition riots are evident in his descriptions of the horror of the times which clearly communicate his desire "to shout his disenchantment with the world."[27] Rushdie, at the other extremity, is farther away in time and can thus easily fantasize his account of the past and drain it of all emotional associations. Rajan, Malgonkar, Attia Hosain and Nahal, all consciously or unconsciously reveal some degree of personal involvement in, or experience of, the nightmarish ordeal of the Partition. The condemnation of human degradation witnessed during that time is clearly discernible in their novels. Bapsi Sidhwa and Gurcharan Das, still farther away, are relatively cool and composed in their depictions.

The problem of the recreation of history in a work of fiction raises the question of technique which certainly deserves attention. A work of fiction may adopt either of the following modes of narration: "telling" and "showing."[28] The novelist may choose to "tell" the reader, facts about the period of history which he wishes to portray through stage setting, explication and interpretation of an action and a summary of thoughts and events. An alternative manner of communicating facts to the reader is "showing"[29] through the heightening of events by dramatization in which the novelist stands at a vantage point from which he can have a broad view of things and approach the immediate scene in a relatively objective manner. In the former mode, the novelist is ever present. His "I" is unmistakable in the perspective that is presented. But in the latter mode, the novelist stands back, so to say, and allows the events to unroll themselves and the characters to play their parts without revealing his hand or presence even as he manipulates everything.

Each of the novelists named here selects his own mode of conveying the facts of history. Khushwant Singh, Attia Hosain,

Salman Rushdie, Bapsi Sidhwa and Gurcharan Das "tell," but in different ways; Rajan, Majgonkar and Nahal "show" in their own characteristic fashions.

History, then is clearly the constant in each of these novels. It is the other co-ordinates that vary according to the interests and literary proclivities of each individual artist. Khushwant Singh cleverly blends history with romance in his novel, thereby giving the work a quality of particularity as well as of universality. The story of *Train to Pakistan* takes place at a certain well-documented time but the love-theme introduced makes it a tale for all times. Rajan in *the Dark Dancer* mingles history with myth, history providing the realistic base to the imaginative superstructure of myths that explore and bring experience to a meaningful expression. The correspondence between the characters in the book and the mythical figures elucidates the various themes in the novel and is indicative of the author's moral purpose. Attia Hosain's *Sunlight on a Broken Column* is a coalescence of history and autobiography. The history of the Indian national struggle for independence and the subsequent partition of the country, fraught with violence, besides providing the background to the personal history of Laila the protagonist, underlines as well, her own struggle for independence from the claustrophobic conditions of a conservative Muslim family. Laila communicates the psychological crisis in her life. A similar crisis prevailed in the life of the novelist who, like Laila, was orphaned early in life. The novel obviously, is a work of fictionalized self-representation.

Malgonkar, in *A Bend in the Ganges*, has a more varied fare to offer. He brings together history, action and romance. On a historical narrative bringing into focus the havoc wrought by the Partition are grafted tales of gentle romance and vertiginous action both helping to establish, by contrast or conformity, the dominant mood of violence. Nahal's *Azadi* is a striking synthesis of history and metaphor, the historical narrative being a metaphor for the theme of forced exile, which the writer himself had suffered at the time of the Partition. Nahal, true to his belief that every historical novel has to move at atleast two levels, realistic and metaphorical,[30] makes *Azadi* communicate on both these planes. Rushie's *Midnight's Children* is a fusion of history, fantasy and autobiography. The novel's presentation of a vast span in the recent history of India is marked not by a strictly factual depiction but by an element of fantasy that enables the writer to convey the aspects of reality that have been painfully experienced by him but are incommunicable in the realistic mode. Yet the novel is also a form of sincere self-depiction which according to the "autobiographical contract"[31] determines the autobiographical nature of the work. Much of the power of the novel comes from the energy employed by the author to strike a harmonious balance between the contrary pulls of autobiographical involvement and the distancing device of fantasy.

Bapsi Sidhwa's *Ice Candy Man* warrants the careful critical attention of those interested in new possibilities for imaginative prose which resorts to viable fictional means—largely realistic—for tracing the pressure of history on individual lives, presenting a collage of the lives and experiences of men and women caught in the web of history. In *A Fine Family*, Gurcharan Das sensitively transposes the unforgettable historical event of the Partition into his fictional universe but he resorts neither to a photographic nor an allegorical representation. His is a narrative, simple and sustained in tracing the impact of the major historical event on three generations of a beleagured Punjabi family.

Each of the novels referred to above is an artistic reverberation of some period of recent Indian history. All these novels include the singular tragic experience of the Partition though there are important differences of emphasis and tone. An in-depth analysis of each reveals it to be a literary apperception of a historical reality illustrative of a novelist's creative transformation of the facts of life into art. The individual communicates to us in his own characteristic mode, the human predicament born of the terrible impact of the partition of India through an aesthetically organized and realistic account of events. He makes the best of what Susan Gearhart calls "the open boundary."[32]

References

1. Salman Rushdie, *Midnight's Children* (London: Picador, 1981, rpt. 1982), p. 435.
2. Salman Rushdie, *Imaginary Homelands* (London: Granta Books, 1991), p. 10.
3. Norman Mailer, cited in "How Is Fiction Doing?" Interview, *The New York Times Book Review*, December 14, 1980, p. 3.
4. Cited in Michiko Kakutani, "Do Facts and Fiction Mix," *The New York Times Book Review*, January 27, 1980, p. 3.
5. *Ibid.*, p. 28.
6. T.S. Eliot, "Tradition and the Individual Talent," *Twentieth Century Literary Criticism*, ed. David Lodge (London: Longman, 1972), p. 72.
7. Comment quoted on the backcover of the Picador edition of *Midnight's Children.*
8. Wilbur Sanders, "Literature as History: With Some Questions About Historical Imagination," *The Dramatist and the Received Idea* (England: Cambridge University Press, 1988), p. 15; Sanders' queries on the apparent contradiction between history and literature are pertinent here: "Is there simply a flat methodological contradiction which leaves one with nothing but a choice of mutually exclusive alternatives. History or literature? Or can the two modes of thought be entertained together? Can the contradiction be forced to yield up a single truth?"
9. William Geddie (ed.), *Chambers' Twentieth Century Dictionary* (1952); rpt. (London: Chambers, 1956)
10. Gore Vidal, "How I Do What I do If Not Why," *At Home: Essays 1982-88* (1982); rpt. (New York: Random House, 1988), p. 300.
11. Eudora Welty, "Place in Fiction," *Critical Approaches to Fiction*, ed. Shiv K. Kumar and Keith Mc Kean (New York: McGraw Hill, 1968), p. 250.
12. Alan Friedman, *The Turn of the Novel* (New York: Oxford University Press, 1966), Introduction, p. XVI.
13. George Watson, *The Story of the Novel* (London: Macmillan, 1979), p. 91, Watson brings to notice Walter Scott's "distilling the essence of a civilization and a cause into a character" and his "grasping personality as an index of place and time" in his historical novels.
14. Eric Heyne, "Toward a Theory of Literary Nonfiction," *Modern Fiction Studies*, Autumn 1987, Vol. 33, No. 3, p. 480.
15. *Ibid.*, p. 489.

16. R.K. Dhawan (ed.), "The Artist as Historian: Three Contemporary Novelists," *Three Contemporary Novelists* (New Delhi: Classical Publishing Co., 1985), p. 4.
17. Chaman Nahal, "Telling of Time Past," *The Hindustan Times Weekly*; March 15, 1981, p. 8.
18. Augustus M. Kolich, "Does Fiction Have to be made Better Than Life?" *Modern Fiction Studies*, Summer 1983, Vol. 29, No. 2, p. 172.
19. *Ibid.*
20. "How Is Fiction Doing?" *The New York Times Book Review*, Dec. 14, 1980.
21. *Ibid.*, p. 30; Jayne Anne Phillips in her interview speaks of the "invention" of history.
22. Ranke referred to the objective of history being to establish "wie es cigentlich gewesen" i.e. "how things really were," cited by M.T. Finley, in *The Use and Abuse of History* (London: the Hogath Press, 1986), p. 13.
23. George Watson, op. cit. , pp. 91-92.
24. Salman Rushdie, *Midnight's Children* (London: Picador, 1982), p. 165.
25. *Ibid.*, p. 435.
26. *Midnight's Children*, p. 435.
27. Extract from the transcript of a talk for the *Australian Broadcasting Commission 'Guest of Honour'* Programme broadcast on 5th April, 1964.
28. Wayne Booth, *The Rhetoric of Fiction* (The University of Chicago Press, 1961), Chapter I, pp. 3-9.
29. Percy Lubbock, *The Craft of Fiction* (London: Cape, 1921), p. 62. Lubbock pointed out the importance of this method seventy years ago [...] "the art of fiction does not begin unless the novelist thinks of his story as a matter to be *shown*, to be so exhibited that it will tell itself."
30. Chaman Nahal, "Writing a Historical Novel," *Three Contemporary Novelists*, ed. R.K. Dhawan (New Delhi: Classical Publishing Co., 1985), p. 40.
31. Sidonie Smith, "Construing Truths in lying Mouths: Truth Telling in Women's Autobiography," *Studies in the Literary Imagination*, Vol. XXIII, No. 2, Fall, 1990.
32. Quoted in "The Lost Instructors" by John Bayley, 'Literature and Criticism,' *Times Literary Supplement*, Feb. 12-18, 1988, p. 167.

3

Tradition and Modernity in Shashi Deshpande's *The Dark Holds No Terrors* and *That Long Silence*

The issue of a woman's quest for identity in a male-dominated world has in the recent past, been addressed by a multitude of writers and there has been a subsequent wave of criticism to highlight the problem and to indicate the modern woman's protest against victimization and marginalization by man. My submission today has a rather different slant in the sense that it focuses not so much on the injustice meted out to Indian women by their male counterparts but on the unrelenting tyranny of customs and traditions in the Indian society. The presentation, however, is not a social or sociological document and hence deals primarily with fiction as art and not as a vehicle of protest.

In the pursuit of art, specifically literary art, it is not desirable to drag in the distinction of moral and traditional values as settled by social standards, prejudice or convention. Particular themes or subjects may not conform to the acceptable norms of society and consequently, may be frowned upon by the bulk of conformists but the magic of the pen may cast upon them a transcendent and unique brilliance so as to make them more than acceptable. It is the artist's subtlety of perception and his treatment of a theme which decide whether his work will flounder in the region of moral and social good in terms of compliance, or rise higher in his attempt to create, his individual perception taking on a new impersonal character as "rasa," the delight of pure sensibility which is the bliss of being.

The Upanishads declare, "By the self one knoweth taste and form and smell, by the self one knoweth sound and touch and the joy of man with woman; what is there left in the world of which the self not knoweth?"[1] So it is the self that creates by a discreet choice, pure bliss for itself. The question that then surfaces is that if what yields ambrosia for the self, threatens the validity and morality of social standards, which way does one turn, to the realism of the moment experienced by the self or the gyrations of the cone which threatens to widen its circumference and to broaden and broaden its base till it engulfs the self and perpetrates absolute disintegration?

Much as the individual would like to celebrate the self and indulge in the exultations of "the river of my mind,"[2] (as Wordsworth puts it in 'The Prelude') the river which reveals the experiential process of individual consciousness, he cannot let slip the present—the physical, the phrenic and the social—in which he inheres and which monitors the problematic nature of his hold on the reality of the self.

A governing concern of the novelist today is that of defining and delimiting the bounds of personal space: of outlining life in the world of *depth*. Without the backdrop of the enduring existence of a *deep* landscape and a vast panorama to give a three-dimensional effect the complex interplay of the self and the society and the balances and tensions between the two would not attain the meaning and anguishing sensitivity indispensable to the grasp of reality, personal as well as social.

According to the Vedic precepts, existence is categorized as that which exists within time and space. "Time is the basic category of Existence,"[3] wrote Heidegger referring to time as experienced by the individual. With reference to the social aspect man experiences time as flux or change but in a more significant manner, he experiences it in terms of the growth of the self. Experientially, time and the self are very intimately related. In literature, time is always different from time in nature; it is subjective, psychological and human.

Time is a perpetual NOW symbolized by the traditional Indian symbol of the "damaru," a double-ended drum. This "damaru" presents diagrammatically the functioning of time in human experience. The larger human reality of man in the social context on the other hand, is recreated by recharging actuality with social and moral significance.

Indian writing in English, besides being a literary experience and a test in literary creativity, is also a documentation of Indian life in all its socio-cultural aspects. It is committed to the Indian consciousness and to the Indian sensibility. The concept of "Indianness" defies all definitions and is more an inherent quality of the mind, a matter of perception and of realization. It is no deliberate pursuit to create a kind of self-mystification—it is the spontaneous flow of the heritage of Indian culture characterized more by surrender and conformity than by rebellion and challenge.

The Indian English novel is firmly rooted in the social and cultural ethos of India and has undeniably been a product of national consciousness from the very beginning. It is India in microcosm and English becomes a supple medium at the disposal of the writer for expressing the complexity and the uniqueness of the Indian voice. In the works of the early writers like Raja Rao, Mulk Raj Anand and R.K. Narayan we find in a subtle and oblique way a sense of India's changing national and social scene, the disintegration of the joint family, the East-West encounter and the mythical past of the nation. Closely linked to these is the theme of the conflict between tradition and modernity, an exploration of the hybrid culture of the educated Indian middle classes and an analysis of the innumerable dislocations and confrontations in a hide-bound and tradition-ridden society under the impact of an incipient industrialization associated with the theme.

The Indian English novel today has graduated to becoming an exercise in the quest for self and there has been in the last decade, an efflorescence of works that treat of the self rather than document the social scenario of the times. And, there is no attempt either, in the Dos Passos (1896-1970) manner at "draining off the subjective"[4] to appear to be objective. Relevant here is Upmanyu Chatterjee's assertion that "All fiction is autobiographical. It's about what you have heard, seen, felt, experienced or imagined."[5] So the action in the modern Indian English novel revolves around the conflict between the ego-centricity of an individual clamouring to be heard and the absolutism of a society seeking to impose indiscriminately on all, a kind of moral and social regimentation clogging personal growth. We catch in it glimpses of nightmares of individuals hemmed in by social and psychological compulsions.

Let us here make a transition from the general "individual" to the specific "woman" in the India of more recent times, in the tradition-bound India that could not remain impervious to the new forces that had started making their impact felt. Among many others, Attia Hosain, over forty years ago, in her novel *Sunlight on a Broken Column*, presented the pre-Partition days in India from the point of view of a Muslim woman, who had led a thoroughly sheltered and protected life till the time she decided to rebel against the claustrophobic condition of her conventional existence and declared her personal independence with total disregard for all the negative pressures and social inhibitions in her life. We have also the compelling portrayals of modern Indian women in the novels of Kamala Markandaya; her rural women, her educated middle-class women and her urban women of the upper strata of society, all reflect the graph of social changes in life in India. The Indian society, so bogged down by tradition, could not remain proof to the new awakenings that had started making inroads into the minds of people. Other women creative writers like Anita Desai, Nayantara Sahgal and Bharati Mukherjee have also tried to re-define the man-woman relationship, and more specifically, the husband-wife equation.

Compared to the others, Shashi Deshpande's is a more vocal expression of the modern Indian woman striving for compatibility between a sought after modicum of self-worth and independence, and a deep-rooted commitment to her various relationships, and primarily to her "dharma" as wife. Even a female slave in some primitive countries has the admitted right to refuse her master the last familiarity. Not so the wife: however brutal a tyrant she may be yoked to in marriage he can compel her to be subjected to the lowest degradation of a human being, that of being made the instrument of an animal function, contrary to her inclinations. And often the decrees of most countries, whether legal or social, are far worse than the people who execute them. If married life were all that it might be expected to be, looking to the social compulsions alone, society would be a hell upon earth. In domestic as in political tyranny, there is scarcely any horror that may not occur under it if the despot, the husband, so pleases. True, the wife, if she can not effectually resist, can at least retaliate but this mode of self-protection is effective only with the least tyrannical of husbands. Thus mere feminine blandishments may work in individual instances but are generally ineffectual in modifying the general tendencies of the situation.

Commonwealth writers have increasingly come to deal with issues concerning the hitherto neglected and often oppressed half of humanity—women. Many of these writers are themselves women and have naturally raised their voices. Colonialism, today, has lost its political power but the "colonial discourse" of power politics which divides the male and the female into the oppressor and the oppressed is still all pervasive. In order to get over this complex, a re-casting of the mental attitudes of men and women is a prerequisite and there needs to be a constant reviewing of masculine and feminine approaches to all aspects of life.

The emancipation of the Indian woman and the Indian English novel has for some time been advancing together. Women, "the disqualified half of the human race"[6] as John Stuart Mill calls them, are the focus of attention in Shashi Deshpande's novels, and illustratively so in *The Dark Holds No Terrors* and *That Long Silence*. It is easier to draw a ludicrous picture of women's disabilities and weaknesses than to answer the arguments for them and speak on behalf of them. Sufferings arising from man's attitude to woman in the Indian context bring to the latter the feeling of a wasted life and the curse of utter helplessness and dry up the principal fountain of human happiness.

Few writers have had as prolific and successful a career as Shashi Deshpande's in terms of her consistent commitment to the valorization of the feminine identity in an amazing and uniformly well-written array of books in the genre of the novel. Deshpande resists her novels being categorized as "feminist" works for she considers this a reductionist approach. She does, no doubt, deal with the predicament of the Indian woman, especially the educated middle-class woman, torn between an assertion of her self and submission to her various roles as daughter, wife and mother; but as she herself puts it, her concern is primarily human relationships, about which she feels "we still know very little".[7] She says:

> Human relationships is what a writer is involved with. Person to person and person to society relationships—these are the two primary concerns of a creative writer and, to me, the former is of immense importance. My preoccupation is with interpersonal relationships and human emotions.[8]

Elsewhere, too, Deshpande is very insistent in her warnings against her works being read as feminist texts. Talking about the dilemma of a woman writer in *The Literary Criterion*, She says:

> A woman who writes of woman's experiences often brings in some aspects of those experiences that have angered her, roused her strong feelings. I don't see why this has to be labelled feminist fiction.[9]

And yet, though not an avowed feminist, her fictional world has at its centre, women clamouring for recognition in a male-dominated society, women straddling the wall between tradition and modernity. Her concern in virtually all her novels is the physical and emotional relationships between men and women, the acute struggle of the Indian woman to survive and create for herself a meaningful life in a man's world and her ardent desire to commit herself to some lasting, satisfying *raison d' etre*. The commitment she has made to emancipating the Indian woman, the commitment she has found most meaningful in the contemporary world is borne out, in principle, by the phenomenal depth of her works, though in range, like Jane Austen, she has confined herself to her "two inches of ivory."

The following extract from Barbara Delinsky's short story "A Woman's Place" epitomizes the quintessential predicament of the modern Indian woman as portrayed by Shashi Deshpande:

> Claire Raphael has managed everything so well. Marriage, children and a thriving business—somehow she has kept it all together. Until now. For now, out of the blue, Claire's world has been turned upside down And suddenly, she finds she is in danger of losing it all.[10]

Saru in *The Dark Holds No Terrors* is a victim of endless misunderstandings at home and in marriage. Her initial conflict is with her mother who is extremely conventional both in her moral and social attitudes. The conflict takes on a particularly poignant quality in as much as Saru's situation is, from the very beginning, of a child—a girl child—that is unwanted, and later, of an adolescent who is despised because she is believed to have killed her brother, Dhruva, for reasons of sheer hatred nursed by her mother's gender discrimination in favour of her sibling. Though married to the man of her choice despite her mother's disapproval and resentment, her initial effervescence and hopefulness in marriage are soon destroyed by the male-ego that raises its inglorious head only to be frustrated and to be put to shame for it fails to come up to the societal expectation of the male being the bread winner in the family. It is she who is now the lady doctor and he her husband! And then, a single question put to Manu lets Hell loose! "How does it feel when your wife earns not only the butter but most of the bread as well?" he is asked by an interviewer of Saru. Later, Saru analyzing her marriage that was on the rocks, introspectively remarks:

> And so the self esteem with which I was surrounded made me inches taller. But perhaps the same thing which made me inches taller, made him inches shorter.[11]

Manu's ego, whittled down to a nought, resorts to a violent sexual sadism that brings to Saru's dark nights misery and torture so that she becomes, literally, a victim of the war of sexes. Despite her withdrawal she is not spared the agony of sexual assault at night and terror is perpetuated. Her repulsion and her sufferings multiply manifold and rise almost as in a crescendo blaring at her the cruelty of the act. Despite all efforts on her part at a compromise she reaches what she feels is a point of no return and then quietly one day, taking the pretext of her mother's death, she runs from her world, runs from it hurt, hurt in some vital part, as it were. Leaving behind her husband, her children and her house, she visits her father after fifteen years only to be at peace, away from all that threatened her. There, taking her father into confidence, she unburdens herself and after intensive self-analysis gains composure and confidence with the passage of time. Now she is ready to confront the facts of life and take things in her stride.

Jaya of *That Long Silence* is another of Deshpande's protagonists who foils all attempts of the male-dominated society to press her to the wall in more ways than one. The novel emphasizes in particular, the sensitivity of insight and intelligence in the contemporary Indian woman whose well run and rational world disintegrates early in life: a partner in a marriage grounded in consent, Jaya finds silence and isolation from her husband more and more a necessity since their relationship lacks so much. It captures the authentic quality of what it is to be a woman, particularly a woman in a man's world and even more singularly a woman who frankly admits her estrangement from her partner in marriage, her disgust at the "speck," the streak of unbearable mediocrity in her husband's character and her refusal to surrender her essential being. What may have been in other hands a depiction of a mere attempt at revolt becomes in Deshpande's novel a sensitive, perceptive, and manifestly universal account of great significance in the growing, changing world of today where women bypass the faceless anonymity of existence and state their predilections with manifest self-dignity.

Shashi Deshpande's third novel *That Long Silence* published by the British feminist publishing house, Virago, brought her to the fore and won for her the Sahitya Akademi Award in the year 1990. Deshpande derives the title of this novel from a statement made by Elizabeth Robins while addressing a world body (i.e. WWSL) in 1907:

> If I were a man and cared to know the world I lived in, I almost think it would make me a shade uneasy, the weight of that long silence.

In the novel the narrator/protagonist, close to her creator in being a woman of literary sensitivity and intellectual proclivities, is greatly conscious of the stifling, social milieu born of the power-relations in the patriarchal structure and the oppressive gender discrimination prevailing in the Indian society.

That Long Silence portrays the protagonist, Jaya's passage through a maze of apprehension and fear towards articulation and an affirmation of the self. It depicts the conflict in her mind between her identity as a writer and her role as daughter, wife and mother. For seventeen long years in marriage Jaya gags her feelings and her desires in order to cultivate the habits (i.e. the characteristic mode of the growth and development of an Indian woman) of being a good wife, of fitting into the paradigm of an ideal woman. If it had not been for the domestic crisis perpetrated by the complicity of her husband, Mohan, in a case of misappropriation of funds in his office, Jaya would never have emerged from the shadow of her husband which had engulfed her from the day of her wedding. Fortunately for Mohan, at the time of incrimination, the children are away on a long tour with family friends. To avoid disgrace, Mohan decides that he and Jaya would go and live in the Dadar flat that belongs to Jaya's maternal uncle. Jaya follows her husband into exile as readily as the mythological Sita did, but resentment, silent resentment had started brewing within her. It is when in her Dadar flat that she is temporarily liberated from the endless monotony of domestic work, "the torture of Sisyphus."[12] as Simone de Beauvoir calls it, that Jaya in retrospect, clears her complexes and indulges in a reconsideration and a reconnaissance of her past and braces herself for confronting her loneliness, her frustrations, her disappointment and her personal failures. Apparently she is a happily married woman with a caring husband, two lovable children and no dearth of material comforts. A closer scrutiny, however, reveals the cost at which her so called fulfilment as a wife and mother has been achieved.

The entire effort of holding on to marital bliss or trying to experience "at least the consciousness of doing right, freedom from guilt,"[13] cast a blight on her career as a writer and made infructuous her relationship with Kamat, earlier only a neighbour but now more than a friend. At the end of the novel the crisis is averted and Jaya receives an "all well" intimation from Mohan who had suddenly left the house angry at Jaya's withdrawal and silence after his being charged with indulgence in malpractices. The end of the novel, however, is notably significant in that it suggests a new beginning, the start of a new relationship for Mohan and Jaya, a relationship not of silence and distance but of two mates trying to reach out to each other.

The two novels under study here have etched Shashi Deshpande out as an unrelenting champion of the urban, educated middle-class Indian woman who is caught in a whirlpool of change and transition and is secure neither with the old-values that are antiquated and exhibit flagrant gender-discrimination nor with the modern, neoteric norms. Such a woman's predicament is clearly that of Matthew Arnold's in the Victorian times:

> Standing between two worlds, one dead
> The other powerless to be born.[14]

Indian women, even today, are hesitant to defy the rigid norms laid down by society and are inclined to buy peace by submitting to the need of the exquisitely handcrafted mat as in Sylvia Plath's novel, *Bell Jar*, being placed in the kitchen to be soiled and trampled.

The earliest memories of Saru, the protagonist of *The Dark Holds No Terrors*, are those of the discrimination shown by her mother in favour of Dhruva, her brother. Her brother's birthdays were occasions for puja to be held in the evenings and a general sense of joyous excitement prevailed. Her birthdays were hardly remembered and acknowledged. This discrimination probably springs from the Indian society's demand of the mandatory presence of the male child in important rituals.

Saru, conscious of this differentiation resents also the traditional practice in her orthodox home when she is treated like a "pariah" during the three days of menstruation every month and is made to sleep on a straw mat.

Again it is in defiance of the traditional social codes that Saru ignores her mother's rigid conservatism and takes up the study of medicine. Ironically, initially, Manu, her husband comes as a saviour who rescues her from the insecurity and callousness of her parents but the façade of happiness in marriage soon gives way. Her recognition and exaltation in status as a doctor is the beginning of the festering of their relationship as husband and wife. Earlier he was the young man and she his bride; now, "I was the lady doctor and he was my husband" (p. 42). One question put to Manu by Saru's interviewer makes the former conscious of his earnings being less than Saru's and then, humiliated, on the rebound he indulges in repeated sexual and physical abuse of his wife in the privacy of their room. A frustrated Manu cannot accept this cognizance of the reversal of traditional roles between marriage partners for "a wife must always be a few feet behind her husband" (p. 137).

So it is Saru who suffers the consequences of the shattering of the male ego and feels "the desperation of a trapped animal" (p. 62) in "a cage of no choices" (*Roots and Shadows*, p. 125), but when objectively analyzing her past and pinning down responsibilities, she finds that she herself is liable to answer for this—"My husband is a failure because I destroyed his manhood" (p. 217) says she.

Ultimately, however the woman has to seek refuge in her "self"—not the 'I,' not the 'Aham' of Hindu religious philosophy and metaphysics but the psychological "self," accommodating all the various other "selves" of daughter, wife and mother, which when gained full possession of, helps one conduct one self with élan and pizzazz.

To quote Sumitra Kukreti, "Sarita in *The Dark Holds No Terrors* depicts the journey of modern woman towards financial independence, emotional balance and social recognition."[15] But what is important is the fact that in the end, she transcends the "I can never do anything, I must endure" (p. 201) attitude to be at peace with herself and is able to confront the realities of life with composure for the dark holds no terrors for her now. The darkness within her has been expelled by her espousal of a positive habitude, she has learnt to connect.

Jaya of *That Long Silence*, essentially modern in her outlook, is however, rooted in tradition but her husband, Mohan, is a retrogressive, die-hard traditionalist, who frustrates all attempts on his wife's part to adjust and co-exist happily. From her earliest days she has been indoctrinated into believing that "a husband is like a sheltering tree" (p. 167) and thus she is painfully conscious of her life revolving around her husband's "needs and desires."

"The truth is that it was Mohan who had a clear idea of what he wanted [...] and I went along with him [...]. To know what you want, I have been denied that" (p. 25) Jaya, trying hard to accommodate herself to the demands of marriage always thought of Mohan and herself as "a pair of bullocks yoked together" (p. 7), and yet, to conform to the traditional role model, she never thought of separation, for that would be "painful". And yet again what was the ultimate purpose of her life in the context of her familial relationships?—(anybody's guess)—for her the answer was always an inexplicable void punctuated with what Anita Desai in *Cry, The Peacock* calls "matrimonial silences."[16]

Marriage in India is an institution that tends to stifle the growth and freedom of the individual by putting him or her into slots and any man-woman relationship other than that between husband and wife is taboo. Jaya's relationship with Kamat, the widower, though marked with understanding and sympathy could not gain ground for want of sanction from a society that looks upon any such extra marital liaison with suspicion and disapprobation. Only one aware of the Indian societal and cultural structures will realize the constraints imposed on the Indian woman in seeking with another a communion of interests and attitudes.

The social network of relatedness within which she has to find her own space, then, determines a woman's identity in the Indian context. The essential inviolable self of the woman can emerge only after she has extricated herself from the prescribed behavioural patterns and allowed expression to her angry, vocal, questioning self. In a society where age-old patriarchal assumptions conflict with liberal ideas of individuation, the birth of the self is a painful process and Jaya goes through the pangs of labour to emerge from her long silence and make life "possible."

Passing now from modernity of content to modernity of form, we observe how Shashi Deshpande abstains from offering any cut-and-dried solutions to the problems posed in her novels. There are no such solutions in life and it is in this that she approximates life to the maximum. Significantly and interestingly enough, her novels may be categorized as what Frank Kermode identifies as "fictions of the End."17 The end of a novel conforming to this category is consonant with the purpose and world view of the particular novelist but also demands active reader participation in visualizing what the actual end may have been. The reader is not offered easy satisfactions but a challenge to creative co-operation.

From the very early days of the novel, its almost intractable form encouraged the belief that there is something inherent in it that is at odds with the needs of form or art. Its representation of life in all its vastness made it difficult for it to be contained within the traditional parameter of a work of fiction. What it required was "an openness of the narrative weave"18 that Bradbury talks of and it is this openness that has now made a bid for the attention of critics. In some ways, this situation breaks up a familiar kind of completeness and elegance that we know as a story, i.e. matters of human interest told, and in being told worked and developed to the ultimate point of its own elucidation. But the novel as traditionally conceived, restrains both artistic and human freedom—the freedom of the creative mind and the freedom of the characters created by it—restrains them because the traditional obligation to provide narrative coherence, to give the entirety of a story, inhibits the larger task of the sensitive comprehension of experience. Thus, the new novel with no traditional poetics of "plot", "character" and "moral sentiment" arouses a great degree of interest and a host of responses and reactions to the various latent possibilities in the fluid and uncrystalline end which suggests an expansiveness of experience which is an attribute of life alone. Traditional ordering in a world of fictional work leans unmistakably towards a well closed, final chapter with a complete and closed form of experience. Conversely, the modern novel today is moving towards an "open"19 form of experience. The expression "open" as made familiar by Robert M. Adams as a term of literary criticism, means the deliberate and major non-resolution of meanings in a work of literary art.

Shashi Deshpande's fiction clearly conforms to the "open" pattern of the novel which reflects and conveys a new attitude towards the process and the goals of experience. It is the flux of experience itself that provides the underlying form of the novels—plot, characterization, technique or point of view are of relatively little importance. In both the novels taken up for analysis here, we witness the earlier process of experience referred to as underlying the novel being disrupted and the new flux of experience that emerges insists on a new vision of existence—a vision of ever-widening openness in the possibilities of life. The central "self," be it of Saru or Jaya, moves through the process of events from a limited experience to a wider one, from relative innocence to relative sophistication, from a narrow to an expanded perception and interpretation. A new relation of the inward Self to the outward world emerges and the protagonist is able to come to terms with even the most distressing and disturbing of events.

The novel traditionally tends to conclude in marriage or death but this is not true of the modern novel of the type written by Shashi Despande. Marriage to Saru and Jaya is an expansion of a sort which lets loose a flood of experiences marked with distraction and disturbances raised to a pitch of complexity and intensity in the mounting climax, and then, there is a release and the protagonist is all geared up to meet the future. Saru like *Daniel Deronda's* Gwendolen Harleth, who endorsed an affirmation of life in her staccato "I shall live! I shall live !" cries out in the end, "Oh yes Baba, if Manu comes, tell him to wait, I'll be back as soon as I can," all set to confront life but with a tacit determination to live life on her own terms now.

Jaya, too in *That Long Silence* looks for possibilities to start life afresh with Mohan. She resolves to break her silence and make a positive gesture of reaching out to him. She interprets his "all well" communication, too, as his efforts at initiating a new understanding of life and marriage. The novel, significantly, ends with a marked resurgence of faith. It is evident that neither *The Dark Holds No Terrors* nor *That Long Silence* adopts a simplistic and reductive approach and it is in the "openness" of each that its worth lies. Adele King's comment on *That Long Silence* beautifully encapsulates the merits of both the novels and is a striking tribute to the novelist herself:

> The richness of the work lies in the refusal to propose any easy resolutions, in the creation of narrators who are not altogether reliable, in the depiction of an atmosphere of doubt."20

Shashi Deshpande has given to her novels a vital quality that makes us conscious of the fact that in *her* vision of life something is intangibly but forcefully modern. She significantly suggests that there is never a close to experience and "The End" is only another opening.

References

1. *Katha Upanishad*, ii, I, 3, Sri Aurobindo's translation.
2. Wordsworth, "The Prelude" II, (1.214)
3. Cited in S.H. Vatsyayan, *A Sense of Time*, (Delhi: O.U.P, 1981) p. 19.
4. Frank Gado, ed., "An Interview with John Dos Passos" *Idol—the Literary Quarterly of Union College*, XI,V (1969), p. 23.
5. *Cited in Sunday*, 4-10 December, 1988, p. 32.
6. John Stuart Mill, "The Subjection of Women" (1869) (essay) (Lucknow: Gurukul Publication, rpt. 2000), p. 99.
7. Geetha Gangadharan, "Denying the Otherness" (Interview), *Indian Communicator*, Sunday Magazine, 20 Nov, 1994, p. II.

8. *Ibid.*
9. Shashi Deshpande, "The Dilemma of a Woman Writer," *The Literary Criterion*, Vol. 20, No. 4, 1985, p. 33.
10. Barbara Delinsky, "A Woman's Place," *Select Editions*, selected and edited by Reader's Digest (Australia: Reader's Digest Pty Ltd., 1998), p. 166.
11. Shashi Despande, *The Dark Holds No Terrors* (New Delhi: Penguin, rpt. 1990), p. 42.
12. Simone de Beauvior, *The Second Sex*, ed. & trans. H.M. Parshley (1953), (Harmondsworth: Penguin, 1983), p. 470.
13. Shashi Deshpande, *That Long Silence* (New Delhi: Penguin, rpt. 1984) p. 84.
14. Matthew Arnold, "Stanzas from the Grand Chartreuse," Poems, 1855.
15. Suman Kukreti, "Female Protagonists in Shashi Deshpande's Novels," ed. R.S. Pathak, *The Fiction of Shashi Deshpande*, (New Delhi: Creative, 1998), p. 195.
16. Anita Desai, *Cry the Peacock*. (New Delhi: Orient Paperbooks, 1980), p. 12.
17. Frank Kermode, "End," *Perspectives on Fiction* ed. James I. Calderwood and Harold E. Toliver (New York: O.U.P 1968), p. 332.
18. Malcolm Bradbury, "The Open Form the Novel and Reality," *Possibilities* (London: Oxford University Publication, 1973), p. 4
19. Robert M. Adams, *Strains of Discord, Studies in Literary Openness* (Ithaca, New York, 1958).
20. Adele King, "Shashi Deshpande: Portraits of an Indian Woman," *The New Indian Novel in English* ed. Viney Kirpal (New Delhi: Allied, 1990), p. 166.

4

Salman Rushdie's *Midnight's Children*: A Quest for Identity

Salman Rushdie, in *Midnight's Children*, has significantly made the vital choice of Indian history as a co-ordinate in his fictional art and has established himself as different from the other writers of the 'history through literature' bandwagon by covering a markedly vaster span of historical facts ranging from the pre-Independence Jallianwala Bagh incident of 1919 to the period of Emergency in 1977 and by adopting a strikingly variant mode of portrayal. The facts themselves have been mapped out by several novelists and historians *ad nauseam* but it is Rushdie's distinctive manner of fantasizing his depiction of historical reality that holds one in thrall. The introduction of the element of the magical and the supernatural has lent the work a dimension that makes it characteristically Rushdie's own for he has his special way of concocting a blend of art and life. Thus, it is in the specific orientation given to facts that his genius lies. By his own admission, it is in *Midnight's Children* that he finds his "true voice."[1]

An in-depth study of *Midnight's Children* reveals three major aspects of Rushdie's characteristic use of history in his novel, namely, (1) the interweaving of autobiography and narrative which clearly shows that the tale is meant to be a yarn spun out of imagination, a blend of truth and fiction; (2) the conspicuous breach of chronology evident from the frequent forward or backward shift in time that makes it difficult to trace the proper sequence of events in the life of the protagonist; and (3) the search for identity and the meaning of life. It is to this search for identity and the desire to "connect" on the part of the protagonist that I will delimit myself here so as to be able to arrive at a narrowing down of focus in order to achieve a clear understanding of the masked purport of the novelist. The quest for identity here is not, however, merely that of the narrator-protagonist, Saleem Sinai, but also that of Padma, a persistent hint of whose self-assertiveness we are conscious of in the novel all through.

Thomas Wolfe, an American dramatist and novelist, begins his first novel, *Look Homeward Angel* (1929), which is largely autobiographical, with the words:

> Each of us is all the sums he has not counted: subtract us into nakedness and night again and you shall see begin in Crete four thousand years ago the love that ended yesterday in Texas.

Each one, despite his individuality, has roots to which he belongs and any severing of these roots leads to a threat of alienation and isolation. One needs intermittently to reaffirm one's sense of "belonging" somewhere and this is often the point from which a literary artist takes off.

The Collins Cobuild English Language Dictionary clearly shows the word "identity" as denoting two related but different meanings, (1) the individuality of a person which makes him *different* from everyone else, and (2) all the qualities, beliefs and ideas which make one feel that one belongs to a particular group of people and is *similar* to them. These two divergent implications, paradoxically enough, converge in the literary artist, who on the one hand, wishes to bring into relief his exceptional character, and on the other, longs for identification with the people he feels he belongs to.

"Identity," in the literary context, refers to the process of creative self-realization in the course of which the artist discovers himself. The artist's struggle for definition conditions and shapes his creative conscience and remains the core of his creative effort. The literary artist is a man speaking to other men, generally, more responsible than others, unwilling to surrender his own identity and reluctant to allow the uniqueness of his personal vision to be subsumed by the received formulae of communication. And yet, for a creative artist to be able to explore the purpose of life and the meaning of experience, re-establishing his identity with others and communicating with them alone make his bid for definition a valid one and the resistance he encounters in it may be a test of creative strength—or even a promise of it.

Any writer of consequence, though professedly objective in his depiction of life and reality, is only relatively so, for the self in the artist is irrepressible and insidiously winds its way through into the creation. A writer, then, is simultaneously, objective and subjective, and is involved in a somewhat paradoxical exercise: an intellectually creative balancing act in which invention and creativity which are largely subjective and judgement which is essentially expected to be objective, co-ordinate to achieve and preserve equilibrium in his endeavour to make sense of experience.

Clearly then, all art, in the ultimate analysis is an expression of man's urge for self creation. An autobiographical work, however, is obviously more inclined towards a projection of the self. "Autobiography," literally translated from Greek, is "self-life-writing." It is an author's attempt to "reconstruct the self," an attempt at making sense of his own life and understanding its purpose and its motivations.

Salman Rushdie, a man of varied sensibility, caught between the cross-currents of the individual and the historical, the personal and the national, and, what Yeats in his poem, "Under Ben Bulben" calls "the two eternities of soul and race," set the trend for autobiographical writing in modern Indian English fiction with his *Midnight's Children* which won him the Booker Prize in 1981. The novel, however, as pointed out before, is an autobiographical work with a difference—it offers a peculiar blend of the factual and the fantastic which characterizes the microcosmic reality of the novel and provides for the varied nuances and contours of individual experience. It demonstrates the author's firm conviction that "it is entirely possible for a novel to be autobiographical and also to be completely fictional. That's what my book is,"[2] says Rushdie. Rushdie undoubtedly found his voice with *Midnight's Children* and the world of the book has a truth of its own, a truth with which he is armed to deal seriously with life as he sees it.

Rushdie's use of the fantastic as a mode of reality is witnessed in his very first work, *Grimus*, in which sheer inventiveness and a sense of the comic pervade the entire work—language, character and situation, all. His use of dream, myth and fantasy to reveal his particular kind of reality in which he sees the individual in relation to the larger historical forces that shape society around him is seen in the subsequent *Midnight's Children*, *Shame*, as well as in the non-fictional *The Jaguar Smile* which is a kind of travelogue based on the Nicaraguan situation of a society recovering from a wave of violence and revolution, a situation paralleled to the one in his own life. "I was myself" says he, "the child of a successful revolt against a great power, my consciousness the product of the triumph of the Indian revolution."[3] Later works, namely, the controversial *Satanic Verses*, *Imaginary Homelands, Haroun and the Sea of Stories*, *The Moor's Last Sight* and the latest *The Ground Beneath Her Feet* are all ample proof of the fecundity of Rushdie's genius, but with *The Satanic Verses* and *The Moor's Last Sigh* one cannot but admit that the novelty of Rushdie's form of a blend of fact and fiction had started wearing out.

However, *Midnight's Children* remains Rushdie's *magnum opus*, his singular achievement in which he appears as a recoverer of what actually happened during the period stretching from the pre-Independence Jallianwala Bagh incident of 1919 to the time of the Emergency in 1977 but what calls for attention is the markedly different mode of depiction that he has adopted in his presentation of history. The facts themselves are of little interest. What is significant is how Rushdie has fantasized his portrayal of historical reality to arrive at a personalization of history that becomes not a mere movement of forces or a sequence of events, but the thoughts and feelings of men. Thus the novel is both, an ingression and entry into the past and a coherent interpretation of that past from a particular individual stand point in the present.

Midnight's Children is clearly, then, a fusion of history, fantasy and autobiography. The novel's presentation of a vast span in the recent history of India is marked not by a strictly factual depiction but by an element of fantasy that enables the writer to convey the aspects of reality that have been painfully experienced by him but are incommunicable in the realistic mode. This experiential truth in the novel characterizes it as a form of sincere self-depiction which, according to what Sidonie Smith terms "the autobiographical contract,"[4] clearly determines the reminiscential and autobiographical nature of the work. Much of the power of the novel comes from the energy harnessed by the author to strike a harmonious balance between the contrary pulls of an autobiographical involvement and the distancing device of fantasy.

Midnight's Children is a literary response to a series of real life situations that have been cleverly fictionalized through allusions, disguised as well direct, to the country's recent as well as not so recent past. The novel has an epic sweep covering about six decades in the history of the Indian subcontinent and Rushdie has cleverly framed his own "literary aesthetic of truth-telling."[5]

At the fictional level, *Midnight's Children* depicts the events and experiences in the lives of three generations of the Sinai family. The account begins with their days in Srinagar and follows their passage through Amritsar, Agra and Bombay to Karachi from where Saleem alone returns hidden in the basket of Parvati, the witch, only to experience the tremors of the Emergency that had been clamped in India. At the semantic level, the novel is far more complex and has intriguing social and political connotations.

We will confine ourselves, here to the semantic reverberations of the novel and trace the protagonist's, as also the author's quest for identity and meaning in life. *Midnight's Children*, published in the post Emergency period much over thirty years after the attainment of freedom, does not indulge in any kind of speculation. It moves from the objective reality to the more comprehensible reality of the self, which is realizable only through fantasy. It does not indulge in ruminations regarding what freedom should have meant but did not come to mean. There is a sense of total alienation of the individual whose quest still continues, not for freedom now but for identity in a society, which presents the picture of a dream turned nightmare. After so many years of Independence, neither the country nor the individual has arrived anywhere; life is beset with estrangement and frustration and there seems to be little hope for the days to come. One has only to "eddy about" and wait to be "sucked into the annihilating whirlpool of the multitude" (p. 463) as the narrator of the novel puts it. The novel thus is not a meditation on the future but a registration of anger at the opportunity lost and anger at the self-alienation from the assumed roots in place and time, that is, in Independent India. The work is also an expression of perplexity at the question of identity becoming problematical both for the country and the unhappy individual who despite their parallel growth, like all parallel lines, never meet. This irreconcilable divide is also cause for anger. For Rushdie thirty-two years have been like a journey undertaken at the end of which he found that it was not that he had lost his way, but something of greater consequence, his identity. Thus began a fresh search for identity. What needs to be marked is that a quest for identity in a country like India is more socially oriented than personal. Unlike that in the West, the individual identity is inseparably intertwined with the identity of the nation. This explains, perhaps, the consistent parallel drawn in *Midnight's Children* between the life of the narrator-protagonist, Saleem, and that of the nation. Rushdie, clearly represented by Saleem, makes of his childhood memories a powerful creative force and in writing about his own life and that of the nation chooses the vantage point of the present to delve deep into the past, which, as he says in *Imaginary Homelands*, he had "some urge to reclaim."[6]

Here, mention must be made of the prominent and sustained metaphor used in the novel in relation to the similar lives of Saleem and the nation, as this metaphor, if rightly interpreted, provides a key to an understanding of the reality that it projects. This is the metaphor of the "chutnification of history" (p. 459), that is, the pickling of time. The "pickles' version of history" (p. 460) as Rushdie calls it in the novel may be "too strong" for some and their smell "overpowering" (p. 461) for others but it preserves time and experience—private as well as public—and makes them available to the generations to come.

"Chutnification"—Rushdie's term for his characteristic fictional mode of depicting a mixture of truth and fiction—may be seen as an attempt to blend and mix ideas and events, individual and public life in such a way as to give life a sense of continuity in the future that he has a longing for, and that he probably feared lost on the memorable midnight. This explains his reference to his son and his son's son carrying on the process begun by him. We normally look back for a sense of continuity but he has brought the past into the present in order to extend his desire for a sense of continuity into the future. For him the past is not over but continues to make itself felt through its impact. So, it becomes a function of his life in the present. No wonder, the boundaries are blurred not only between past and present but also between fact and fiction, imagination and reality. Rushdie dreams his desire into reality—the reality which consists of his life and his country's. The desire for immortality as well as that for continuity are parallel desires, both of which Rushdie cherishes and expresses forcefully. This promptly brings to mind Carlos Fuentes' assertion:

> It is important to realize that we remember in the present, that memory is a celebration of the present. It is in the present that we remember and we desire which are two things that come together in writing—memory and yearning. Wanting. Trying to identify with something.[7]

Midnight's Children, like the later *The Satanic Verses*, is written from what Rushdie himself calls "the experience of uprooting"[8] that comes from the migrant condition. In an interview by the B.B.C. in 1988 Rushdie refers to the "aspects of personal history"[9] contained in *Midnight's Children.* "A man from too many places"[10] he calls himself. Born in India and living in Britain, he is "a product of biethnicity"[11] which, according to Suryanarayana Murti is "the creative matrix of his fiction."[12]

That Rushdie's migrant condition is the creative matrix of his fictional work is borne out by the author's own statement in the title essay of *Imaginary Homelands*, which refers to the expatriate writer's need to imaginatively reconstruct his roots. For the immigrant angst and solicitude he recommends an antidote of "mingle and mix."[13] He writes, "Our identity is at once plural and partial. Sometimes we feel that we straddle two cultures; at other times, that we fall between two stools. But, however ambiguous and shifting this ground may be, it is not an infertile territory for a writer to occupy."[14] It breeds, perhaps a healthy eclecticism such as Rushdie's own.

Dr. Alistair Niven, referring to Rushdie and all those Indian writers who live in England but write about their own subcontinent, describes what they would term "detachment" in their works as actually "a deracinated loss of identity."[15] "[...] it is hard to see where they belong"[16] says he. Rushdie himself confirms this "sense of deracination"[17] experienced by him while studying at Rugby School, where racial prejudice was so strong that for the first time he realized that he belonged to "a race." "Suddenly in England I became an Indian,"[18] says the author. The irony, however, lay in the fact that while in England he felt like an alien, in India his family felt discriminated against and moved to Pakistan. But even that move failed. So when he settled down in England he began to search his roots, and *Midnight's Children* became the medium of the quest of one who could never really "belong" anywhere.

Ashutosh Banerjee in his article, "Narrative Technique in *Midnight's Children*," calls Saleem, the central character in the novel, "Rushdie's fictional alter ego."[19] Saleem, having been born at the precise moment at which India attained her Independence, establishes a kinship with his creator in that the latter, too, was born about that time, that is two months before that day of Indian Independence, in June 1947, in Bombay.

Rushdie deliberately fictionalizes his date of birth in his novel for narrative purposes, for it is the time of Saleem's birth that subjects him to a more difficult fate by giving his identity a larger dimension. It is as "midnight's child" born on August 15, 1947 that Saleem is "mysteriously handcuffed to history" (p. 9). He becomes, as M.K. Naik observes, conscious of his "larger identity."[20] rather early in life. Naik draws attention to "the protagonist's identity crisis"[21] and comes to the conclusion that *Midnight's Children*:

> illustrates the permanent plight of individual identity in the hostile modern world which makes it impossible for anyone to remain an island but compels everyone to be part of a continent, with the result that the individual is inevitably handcuffed to history.[22]

Thus, the central theme of the novel, according to Naik, is the fate of individual identity is a hostile world, which causes it to suffer fragmentation and sterility.

Saleem is the central consciousness in the novel whose ordeals and tribulations are closely followed and analyzed. He is an extremely sensitive and self-conscious narrator (like his creator), and, inspite of all other weaknesses, is confident of his competence as a story-teller. He knows that Padma, who represents the reader-response to the narrative will be disarmed by his narration. Yet she is fully aware of the "constructedness"[23] of Saleem's narration and regards his autobiography as fiction. Thus Saleem, like his maker, is, as Nancy E. Batty avers "creator rather than recorder of his own history"[24] and this history is more tentative than unalterable or final because it deals in "broken mirrors, some of whose fragments have been irretrievably lost"[25] and thus, the gaps in memory have to be filled up by the imagination.

Despite the tentative nature of the narrative that Saleem weaves out of his fractured human perception, he never, during the course of the narrative, abandons his pursuit of the meaning of life for in the absence of import and direction, identity and existence have no substance. Meaning, he knows, as Rushdie himself does, "is a shaky edifice that we build out of scraps, dogmas, childhood injuries, newspaper articles, chance remarks, people you love, people you hate, old films, small victories."[26]

Saleem is conscious of the whirling speed with which time is passing and in his search for identity and "meaning" he races against time which is "running out" (p. 9). He never gives up the quest for meaning, though, he has to maintain all along, a certain degree of caution, for, in his desire to place himself in a central role, he is inclined to misrepresent things and this apprehension is revealed in his protagonist's self-analysis later in the novel:

> Am I so far gone in my desperate need for meaning, that I'm prepared to distort everything to rewrite the whole history of my times purely to place myself in a central role? Today, in my confusion I can't judge. I'll have to leave it to others [...]." (p. 166)

But soon, "after years of yearning for importance" (p. 350) Saleem, the Buddha, who had abandoned consciousness and deliberately severed himself from history, comes to the realization that any determination to espouse a historical role is futile for every individual is nothing but a drop in the river of human life, and yet, human life is what it is merely because of the presence of that one drop and many other such drops:

> Who, what am I? My answer: I am the sum total of everything that went before me, of all I have been seen done, of everything done to me, I am everyone, everything of whose being-in-the-world affected was affected by mine. I am anything that happens after I have gone which would not have happened if I had not come. Nor am I particularly exceptional in this matter; each 'I,' every one of the now—six hundred million—plus of us, contains a similar multitude. I report for the last time, to understand me, you will have to swallow a world." (p. 383)

Thus having come full circle and returning to the premise from which we started, each individual can claim an identity of his own, and yet, he has to submit to a final merger with the milling myriads who make their respective contributions and then pass into anonymity leaving behind invigorated roots for posterity to belong to.

Saleem, like his creator, believes firmly in the ultimate merging in of the individual with the multitudes so that he is no longer a separate entity but an inseparable part of the "many." This faith is harboured with unflagging conviction from the first to the last page of the novel. In the beginning Saleem tells us:

> I have been a swallower of lives; and to know me, just the one of me, you'll have to swallow the lot as well. Consumed multitudes are jostling and shoving inside me, [...]" (p. 9).

At the end, too, his faith remains unchanged and he reaffirms his belief. "[...] I have been so many too-many persons" (p. 463).

Attributing Rushdie's protagonist's problems of identity to the writer himself, one would be inclined to think that throughout the novel Rushdie is preoccupied with a search for identity. There is, I feel, justification enough for this though Rushdie himself would have us believe that he is engaged in no such quest: "I know who I am" says he, in an interview published in the *Northern India Patrika*, "and I don't have a sense of having an identity crisis. But people keep telling me I should."[27]

But, an assertion is no proof and the chinks in the armour soon begin to show. We cannot always take the writer's word as the ultimate authority for he may be deliberately misleading us in our attempt at interpretation, or he may himself be unconsciously trying to establish his identity. This will become clear presently. Such close parallels and correspondences between the life of the protagonist and that of the nation can be drawn only by one who himself is deeply involved in matters relating to the community of people to which he belongs, and thus finds it difficult to maintain distance and objectivity in his art inspite of every distancing device adopted. Saleem, clearly filters for us the author's own poignant experiences which could be represented or re-enacted better in Rushdie's modernistic device of fantasizing mixed with first person narrative than in a simple narration of the realistic novel type. However, as Rushdie himself draws our attention to it, a point of caution to be marked here is that "the point of view of the narrator is not entirely that of the author,"[28] and hence, a total identification of the two may lead to errors of interpretation and judgement.

The central query in *Midnight's Children*, then, is: what is the compulsion—aesthetic or personal—that makes the novelist assiduously weave such a complex web of parallels between the life of the protagonist (who, as said before, may very well be identified with the novelist himself) and, that of the nation? Could it be the artist's own way of reconstructing meaning out of the chaos of the times, of discovering his identity in the context of a large perspective? Inspite of the novelist's repeated denial one has little doubt that the work is a verbalization of the writer's quest for identity, his desire to "belong" somewhere and to discover where he belongs, an expression of his urge to know how he came to be what he is and how he came to be where he is. To Keats, "what the imagination seizes as beauty must be truth"; to Rushdie, what the fancy apprehends as content must be the meaningful truth. The apparently fanciful images and constructs must merge into a significant whole. Thus, what Rushdie embarks upon in this novel is an exploration of his life, which he identifies with the life of the state, and more specifically, with the life of the particular community to which he belongs, namely, the Indian Muslims, the word 'Indian' here having greater import and significance for him than the latter word for he has always been full of what he calls "Bombayness" in *Midnight's Children* and "the India-idea" elsewhere. Multiplicity, plurality, incompatible realities and different faiths—this is what modern India is all about and Rushdie is very much a product of it—what he needs is reassurance and understanding and a re-acquaintance with Bombay, his "lost city."[29]

Initially, Padma, categorically meant to be a conceptual "woman" in the novel, is not defined as a subject in her own right but merely as a being or a presence that has bearing on either the real or the fantasized life of Saleem. There is little cognizance taken of the actuality of her life-situation and the humiliations and traumas that she is made to endure. Human experience, for centuries, has been identified with masculine encounters and exposures alone and consequently, the image of humanity projected has always been deficient and partial. A feministically read text can help one acquire a better understanding of the woman condition and thereby devise a course of action for confronting the male strategies of oppression. *Midnight's Children*, read from the feministic point of view, underscores the significant communication that Padma with her determination and persistence succeeds in demolishing the traditional concept of woman as a mere sex-object and affirms the dignity rightfully hers in the context of familial and extended social relationships.

The strong wave of feminism that swept the world in the 1960s and 1970s can clearly be discerned in the oblique but meaningful reflections and pronouncements that Rushdie's protagonist, Saleem, makes in *Midnight's Children*. The female quest for identity and self-assertiveness is thus represented in the novel by Padma whom Nancy Batty calls "the index for reader-response to the framed narrative."[30] Uma Parameswaram, too, emphasizes the centrality of Padma in the narrative in pointing out that the latter "is many things within the novel and certainly deserves a full-length study."[31] Among the "many things" that Padma stands for, the robust vein of pulsating feminism is, perhaps, the most strident and cannot in any way be repressed into conformity.

The conventional distribution of social and sexual roles in Indian society clearly highlights man as ambitious and dynamic and woman as domesticated quite like the Victorian concept of "man for the field and woman for the hearth."[32] Padma, primarily a woman, is a victim of male dominance and there are flagrant derogatory comments about her. Saleem, with whom she is soulfully in love, has no compunction and reservations about calling her "a bitch-in-the-manger" (p. 24). This damaging insinuation negates all her positive qualities and she is completely devalued. Reductive and deprecatory details are piled up one after another to give her nothing more than a comic identity. She is described as "thick of waist" (p. 24) and "somewhat hairy of forearm" (p. 24). Saleem, to assert his dominance over her, tries "to educate her" (p. 38) as he puts it, but she is good only as an audience, as a receiver and Saleem is the giver. He, though himself incapable of giving Padma any emotional security and physical and sexual fulfilment, gives the impression of her being a mere bundle of sexual urges.

Kate Millett in her work, *Sexual Politics*, in her discussion with regard to Henry Miller's *Sexus*, writes of a male contention of ascendancy over a submissive and not so intelligent female and refers to it as "a case of sexual politics at the fundamental level of copulation."[33] Padma's is a similar case where the sexist bias in the novel operates against her. Saleem, setting himself as the human benchmark allows her only the status of the comic and her simplicity, illiteracy and ignorance are made sources of fun and laughter. She is taken too much for granted and the labours she performs, though indispensable, are completely devalued. A reading of the novel convinces one that Padma is an individual of ethical principles as against Saleem who has been visiting whores. Charu Verma, in her feminist analysis of *Midnight's Children* gives full credit to Padma for being "ready to accept his inadequacies without condescension."[34]

Padma has no active role to play in the novel and figures only with respect to the narrational aspect of Saleem's tale and in this, too, she is ignored at moments of critical resolutions like when, at the very start, he decides to begin the narrative, and when, later in the narrative in Chapter 29, he is hesitant to come out with revealing facts about the Emergency period. At all such moments he dismisses her as irrelevant and decides that she "must take a back seat" (p. 385). Padma, thus, is given no independent identity and is often discarded as dung. Saleem does not even feel the need to place her in time or space and treats her as existing almost in a vacuum.

Padma then, is persistently marginalized in the novel. She is despised, used, exploited and turned into a commodity. Though Saleem needs her desperately during her absence, as a man he hates to acknowledge his need. He gives her no credit for the discrimination and intelligence she displays. As a surrogate of the reader he considers her to be completely taken in by his narration—"No doubt about it; my story has her by the throat," (p. 38) says he. He, however, is sadly mistaken for

Padma as "narratee" does offer attention in exchange for information but seems well aware of the fabrication and "constructedness" of Saleem's narration as she can seldom comprehend any connection between Saleem's stories and his so-called "real" existence. "There is reason to believe," says Nancy Batty, "that even Saleem's explicit audience, Padma, regards Saleem's autobiography as a fiction."[35] The disbelief that Padma shows in Saleem's narrative is clearly indicated in the latter's observation of her "jutting a careless hip in my general direction." "Her shrug," says he "cuts me off" (p. 38). But Padma remains unaffected and nonchalantly remarks, "To me it's a crazy way of telling your story" (p. 38). Everything he tells her of his past is dismissed as "just so much fancy talk" (p. 444).

Padma, surely, is learning to assert herself. She challenges and resents the break in chronology in Saleem's story and advocates what the latter himself calls "what happened-nextism" Padma now "complains" against, "bullies" and pressurizes Saleem into doing things her way; she even takes the initiative in trying to arouse him to make love to her. Dieter Reimenschneider is sadly mistaken when he writes, "Salman Rushdie's *Midnight's Children* [...] is essentially concerned with man's quest for identity."[36] The novel is also majorly about Padma as a victim of male dominance who eventually rebels and protests against her marginalization in no uncertain terms.

This then is the story of Padma's rise from submission to assertion. Like a true Indian woman, in the beginning, she stoically braves all the humiliation meted out to her but in the process "her majestically unshakeable resolve" (p. 444) and her "powerful as oil" (p. 443) determination propel her into a proposal of marriage to Saleem who is completely overpowered. He knows fully well that she will not take 'no' for an answer and thus surrenders to her now superior will. This is Padma's achievement.

References

1. Anon, "Raj Reversal" (Cover Story), *Sunday*, Dec. 4-10, 1988, p. 30.

2. Salman Rushdie, "*Midnight's Children*: Memory's Recesses," *Northern Indian Patrika*, January 16, 1983, p. 6.
3. Cited in "Interpreting Reality," *The Hindustan Times*, February 22, 1987, p. 8.
4. Sidonie Smith, "Construing Truths in Lying Mouths: Truth Telling in Women's Autobiography," *Studies in the Literary Imagination*, Vol. XXIII, No. 2, Fall, 1990.
5. David Lodge, "The Novelist at the Crossroads," *The Novel Today*, ed. Malcolm Bradbury (Great Britain: Fontana, 1977), p. 85.
6. Salman Rushdie, *Imaginary Homelands* (London: Granta Books, 1991), p. 10.
7. Carlos Fuentes, "Modern Literature Conference: The Politics of Experience," *The Centennial Review*, Vol. XXX, No. 2, Spring, '86, p. 135.
8. Salman Rushdie, "Not Guilty!," *Sunday*, February 18-24, 1990, p. 27.
9. Salman Rushdie, Interview, *B.B.C.*, September 2, 1988.
10. *Ibid.*
11. V.K. Suryanarayan Murti, "Secular Fantasy: Salman Rushdie's Fiction," *Kohinoor in the Crown: Critical Studies in Indian English Literature* (New Delhi: Sterling Publishers, 1987), p. 71.
12. *Ibid.*
13. Tarun J. Tejpal, "Essays in Criticism," Book review of 'Imaginary Homelands' by Salman Rushdie, *India Today.*
14. Salman Rushdie, "Imaginary Homelands," *Imaginary Homelands.*
15. Dr. Alistair Niven, "Indian Writing in English: Past and Present," Sahitya Akademi International Seminar on *Indian Literature in English Translation*, February 25-28, 1986.
16. *Ibid.*
17. Cited in Bryan Appleyard, "Portrait of the Novelist as a Hot Property," *The Sunday Times Magazine*, September 11, 1988, p. 31.
18. *Ibid.*, p. 28.
19. Ashutosh Banerjee, "Narrative Technique in 'Midnight's Children,'" *Three Contemporary Novelists*, ed. R.K. Dhawan, (New Delhi: Classical Publishing Company, 1985), p. 196.
20. M.K. Naik, "A Life of Fragments: The Fate of Identity in 'Midnight's Children,'" *Studies in Indian English Literature* (New Delhi: Sterling Publishers, 1987), p. 51.
21. *Ibid.*, p. 52.

22. *Ibid.*, p. 54.
23. Gerard Genette, *Narrative Discourse: An Essay in Method*, 1972 trans. Jane E. Lewin (New York: Cornell Press, 1980). Genette, in the discourse, implies the "constructedness" of all narrative.
24. Nancy E. Batty, "The Art of Suspense: Rushdie's 1001 (Mid-) Nights," *Ariel*, Vol. 18, No. 3, July, 1987, p. 59.
25. Salman Rushdie, "'Midnight's Children': Memory's Recesses," *Northern India Patrika*, January 16, 1983, p. 3.
26. *Ibid.*
27. *Ibid.*
28. Salman Rushdie, *Imaginary Homelands*, p. 16.
29. *Ibid.*, p. 9.
30. Nancy Batty, "The Art of Suspense: Rushdie's 1001 (Mid-) Nights," *Ariel*, p. 53.
31. Uma Parameswaram, "Salman Rushdie in Indo-English Literature," *Journal of Indian Writing in English*, 12 (July, 1984), p. 23.
32. Alfred Tennyson, "The Princess" (1847).
33. Kate Millett, *Sexual Politics* (London: Rupert Hart-Davis, 1969, rpt. 1971), p. 6.
34. Charu Verma, "Padma's Tragedy: A Feminist Deconstruction of Rushdie's *Midnight's Children*," *Feminism and Recent Fiction* ed. Sushila Singh (New Delhi: Prestige, 1991), p. 159.
35. Nancy Batty, op. cit.
36. Dieter Reimenschneider, "History and Individual in Anita Desai's *Clear Light of Day* and Salman Rushdie's *Midnight's Children*," *World Literature in English*, 23 (1984), p. 196.

5

Vikram Seth's *The Golden Gate*: Celebrating the Californian Way of Life

Despite the current fascination for and preoccupation with magic realism in Indian English fiction, a trend popularized by Salman Rushdie, there still flourishes alongside a vibrant school of social realism led by Vikram Seth for there is no gainsaying the fact that the novel is born of social and circumstantial reality that remains an eternal source of artistic inspiration. Vikram Seth's *A Suitable Boy* (1993), published almost twelve years after Rushdie's *Midnight's Children*, drew almost as much attention on its publication as the latter did.

Vikram Seth's first work of fiction, a novel in verse, was *The Golden Gate* (1986), which is set entirely in California. His second novel, *A Suitable Boy* (1993), this time a work of prose, is conceived as an imaginative endeavour of large dimensions in the manner of Tolstoy's *War and Peace* and George Eliot's *Middlemarch*. As indicated by the title, the action of the novel revolves around the search for a suitable match for her daughter by Mrs. Rupa Mehra, a middle-aged lady markedly influenced by prevalent societal attitudes. What is of greater interest, however, is the novelist's depiction of the social scene in India in the decade after Independence. The novel running into about thirteen hundred pages has "a surprisingly well ordered structure."[1]

Seth's next novel, *An Equal Music* (1999), is a high-spirited venture in which he experiments boldly by punctuating the narrative with frequent discussions of the technical aspects of Western music. The discussions, however, often have a cloying effect in that they are incomprehensible to the common reader who is not acquainted with the technicalities of a maestro's art. The story is set entirely in the West, and all the characters are European as they were in *The Golden Gate*. The title, *An Equal Music*, is derived from a poem of Donne. Music, here, is the food of love and it plays a significant role in a narrative of love twice lost.

Seth is currently busy completing his work, *Two Lives*, categorized as "a history-cum-fiction." The protagonist of this novel is born in 1908 and lives in India till he is twenty-three years old and then leaves for Germany to study medicine. Several relatives of Seth figure in this semi-biographical work of fiction.

In the last decade or so, the immigrant or diasporic novel of which Vikram Seth is an exponent has emerged as a vocal sub-class of Indian English fiction. A major part of this fiction is now increasingly portraying the migrant experience of Indians, primarily in the United States or in Britain. The new diasporic writers do not focus on the trauma of displacement and dislocation. The New World not only offers attractive professional lures and financial betterment but also advocates an acceptance of and a merger with the new milieu. Barriers in adaptation, a longing for home, inability to relate to life in India owing to long absence, a schizophrenic feeling of being cursed with a dual identity—Indian and Western, and an enervating lack of a sense of belonging somewhere remain persistent features of the psycho-cultural expanse that the Indian immigrant inhabits. Seth, however, is different from other diasporic writers in that these predominant themes are not central to his work. In his fiction, Seth drains the texts of ethnic peoples and immigrant problems. His only novel located specifically in his native-land is *A Suitable Boy*, which deals with India of the 1950s. Generally, in his work, Seth does not address issues born of a conflict of cultures. In fact, he nurses the pleasure of having experienced a multiplicity of homes and is equally comfortable in each of the four vastly different geographical and cultural contexts that he has been a part of—Indian, English, Chinese and American. He is, as Mala Pandurang establishes, a man of multiple locations and a multivalent identity.[2]

Vikram Seth as a creative writer emerged as a marvel nonpareil in subliminal advertising and in the portrayal of the subconscious. Having reportedly received an unbelievable advance of two crores of rupees from his publisher, he became a name overnight. As a critic jocularly put it, with the fabulous amount forwarded to him "Vikram became a Seth." Critics of a varied standing including C.D. Narasimhaiah[3] have assessed *The Golden Gate* as a work highly over-estimated merely because of the reviewers' penchant for novelty, but the novel certainly cannot be dismissed as a work without a learning experience.

Vikram Seth is often held accountable for not having any identifiable "Indian" features in his work. He is censured by C.D. Narasimhaiah for being deficient in the highly desired "Indianness of spirit"[4] that a common reader looks for in the literary pursuits of Indian English writers. Narasimhaiah takes a dim view of what he believes Seth proposed to do and did in *The Golden Gate:*

> At a time when the American public was in a state of despondency, Vikram Seth, then living in America, should have felt called up to remind them by way of reinforcement as was expected of a well-bred Indian [yet] [...] he chose to commend to the American youth in his bizarre book, *The Golden Gate*, a very un-Indian piece of advice: 'not to look for meaning in life,' but, in effect, learn to do what others did.[5]

Vilas Sarang, however, absolves Seth of this charge of "un-Indianness" and does not demur at the idea of accepting the latter as an Indian poet despite his choice of writing about

Californians and their way of life. He emphatically says that Seth has no:

> neurotic anxiety about being Indian [...] nor does he make any self-conscious attempts to underscore a national, or sectarian allegiance.[6]

Though the novel in verse is as old as Kshemendra's *Padyakadambari* and *Lavanyavati* written in India in the eleventh century, the novel is certainly a relatively new form in English and the novel in verse is assuredly a novelty. Seth, in writing *The Golden Gate* was professionally inspired by Pushkin's *Eugene Onegin*, which he read in its English translation.

There were a couple of translations of Pushkin's *Eugene Onegin* from Russian to English that were available to Seth for comparison and study. They fired the writer's imagination and motivated him to write *The Golden Gate* which is set in San Francisco of the 1980s and is written entirely in the sonnet form when most of contemporary poetry is being formulated in free verse. The novel comprises 594 sonnets in iambic tetrameter and each sonnet follows the fourteen-line stanza pattern of Eugene Onegin, the rhyming scheme being ababccdd effegg. So, having made the choice of his medium with discrimination and prudence all other things fell into place unerringly:

> the idea of the novel, the actual structure, the classical structure of the stanzas, and the idea of writing about California and the life there.[7]

The novel is divided into thirteen chapters and is neatly balanced in its presentation of the episodes that are carefully conceived segments of the essential communication of the work. The span of the tale covering a period from the month of September to that of November next is a little over a year and the passage of time is recorded in terms of depictions of the passing seasons typical of the Californian Bay area. The brisk and unimpeded flow of the narrative and the considered use of the present tense lend a compelling sense of immediacy to the novel. The work, however, is not merely about tie-ups and relationships. It is not just a tale about a 'John' or a 'Janet' in terms of love, reunion and deprivation. Ashok Jha identifies the author's central ground as something far more consequential and comprehensive. Seth, he asserts, "dramatizes existential anguish within the framework of a narrative in verse."[8] and offers the alternative of inviolable family bonds and communal solidarity to confront loneliness and hyper-individualism. One must not fail to note here that in this oblique option offered, Seth is Indian to the core and would have us fall back upon the family emotional sap reserve to revive ourselves and emerge out of despondency and sorrow.

In *The Golden Gate* Seth takes pains to portray an intimate understanding and grasp of the Californian way of life. Leslie reports that:

> [...] it was not his detachment but rather his love of California that was the most valuable to him in writing the book [...]. One can't come with a cold and objective eye from outside and then write with affection about a place. One must have lived years in that place and not just observed for years.[9]

In Seth's depiction of California there is a multitude of details that pass from the apparently insignificant to the relatively graver issues such as the sexual mores prevalent in the society. Housewarming parties, wine-making picnics and week-end excursions represent regular social activities of the people of the place. Seth's Californian characters also share a special kind of relationship with their pets, which include a Siamese cat called Charlemagne and an iguana called Schwarzenegger. The favourite pastimes of youngsters include their fascination for star wars, art exhibitions, classical music and renditions of a rock band called *Liquid Sheep*. Seth, to project his desired identity as a Californian, uses as many culture-specific signifiers as are available to him so as to convince the reader that he is an insider. As observed by Leslie, again, he refers to details about California "that natives sometimes overlook because of excessive familiarity."[10]

When interviewed by Bobb and Digirolamo in 1986 Seth admitted that the icons of pop culture and the idols of the world of advertisements that he intersperses his narrative with, may not be accessible to the Indian reader for whom the entire scenario stands far removed from the actual life conditions that prevail. Seth, then, had unhesitatingly stated that:

> the problem of search for meaning in the midst of plenty is not one that people have in the Third World. The main problem is to just make ends meet.[11]

Today, however, after almost two decades of the publication of *The Golden Gate* things are very different. The policy of economic liberalisation and the consequent entry of multinationals into the corporate life of the Indians as well as the growing upward mobility of young professionals in India has led to fast changing life-styles among the middle-class Indians themselves and their horizon of awareness has widened inconceivably.

There are five principal protagonists in the novel who interact with each other at one or more planes. Each of these characters is defined, as has been discriminatingly marked by a particular critic, "within the parameters of profession, personal ethics, eccentricities, family and social connections."[12]

John Brown is a twenty-six year old graduate who is a successful but extremely lonely computer executive in a computer and electronics industry in the Silicon Valley. A dedicated worker, his area of interest is nuclear research. Seth offers us glimpses of John's childhood and elicits from the reader an empathetic understanding of the deprivations suffered by the latter. His mother's love he had never been fortunate enough to enjoy.

Janet Hawakaya, the only character in the novel carrying with her traces of the "ethnic," is a girl of Japanese descent. Earlier John's girl friend, Janet becomes now his confidante and subsequently his beloved once again. The artistically inclined Janet thus changes her positional stance from ex-girl friend to confidante to beloved. Essentially a sensitive sculptor, Janet is also a drummer in the punk band, *Liquid Sheep*. As a friend she tries to recondition John's incommodious mind and constricted attitudes. It is Janet who gives the matrimonial insert for John in the newspapers.

Liz Dorati, who responds to John's matrimonial insert, is a twenty-seven year old Law School attorney. Coming from a family of Italian immigrant wine-growers, she impresses John with her hand-written reply to the matrimonial advertisement. John and Liz share a brief relationship that is soon destroyed by personal biases, politics and Charlemagne, the latter's pet cat. Invited to a protest meeting organized by anti-nuclear presentations, Liz speaks vehemently against nuclear bombs.

Phil, twenty-eight years old, is John's former room-mate from Berkeley. Once a nuclear engineer in Datatronics, he opts out of the mainstream to devote himself to the anti-nuclear movement. He is a Jew and has a six-year old son by his now divorced wife, Claire, whose Protestant family had never really approved of Phil.

Twenty-three year old *Ed Dorati* is caught in a bind between his religious duties and his homosexual inclinations. He is in a relationship with Phil but pulls away from it because of a sense of guilt engendered by his Catholic upbringing.

The characters in *The Golden Gate*—John, Janet, Liz, Phil, Claire, Ed, Sue and the cats, Liz's Charlemagne the Great and Janet's Cuff and Link, the less worthy representatives of the feline fraternity as also Phil's Iguana named after Mr. Universe, Arnold Schwarzenegger—all pale in significance before California itself, symbolized by the Golden Gate Bridge, which connects individuals and is a link between geographical areas as well. Like Hardy's Egdon Heath in *The Return of the Native* California here is the overawing presence against which the whole human drama is enacted. Thus *The Golden Gate* is, as S. Ramaswamy puts it, "a Californian novel in the best sense of the term."[13]

The fact that *The Golden Gate* is written in altogether five hundred and ninety-four sonnets has made it a technical feat. Rowena Hill, in her paper on this verse novel subtitled, "A Quick Look,"[14] has analyzed the novel's structure in terms of the 'Sonata Form,' keeping firmly entrenched in mind that the real protagonist of the novel is California, the towering C-Major, to borrow a technical expression from Western classical music.

A unique novel like *The Golden Gate* cannot be analyzed with regard to the traditional concepts of plot, characterization, dialogue, style etc.; it deserves, according to Rowena Hill, an unconventional treatment like the interdisciplinary approach taken up in her article. The idea, perhaps, came from Seth's various references to Western classical music in his novel—there are four references to Mozart (pp. 40, 67, 68, 149), four to Bach (pp. 62, 76, 82, 180), four to Brahms (pp. 65, 69, 71, 210), three to Shonberg (pp. 67, 68, 70) and one to Vivaldi (p. 73). Discussions on these composers are not incidental but correlated to the prevailing moods of the characters in the particular scenes depicted. For example, when Phil meditates on his separation from his wife, Claire, he indulges fondly in memories of his early days with her in terms relating to music:

> Sometimes we would light a fire
> I at the keyboard, and you'd sing
> Like the old days in the Bach choir
> Where we first met. (p. 62)

In the ultimate analysis, however, despite the graphic descriptions of the pivotal characters and the variedly different modes of their depiction, California remains, unmistakably, the chief protagonist of the novel. The description of San Francisco in the introductory stanzas establishes firmly the locale of the fictional work and offers a picture of California sketched with amazing verisimilitude. The entire far-west Pacific panorama comprising the Golden Gate Bridge, the Golden Gate Park, and in fact, the entire "Golden State" of California, is the central character in the novel just as Dublin is in the title role in James Joyce's *Ulysses*. "The mystery of San Francisco's restless history" (p. 5), as Seth puts it, is explored and the identity of the place established. Every nuance of life in San Francisco is adeptly conveyed in the minimum of words and the essential sense of liberation and joy which is part of the experience of living in this city unerringly communicated: "The unfettered city/

Resounds with hedonistic glee" (p. 6). The Berkeley campus and the Silicon Valley are integral to the place. The Chinese restaurant with the waiter "muttering in Cantonese" (p. 22) is as much a part of San Francisco as is the freeway that defines it—the freeway on which

> Above the rush-hour droves, commuting
> Bumper to bumper horns are hooting. (p. 29)

and people in a tearing hurry are driving at breakneck speed giving "no quarter, grace or leeway/to lesser cars within the law" (p. 28).

With the stage set in California, Seth introduces in *The Golden Gate* the theme of loneliness. John, Janet, Phil and Ed are all "lonely." John is depicted as "lonely" in the very first sonnet of the book:

> A linkless node, no spouse or sibling
> No children, John wanders alone. (p. 106)

Elsewhere, Janet remarks "It's sad to see you look so lonely" (p. 21). Even the newspaper matrimonial insert framed by Janet for inviting a suitable match for John is significant:

> Young handsome yuppie, 26
> Straight, forward, sociable, but lonely,
> Cannot believe that he's the only
> Well-rounded and well-meaning square
> Lusting for love. (p. 25)

So, in Seth's San Francisco there are these winsome but "lonely" youngsters "lusting for love" (p. 25). Janet is forlorn but like many others in California she is preoccupied with professional pursuits to the point of being what Seth terms "workoholic." Phil is lonely because his wife, Claire, has left him and he seeks first the companionship of Ed in a homosexual relationship and then turns "normal" to marry Liz. All this action takes place in California which fascinates all and sundry. Ed, too, is enchanted by the city:

> Subdued and silent he surveys it—
> The loveliest city in the world.
> No veiling words suffice to praise it

[...] Even tonight as Ed, alone,
Makes out Marina, plaza, tower,
Fort Point, Presidio—he feels
A benediction as it steals
Over his heart with its still power. (p. 104)

John, who is initially introduced as "lonely" is still "lonely" at the end of the novel after having lost Janet to the inexorable clutches of death.

In contradistinction to the theme of loneliness in *The Golden Gate* is the all-pervasive theme of love—John's love for Liz and Phil's love not only for Claire first and then Liz., but also his passion and yearning for Ed. Thus, the human story of love and loneliness is unravelled against the captivating backdrop of the city of San Francisco, the city of the Golden Gate Bridge. In Seth's realization of the theme of love there are the inevitable eternal triangles but with a difference, the difference stemming from the introduction of humour and irony in the depiction of love-ties. John's love relationship with Liz is impeded by the latter's love for Charlemagne, the cat. In the homosexual affair between Phil and Ed, it is Phil's former wife, Claire, who forms the third party. The third predicament is that of Liz deciding to abandon John and marry Phil.

Despite all the developments through which the narrative winds its way John's situation, in the main, remains unaltered. With life come full circle, he is again alone as he was at the start of the saga, embittered and cynical but comforted by Janet coming back into his life as a whiff of fresh air, this time as his prized beloved and not merely his friend and well-wisher. His life, however, seems jinxed and the novel ends on a tragic note as Janet is killed in an automobile accident just before their marriage is to be solemnized. Liz and Phil try to remain friends with John , who has yet not been able to come to terms with the fact of their having "betrayed" him, betrayed him when he trusted them most. And, San Fancisco has once again been a witness to the human drama enacted on its terrain and has communicated its silent cryptic comment on the nonchalance of nature through the hieroglyphs that define its essential spirit:

[...] the blue Pacific
Unwrinkled as a pond, defines
With wharves and cypresses and pines
Three edges of the hieroglyphic
Of San Francisco, still and square
And sun-bleached in the ocean air. (p. 257)

Section Thirteen, the last section of the novel, concludes the tale with the idea that life goes on, it *has* to go on despite everything. Janet is no more but John still has miles to go. Despite the exposition of the mechanics of existence the novel significantly ends on a personal note with John's remembrance of Janet. Thus one may appreciate the fact that Seth opts for California as a construct for wider human significance than merely as an extension of yuppiedom in the Silicon Valley.

The American reviewers identify the "American qualities" of *The Golden Gate* and largely agree that the novel presents the quintessence of life in California. Seth in celebrating the Californian way of life signalizes his novel with the presence of unmistakably Californian characters who live a typically Californian life. He presents the very texture and colour of life as lived in California. And yet, despite all this talk about Seth confining his scene of action to California, one is inclined to believe with Makarand Paranjape[15] that Seth does present an intimate picture of Californian locales but his moral world is a larger and vaster one and extends to the entire globe. The central theme of the book, he suggests, is world peace. So, California becomes a substructure for a world with extensive human relevance though at the strictly textual and experiential level *The Golden Gate* remains a novel about California.

References

1. M.K. Naik and Shyamala A. Narayan. *Indian English Literature: 1980-2000 (A Critical Survey)* (Delhi: Pencraft International, 2001), p. 54.
2. Mala Pandurang, *Vikram Seth: Multiple Locations, Multiple Affiliations*, Series editor, Jasbir Jain (New Delhi: Rawat Publications, 2001), pp. 13-17.

3. C.D. Narasimhaiah, "Spurious Reputations: Vikram Seth, Salman Rushdie and Shashi Tharoor," *Essays in Commonwealth Literature* (Delhi: Pencraft International, 1995), pp. 119-22.

   Narasimhaiah has drawn attention to the fact that the Chairman of the Booker Prize Committee rejected *The Golden Gate* as a novel with no "compulsive passions" and as one where the characters are seen throughout at the "level gaze" without being subjected to the scrutiny of the novelist. p. 121.

4. Cited in Mala Pandurang, *Vikram Seth: Multiple Locations, Multiple Affiliations*, p. 24.
5. C.D. Narasimhaiah, "Makers of Indian English," Address at the Inaugural Session of the Conference of "Makers of Indian English." Dhvanyalok, June, 1998. *Literary Criterion*, XXXIV/99/1.
6. Cited in G.K. Bansiramani, *An Assessment of Modern Indian English Poets and Poetry* (Mumbai: Vipul Prakashan, 1998), pp. 217-18.
7. Suresh Kohli, "Another Suitable Boy," *Hindu Literary Review*, Sunday, May 16, 1999, pp. xiii-xiv.
8. Ashok K. Jha, "Vikram Seth: *The Golden Gate* and Other Writings," *Recent Indian Fiction* ed. R.S. Pathak (New Delhi: Prestige, 1994), p. 63.
9. Jacques Leslies, "Rhyme and Reason," *Span*, Nov. 1986, pp. 4-6.
10. *Ibid.*
11. Dilip Bobb and Vincent Digirolamo, "I Am Looking Forward to Non-entityhood," Interview with Vikram Seth, *India Today*, June 15, 1986, pp. 152-55.
12. Sahana Misra, "The Reader and the Point of View: The Narrative Technique of *The Golden Gate*" (M.Phil. Dissertation, Department of English, Mumbai, 1990), p. 15.
13. S. Ramaswamy, "A Sonata in C. Major: Vikram Seth's *The Golden Gate*," *Essays in Criticism on Indian Literature in English* ed. Nagarajan, Eakambaram, and Natarajan (New Delhi: S. Chand and Company, 1991), p. 152.
14. Rowena Hill, "*The Golden Gate*: A Quick Look," *The Literary Criterion*, Vol. XXI, No. 4, 1986.
15. Makarand Paranjape, "*The Golden Gate* and the Quest for Self-Realization," ACLALS Bulletin, Eighth Series, No. 1, *Contemporary Commonwealth Fiction*, ed. John Thieme, Aarhus, 1989.

Note: All references to the text are from Vikram Seth, *The Golden Gate* (London: Faber and Faber, 1999 edition).

6

Family and Society as Operative Determinants in Manju Kapur's *Difficult Daughters*

There are problems galore at every stage of life, which offers a constantly changing scenario. The solution to a problem is not to be found in isolation, in withdrawal, but in understanding the whole predicament of ourselves in relationship. As J. Krishnamurti puts it, "you cannot live in isolation; to be is to be related."[1] To meet the challenge of our ever changing world, we need to understand the whole structure of ourselves which is primarily the consequence of our environmental and social conditioning in the past. We cannot live in abstraction; we need to know ourselves in our daily conduct, in action, in conformity and in conflict. This is where the relevance of a social edifice inexorably proclaims itself.

The family and the society represent a kind of bonding which provides, among many other things, a sense of psychological security. This inward security, when pursued as a passion, often leads to an exclusion and a kind of separatism, which, in turn, leads to catastrophe, personal and social. This self-enclosing nature of these social units tends to take on a prescriptive sovereignty which treats the individual like putty to be fitted into a matrix. A person is "good"[2] and can become respectable only by doing what society demands no matter what values the society upholds. A psyché moulded by firmly entrenched social beliefs and shaped by antiquated preconceived concepts can never be blessed with a truly free way of thinking. It is bound to flounder in the world of relationships. It is these very relationships born of social sanction and social constraints that are the primary concern of Manju Kapur's debut novel, *Difficult Daughters*, which won the Commonwealth Writers' Prize for Best First Book (Eurasia region).

Difficult Daughters focuses on the intellectual and emotional dilemma faced by an educated daughter of a conservative joint family of India in the context of the socio-cultural situation that prevailed. With the tumultuous years of the World War II as a distant backdrop and the period of the struggle for Independence culminating in the partition of India as an immediate setting to the human drama enacted, the novel offers a realistic portrayal of women of three successive generations with Virmati, the difficult daughter of the second generation, holding centre-stage. The opening sentence of the novel, "the one thing I had wanted was not to be like my mother,"[3] sets the tone for the mother-daughter confrontation that had prevailed. Had the daughter begrudged her mother the interference or the indifference with regard to her personal life? Had she tread the path her mother carefully chose for her or had she deliberately set off in the opposite direction? Women at a relatively advanced stage of life, labouring under the various compulsions, enjoy less social and psychological freedom than men and are forced to live their lives in the shadow, first, of parental dominance, and then, of patriarchal oppression.

The position of a woman in the community is socially construed and is, as stated earlier, apt to change with the times. Freedom and censure have both been integral parts of a woman's life and women who have refused to buckle under patriarchal pressure have very often succeeded in changing their own lives and those of others dependent on them. One such woman is Virmati in *Difficult Daughters* who has been placed in a private, domestic world where emotions and feelings are her bridge to experience but with education bringing enlightenment and empowerment she is equipped to challenge confidently the traditional framework of knowledge and to steer her way through the boulevards of familial and social oppression and discrimination to arrive at a new consciousness of her own worth and place in society. As Virginia Woolf puts it, initially, "Nothing follows a regular course. The paths wind between bogs and precipices; the trees roar and rock and fall in ruin,"[4] but then, everything falls into place. Virmati strives to overcome the prescriptive norms of her family and society and eventually emerges from the shadow of patriarchal dominance with a transcending awareness of a new identity, an identity that gave her space, which she had never enjoyed till this moment of being.

Ida, the narrator, a divorcee and a childless woman, when making the intriguing statement of not wanting to be like her mother, is conscious of her own lapse in having failed to understand her mother, to connect with her and to empathize with her in the reported traumatic progress of events in her life. Ida's inability to commiserate with her mother takes the form of a mother-fixation, an obsession that persistently gnaws at her till she is able to reconstruct and reinterpret her own fragmented bygone times by exploring the sequence of events in her mother's life. Her mother, apparently, had always been evasive about her past and any scrutiny of her personal history had been frustrated by her neatly side-stepping the queries put to her. At the end, the certainty of knowledge that comes to her regarding her mother's past leads her to a kind of purgation which she hopes will now enable her to live in peace:

> This work weaves a connection between my mother and me, each word a brick in a mansion I made with my head and my heart. Now live in it, Mama, and leave me be. Do not haunt me any more.[5]

This kind of love-hate relationship between mother and daughter invariably emerges as a consequence of the mother's efforts to introduce checks and restraints in the unbridled activities of the daughter. The novelist herself, conscious of the autobiographical resonance of the alternation between friction and resolution in her relationship with her daughter, asserts that:

> conflict between daughter and mother is inevitable and I suppose I was a difficult daughter. The conflict carries on through generations because mothers want their daughters to be safe. We want them to take the right choices—right in the sense that they are socially acceptable. My mother wanted me to be happily married, I want my daughters to have good jobs.[6]

Objectives and choices change with the passage of time but there is no let-up in the conflictive situation that prevails perpetually between mother and daughter. It is interesting to note that the persistent mother-daughter interface that we witness in *Difficult Daughters* is a relationship damned with confrontation but blessed with a subterranean emotional bond that ever tugs at the hearts of both. Together at Dalhousie for Kasturi's confinement, "the peace that both mother and daughter felt"[7] was unprecedented for Virmati had never had Kasturi so much to herself; but, soon after came the realization that her mother was inaccessible and "the language of feeling had never flowed between them."[8]

The central consciousness in the novel is that of Ida which alternates between the present and the past as she investigates her mother's antecedents and experiences of the time gone by through her visits to the different places and the different individuals who were in anyway and at any time in the past associated with her mother, Virmati. In retrospect, when assessing her mother's competence in confronting her predicament, she feels that her mother had been rather simplistic, tacky and jejune in her mode of self-assertion and had failed to create the requisite space for herself. Virmati's contention at the close of the novel that she "had never had so much space around her"[9] till then, is, perhaps, a compromise with life in resigning herself to whatever happiness there is in store for her. It is, perhaps, a joyous acceptance of a situation which is not within the purview of an individual to change.

The novel, then, is "a daughter's reorganization of her fractured and fragmented past hinging on her mother's story."[10] Ida, looking back, never forgives her mother for her semi-acquiescent attitude in accommodating her hopes and aspirations to familial and social considerations, especially after she had initially braced herself to face the consequences of violating the socio-ethical code and had finally taken the plunge with total indifference towards the consequences. Her impatience with her mother's lapses is a statement of assertion spelling out her supercilious disregard for societal norms. But, a mere rejection of these norms is not enough. A woman must have the tenacity of purpose to bring things to their logical conclusion, she must be rational and self-reliant and must continue to have faith in herself despite the various compulsions she is subjected to. The untenable, the unjust and the unethical should always be challenged and demolished by her. The prime determinants of her options in life should be, not the framework constructed by men but her own experiential knowledge and perceptions. "Women," as Kalpana R.J. puts it "must be given freedom within their chosen life patterns and freedom in choosing alternative life patterns."[11]

Ida could never really bring herself to approve of the course of action chosen by her mother in the past for the latter, she believed, lacked the courage of her conviction except when she first walked out of her house trampling patriarchal norms and hoping to achieve self-fulfilment. But, in this act of individual assertion and belying of societal expectations she is ultimately a loser for she opts out of the security of her maiden home and is unable to entrench herself satisfactorily in the domestic domain provided by her husband. Seema Malik, in her essay on *Difficult Daughters*, refers to her as the deprived one "whose acts totally alienate her from her family and she fails to create a space for herself for which she has been striving all along."[12] The hiatus between what she does achieve at the end and what she really wished to achieve is immense.

Ida is not prepared to accept Parvati Masi's attribution of simplicity to her mother. "I hate the word 'simple,'" says she. "Nobody has any business to live in the world and know nothing about its ways."[13] No woman, she believes, can explain away her violation of patriarchal norms and her rejection of the security of familial bonds by characterizing herself as simple and naive. Ida, herself, breaks up with her husband, Prabhakar, because he compels her to have an abortion, "denying that incipient little thing"[14] in her belly. How, then, could she approve of Virmati's opting for an abortion because the Professor was not prepared for an immediate alliance?

Coming to the chronological account of events in the narrative, Virmati, the eldest of ten siblings in a conservative and esteemed Punjabi family of Amritsar, is weighed down by the charge she is given of looking after her mother during her successive pregnancies. From the earliest days, Virmati has been conditioned to the idea that every girl "is to get married" and that the woman is for the hearth and not for the field or a job outside the house. Though already engaged to be married to Inderjeet, a canal engineer, Virmati is inspired by her cousin, Shakuntala, to experience freedom and lead a life of her own so that she can shoulder responsibilities other than those of a husband and children. To go in for further studies she has "to fight her mother who was so sure that her education was practically over."[15] With consent reluctantly given, she enters A.S. College, "the bastion of male learning."[16] It is here that she notices and is noticed by the Oxford-returned Professor, Harish Chandra, her neighbour. And then onwards, there is no looking back. Swayed by passion for the already married man, Virmati rejects the pre-arranged marriage, attempts suicide and as a punitive measure and is confined to the four walls of a storehouse. Despite all this, deep within herself, she does realize the hopelessness of her illicit love when she learns that the Professor's wife is with child. At this point, there is a consciousness of being deceived and a spurning of the man she loves. "You think you can do what you like so long as you go on saying you love,"[17] she tells him and promptly leaves for Lahore for advanced studies.

Here, at this point in the narrative, emerges the "New Woman" in Virmati who refuses "to be a rubber doll for others to move as they willed."[18] Defying patriarchal constraints she asserts herself to attain self-reliance through education. Conscious of the Professor's incompetence to deal with the domestic tangle, she takes control of the situation, decisively shunning the Professor and ignoring his pleas. She braces herself to be "strong to bear the pain, silently, without anyone knowing"[19] and to sever herself from her past she determinedly burns the Professor's letters.

Unfortunately, however, the assertive and resolute Virmati never blossoms to the full. Inspite of her initial determination to be brusque with and ignore the Professor, she eventually succumbs to his implorations to grant him clandestine meetings, in the course of which she comes to be with child. A sense of guilt at this loss of virginity and at an unwed pregnancy is first dismissed by her as "an outmoded morality"[20] but then distress and uncertainty begin to gnaw at her mind. From this point onwards begins the down-slide. She gets the child secretly aborted, no doubt, but the tenacious and assertive woman has now, with the passage of time, become a dupe who is mesmerized by the Professor, who has come to be her sole guide in "just what to look for, what to admire, what to criticize."[21] Like Swarnalata, her roommate, she wants to indulge in "meaningful activities" like those of the freedom movement but the Professor dissuades her from such indulgence. As far as their marriage is concerned the Professor keeps deferring it, pleading only for furtive rendezvous with her. Later, too, when he does marry her at a friend's instance she is not given the status due to her. In her effort to please him, she is reduced almost to a non-entity. Even the choice of the subject for her post-graduation is the Professor's though she herself finds the subject dull and meaningless. She felt, "it was such an uphill task being worthy of him."[22] For her own people, however, she remains a "difficult" daughter throughout.

In her relationship with the Professor, Virmati is aware of the possibility of her saying to him that, "she will be her own mistress and relate to him with dignity or not at all,"[23] but she is not able to do so because, perhaps, her mind had gone "soft and pulpy with repeated complying."[24] Thus, the rebel in Virmati seems to have lost confidence. She now feels emotionally, intellectually and psychically roofed in and is unable to emerge out of what Chaman Nahal calls "the dependence syndrome,"[25] that is, the need to fall back on someone in times of crises. Even after she has married the man of her choice life is no triumph for her.

> As second wife she must fight social ostracism outside the house, and compete for the kitchen and conjugal bed with Ganga, the first wife, inside it.[26]

So, ironically enough, though Virmati has been one of the fortunate ones in availing herself of higher education despite social constraints, she craves to be a down-to-earth housewife looking after the mundane needs of her husband. Another instance that seems incongruous is the fact that though Virmati herself violates age-old family traditions, she tries to persuade Ida to conform to the values upheld by the family. And again, she makes a futile attempt to curb Ida's energy for the latter develops into an intractable woman, never making an effort to understand her mother.

Swarnalata seems to be the novelist's ideal woman in the Indian context, a woman who can assert her individuality and pursue her interests without threatening the family structures. The partnership in marriage, the writer seems to suggest, should be one of interdependence but if there is any undue shift of power to one partner, there should be a total breaking away from the relationship. A woman, especially, needs to extricate herself from her cumbrous circumstances and emerge from the psychic detention she may find herself in. Giving credit to the novelist, Jaidev observes the she "has understood a woman both as a woman and as a person pressurized by all kinds of visible and invisible contexts."[27] It is not gender equality as a prerequisite to an ideal marriage that she advocates for a woman but a certain freedom within the community of men and women that will fulfil them. Like Anita Desai's women, Manju Kapur, too, wants her female protagonists "to explore their own potential or to live on their own terms regardless of the consequences that such a rebellion may have on their lives."[28] Their predicament—Kasturi's, Virmati's and Ida's—is not a predominantly private one but a braided synthesis of the complex social context, family attitudes and the relationship with the man in each one's life.

Social life in India swarms with problems—"vagaries and varieties"[29] as Iyengar refers to them, and an observant novelist like Manju Kapur deals with the most conspicuous and relevant of them today, namely an individual's search for identity and space. She depicts the issue with an acute awareness of what Shiv K. Kumar identifies as "a gradual shift in values that has been taking place in this sub-continent during the past two decades or so."[30] It is in such a context that the relationship of literature to society becomes vital and the literary work produced "involves a creative interaction between the writer and the social milieu."[31]

Difficult Daughters, which is largely autobiographical in content and perspective, evokes the atmosphere of the times as reflected in the life of a "high-minded" Punjabi family of Amritsar. Virmati, the chief protagonist is, perhaps, modelled on the novelist herself. The world portrayed here is that of the pre-Partition days in India but while human experience in the novel is grounded in historical events, the depiction of history in its various dimensions is not the concern of the novelist. It appears that Virmati's own struggle for independence from the shackles of form and seemingly claustrophobic traditions is reinforced by the history of India's struggle for Independence and the subsequent partition of the country. Virmati too, like the country, seems to be "torn" between her private life and her social existence as a member of a family, a community and a society. The earlier part of the novel maintains the primacy of the individual tale whereas the latter part demonstrates how social and political events determine the course of the lives of the various characters. For example, the departure of Ganga from Amritsar enabling Virmati to gain space is a compulsion brought about by the exigencies of the historical situation.

The narrative starts as a quiet tale involving outwardly insignificant events and personal relationships. It is only later when the Professor insidiously makes his presence felt as a neighbour, and more, that the central figures begin to get embroiled in the mesh of circumstances. Compelled to lead a life subjected to a host of negative pressures, Virmati has to confront painful compulsions that drive her to build up resistance which eventually ends in total rebellion. The rebellion, however, leaves her deprived of her dear ones, who together provided her a sense of security, which she is now striving for, though even when amidst them, as the eldest child, she sometimes "yearned for affection, for some sign that she was special"[32] for she was ever-burdened with familial responsibilities that weighed her down. Her mother, Kasturi, too, before her, had succumbed to the familial demand for more and more children and thus endangered her health. "She had filled the house as her in-laws had wanted, but with another child there would be nothing left of her."[33] According to the Indian ideological and sociological underpinnings women are to conform uncomplainingly to the demands of the family and the social structure.

Kasturi, sworn to compliance with social norms, disapproved of her niece, Shakuntala's emancipated views and her decision to remain single without regard for her parents' desire to see her "settle down" in life. Study, she feels, is not for liberation and total absence of social restraints: "Study means developing the mind for the benefit of the family. I studied too, but my mother would have killed me if I had dared even to want to dress in anything other than was bought for me."[34] So, it is the family that remains the frame of reference and what matters is the opinion of the members of the family. Yet, Shakuntala, conscious of the shifting times, exhorts Virmati to accommodate her ways to the changing times: "Times are changing, and women are moving out of the house, so why not you?"[35]

Kasturi remains firm in her indifference towards changing times. What she had been schooled in were traditional Indian values that defined "propriety" with reference to social worth and societal norms. Sibling relationships, too, as portrayed in the novel, are those of interdependence, love and caring; despite her inclination to pursue her own aspirations, Virmati did not wish to ruin the "marriage chances" of her siblings. So the thought of marriage to the already married Professor and the frequent clandestine meetings with him were preying on her mind, "splitting her into two socially unacceptable pieces,"[36] each, perhaps, to clamour for admissibility and acceptability for years to come. Social values in India would have the social institutions subsume the individual for practices were always judged by their conformity with or contrariety to "family spirit."[37] Family unity was a source of strength and vigour: "United the family talked. United, they raged and grieved, united they questioned."[38] Besides, as Virmati writes to the Professor, "the family protects you if things go wrong."[39] On the other hand, the Professor believes that tradition has a stultifying effect on the individual and is responsible for all one's miseries:

> Who is responsible for this state of affairs? Society, which deems that their sons should be educated, but not their daughters. Society that decides that children—babies really—should be married at the ages of two and three as we were.[40]

But then, one is so overpowered and so overawed by the collective strength of the society that one can only, as Virmati, did "adjust, compromise, adapt."[41] "That," Ida says "is my female inheritance. That is what she tried to give me."[42]

The family and the society, then, in the ultimate analysis, become intimidating prescriptive factors in life and are largely responsible for the rigid standards of morality imposed upon the Indian woman, who, instead of emerging as a self-determining individual is cursed with playing a subordinate role in every field of life. Though, there is no gainsaying the fact that the social structure in India does provide the individual with a strengthening sense of security, the tradition-bound, male-dominated society is her cross. It does not let her grow. It courts her to the point of wreckage and then leaves her to piece the shards together. This is the juncture at which, at the level of content, literature and sociology slip into a concentric conspectus and establish a vital relationship.

References

1. J. Krishnamurti, *On Relationship* (Chennai: Krishnamurti Foundation India, 1999, rpt. 2002), p. 26.
2. J. Krishnamurti, *What Are You Doing With Your Life*? (Chennai: Krishnamurti Foundation India, 2002, rpt. 2003), p. 172.

   Krishnamurti, here, defines "goodness" in terms other than the socially acceptable ones.

3. Manju Kapur, *Difficult Daughters* (New Delhi: Penguin Books India Pvt. Ltd., 1998), p. 1.
4. Virginia Woolf, Harriette Wilson, *Collected Essays*, ed. Leonard Woolf (London: Hogarth Press, 1966), Vl. III, p. 227.
5. Manju Kapur, *Difficult Daughters*, p. 259.
6. Cited in Suman Bala and Subhash Chandra, "Manju Kapur's *Difficult Daughters*: An Absorbing Tale of Fact and Fiction." *Fifty Years of Indian Writing* (New Delhi: IAES, 1999), p. 107.
7. Manju Kapur, *Difficult Daughters*, p. 10.
8. *Ibid.*, p. 11.
9. *Ibid.*, p. 253.
10. Gajendra Kumar, "Manju Kapur's *Difficult Daughters:* A Postcolonial Analysis," *The Indian Journal of English Studies*, Vol. XL, 2002-03, p. 197.
11. Kalpana, R.J., *Feminism and Family* (New Delhi: Prestige Books, 2005), p. 25.
12. Seema Malik, "Crossing Patriarchal Threshold: Glimpses of the Incipient New Woman," *Indian Writing in English: The Last Decade*, ed. Rajul Bhargava (Jaipur: Rawat Publications, 2002), p. 175.
13. Manju Kapur, *Difficult Daughters*, p. 207.
14. *Ibid.*, p. 144.
15. *Ibid.*, p. 17.
16. *Ibid.*, p. 41.
17. *Ibid.*, pp. 98-99.
18. *Ibid.*, p. 85.
19. *Ibid.*, p. 101.
20. *Ibid.*, p. 114.
21. *Ibid.*, p. 119.
22. *Ibid.*, p. 237.
23. *Ibid.*, p. 236.
24. *Ibid.*, p. 236.
25. Chaman Nahal, "Feminism in English Fiction: Forms and Variations," *Feminism and Recent Fiction in English* ed. Sushila Singh (New Delhi: Prestige, 1991), p. 17.
26. *The Pioneer*, New Delhi, August 1, 1998.
27. Jaidev, "Problematizing Feminism," *Gender and Literature*, ed. Iqbal Kaur (Delhi: B.R. Publishing Corporation, 1992), p. 68.

28. Anita Ghosh, "Woman on Top: A Study of Feministic Consciousness of Modern Indian Women Novelists," *New Lights on Indian Women Novelists in English* (Part II) ed. Amar Nath Prasad (New Delhi: Sarup and Sons, 2004), pp. 250-51.
29. K.R.S. Iyengar, *Indian Writing in English* (Bombay: Asia Publishing House, 1973, 2nd Edition), p. 327.
30. Shiv K. Kumar, "Tradition and Change in the Novels of Kamala Markandaya," *Osmania Journal of English Studies*, 7/1 (1969), p. 1.
31. R.S. Pathak, "Kamala Markandaya's Sociological Concerns" *Modern Indian Novel in English* (New Delhi: Creative Books, 1999), p. 70.
32. Manju Kapur, *Difficult Daughters*, p. 6.
33. *Ibid.*, p. 7.
34. *Ibid.*, p. 14.
35. *Ibid.*, p. 16.
36. *Ibid.*, p. 60.
37. *Ibid.*, p. 51.
38. *Ibid.*, p. 79.
39. *Ibid.*, p. 101.
40. *Ibid.*, p. 95.
41. *Ibid.*, p. 236.
42. *Ibid.*

7

Mahesh Dattani's *Final Solutions and Other Plays*: "A Living Dramatic Experience"

Indian English literature, Professor G.N. Devy points out,[1] is not one of the condescendingly designated "New Literatures" for it cannot adequately and comprehensively be defined as merely "post-colonial" in the sense that African and West Indian literatures can. Not only is there a two hundred year history of Indians writing in English but also a significant bulk of Indian writing that endorses any literary culture that is truly Indian in core. All Indian literature including Indian English represents the typically complex Indian experience which is historically multilingual and multicultural but does not fail to underscore well-defined concepts of national identity. Indian English literature has steadily moved towards self-assertion and self-definition and acquired an unmistakable sense of "selfhood."[2]

The origin of Indian drama can be traced back to the Vedic period. As a manifestation of our national sensibility Indian drama came into existence as a means of exploring and communicating the truth of things and was popularly hailed as the "Fifth Veda."[3] Iyengar, defining the scope of Indian drama, said that it was envisioned to "comprehend the whole arc of life, ranging from the material to the spiritual, the phenomenal to the transcendent and provides at once, relaxation and entertainment, instruction and illumination."[4]

Bharata's *Natyashastra* in Sanskrit discusses the minutiae of ancient stagecraft and displays consciousness of all major aspects of drama, namely, stage-setting, music, plot-construction, characterization, dialogue and acting. Sanskrit drama flourished under the patronage of the court till the twelfth century but gradually ceased to be performed on the stage and entered a period of decadence which led to its virtual extinction. What replaced it was the theatre of the people and music, dance and drama was witnessed in varied forms. The "jatras" of Bengal, the folk plays of Tamil Nadu like *Satharam*, the "yakshaganas" of Andhra and Karnataka, the "kathakali" of Kerala, the "kirtaniya" of Mithila, the "Bhavai" of Gujarat and the Ramlila plays of North India—all these forms of entertainment had little value as literature but were characteristic of Indian culture, and represented a transition from the classical Sanskrit drama to the modern Indian drama. By 1920 a new drama in almost all the Indian languages came to the fore, it was a drama largely influenced by prevailing movements like Marxism, psychoanalysis, symbolism and surrealism.

For certain reasons which need to be identified the development of Indian English drama has not been able to keep pace with that of poetry and fiction. The theatre movement in English has always trailed along far behind the flourishing prevalence of Indian poetry and fiction in the same language. It was as early as 1871 that Michael Madhusudan Dutt wrote the first Indian play in English, *Is This Civilization?* There was, however, no follow-up creative dramatic activity for years, one reason, perhaps, being that the total commitment required on the part of the playwright, the actor and the audience could never really be co-ordinated for a living dramatic experience. Also, it is difficult to lend conviction to a dialogue in English between two Indians who normally converse in their mother-tongue. The difficulties, however, have been overcome by many and the pre-Independence era saw the emergence of literary giants like Rabindra Nath Tagore, Sri Aurobindo, T.P. Kailasam, Harindranath Chattopadhyaya and Bharathi Sarabhai, who, through their plays, gave a fillip to the growth and development of Indian English drama and opened up new vistas in the genre.

This pre-Independence crop of dramatists, despite the poetic excellence, thematic variety, technical competence and symbolic and moral significance of their works, did not give enough weightage to the actability and "stage worthiness"[5] of their plays.

One of the earliest Indian dramatists to show interest in producing drama for the stage was Asif Currimbhoy, hailed by many as "India's first authentic voice in theatre."[6] His plays—'The Hungry Ones,' 'The Captives,' 'An Experiment with Truth,' 'The Refugee' (1971) etc. reveal a social purpose, a philosophical basis and dexterous stagecraft. Currimbhoy is fully alive to the basics of theatre and maintains that "good theatre does not depend upon language or geography; rather it depends upon inherent situations, and of course, conflict [...]."[7] M.K. Naik, equally conscious of the prerequisites of good theatre visualizes the plight of still born playwrights who lack viable dramatic action.[8]

Some notable contemporaries of Currimbhoy known for their contribution to Indian English drama are Nissim Ezekiel with a volume of three plays to his credit, Gurcharan Das, who based his "Larin Sahib" (1970), a play in three acts, "on events in the Punjab in 1946-47 [...] reconstructed from documents and letters exchanged by the principal characters"[9] and Girish Karnad (in the 1970s), who originally wrote in Kannada and then translated his plays into English himself. Shyam Asnani, critically evaluating the works of these playwrights, draws attention to the prevailing misconceptions about the nature of drama.[10] Drama, he says, is not just good literature, it has to be effective as theatre. To endorse his belief he quotes J.K. Styan's assertion that drama is a dramatic construct "realized"[11] in theatre, where the word in the play-text becomes "fleshed out"[12] as it were. A play is a living experience and needs a real theatre and a live audience. Recent attempts at experimentation in theatre-oriented plays are commendable and include works like Pratap Sharma's *A Touch of Brightness*, Shiv K. Kumar's *The Last Wedding Anniversary* and Balwant Gargi's *The Knife*.

Contemporary Indian drama in English translation has made striking innovations and successful experiments in terms of thematic concerns as well as technical virtuosities. It has been increasingly resorting to history, legend, myth and folklore drawing sustenance from their springs of vitality. Mohan Rakesh, Badal Sircar, Vijay Tendulkar and Girish Karnad are vibrant representatives of the Indian drama of the present times in Hindi, Bengali, Marathi and Kannada respectively. They do, however, also represent Indian drama at the national level for they dramatize universal aspects of modern human life in India.

While Mohan Rakesh presents the total absence of communication between one man and another in contemporary life Badal Sircar depicts the existential attitude of modern man in the present times. Tendulkar focuses on middle-class life in India and shows the isolated individual's confrontation with adverse circumstances and hostile surroundings. He strongly believes that ideas are firmly entrenched in our psyche at an early age and "our attitudes have a lot to do with what we internalize in our early formative years."[13] With the help of various myths and legends, Girish Karnad, the Kannada playwright, shows the absurdity of modern life and its passions and conflicts his objective being the re-interpretation of the past from the vantage-point of the present.

Often compared to luminaries like Henrik Ibsen and Tennessee Williams in his practice of stagecraft, Mahesh Dattani, the thirty-eight year old playwright from Bangalore, alongwith Manjula Padmanabhan has given a fresh lease of life to Indian drama in English. Whereas Padmanabhan presents in her plays (for example, in 'Harvest' where we see mothers selling their sons for the price of rice) a dehumanized and unpalatable world. Dattani's works are less grim and forbidding though generally about the unwelcome and unpleasant things of life. What is most notable about Dattani's dramatic art is that the stage for him is no plain expanse of space but a complex multidimensional area in which vital incidents placed in time may be viewed and re-assessed, an area in which atmospheric details related to humidity and air-temperature, insignificant though they may seem, are not overlooked. The arena of performance for him is a space in which the written text of a play assumes the form of an enactment and the use of masks represents a deep ritualistic meaning.

Dattani confidently challenges the traditional denotations and connotations of the words "India" and "Indians." He places on them constructs that are far removed from the ones prevalent in modern theatre but are meaningfully related to social, cultural, sexual and religious issues that hold centre-stage in life in the present times. In his plays, Dattani explores what he calls "invisible issues" of Indian society. He believes that there are certain issues which cannot be addressed because they are taboo and are what he calls "confrontational."

Dattani's theatre group, Playpen, was formed in 1984 and he has directed several of their plays ranging from classical Greek to contemporary works. It was in 1986 that he wrote his first full-length play, *Where There's a Will*, and since then, there has been no looking back. In 1998, he set up his own theatre studio for the grooming of new entrants in acting, directing and stage writing. In the same year he won the Sahitya Akademi award for his anthology of plays, *Final Solutions and Other Plays*, published by East-West Books, Chennai, thus attaining the honour of being the first English language playwright to win the award.

Mahesh Dattani has an array of themes to offer in his plays and the issues he chooses to project are the most topical but also the most controversial ones. "We're living in the present and there are so many challenges facing us [...]."[14] says Dattani. *Seven Steps Around the Fire* (a radio play) is the heart-rending story of a "hijra" Kamala, who happens to fall in love with Subbu, the son of an affluent minister. When the fact of her being a "hijra" is revealed to people she is mercilessly murdered. Her deprivation in terms of essential femininity instead of arousing sympathy and a feeling of compassion is looked down upon; she is discriminated against and ultimately murdered. A sense of horror and injustice prevails for it is not by choice but by sheer misfortune that she is what she is. The play, thus, is about class and gender based power implications and also a study of class- and gender-related violence.

On a Muggy Night in Mumbai is a tragi-comedy that deals with the travails of the gay community. The play is like a charter of demands for homosexuals whose activities are absolutely taboo in the Indian society. Their sexual proclivities are still strongly forbidden by social custom and are greatly offensive to the prevailing moral and social code. Kiran in the play innocently remarks, "I really wish they would allow gay people to marry." Dattani, here, clearly pleads for social sanction to homosexuals.

Do the Needful is another of Dattani's plays that deals with the problem of homosexuality but what makes it different is that there is grafted onto it a love interest which cannot culminate in marriage because of communal consciousness in the Indian society. The play is a fabric of complex relationships, which expose the fact that the institution of marriage today has lost its sanctity and is nothing but a compromise to promote personal ends. Lata and Alpesh both pursue their extra-marital love liaisons even after they have tied the knot, marriage being only an expedient mode of coexistence.

Bravely Fought the Queen deals with women from affluent homes fighting against patriarchal dominance as it prevails in India. The title of the play is derived from a poem in Hindi ("Jhansi Ki Rani"—by Subhadra Kumari Chauhan) about the indomitable Rani of Jhansi. Dolly Trivedi, the chief protagonist, has to brave the onslaughts from her violent and unfaithful husband and her tyrannical mother-in-law, who, even in her paralytic, diseased state, holds on to the reins of domestic governance. The technical achievement of Dattani in this play deserves special mention for his realization of the stage as a multi-level space in which time is perceived in its simultaneity and is projected as stratified and tiered. The opening set for the play is furnished with three white blocks representing the Trivedi office and two separate rooms in the family's residence.

Tara, is predominantly a play about gender discrimination and about the Indian parents' preference for a male child over a female one. It is the story of a pair of conjoined twins, a boy, Chandan, and a girl, Tara, who are "separated" (a physico-medical separation) from each other by manipulation and design but they love each other immensely. The twins born with three legs, got one leg each but the third leg, though it got a major part of its blood supply from the girl, was, at the instance of the mother, Bharati, and the influential maternal grandfather, deliberately given to the boy so that he could live with two legs. The third leg however atrophied and had to be amputated as Chandan's body could not sustain it. Tara would very well have lived with the third leg but as a consequence of being insistently discriminated against by her mother, she eventually dies. Through her death Dattani demonstrates the unfortunate consequences of differentiation between children on grounds of gender.

Dance Like a Man is a play set in Chennai where dance is an integral part of life and a favourite mode of aesthetic expression. Ratna wants her daughter Lata to achieve distinction as a danseuse as she herself had been thwarted in her desire to make her mark as a dance artist because of the repressive patriarchal dominance exercised by her father-in-law, Amritlal, who expected all the members of his family to prostrate themselves before him. Rebellion surfaces in the family the very moment Amritlal breathes his last.

Where There's a Will is another play in which Dattani's recurrent motif of patriarchal paramountcy appears. A woman is generally looked upon as a commodity; her prime functions in marriage are to dance attendance upon her husband and to be an exciting partner in bed. This undemocratic nature of man is what repulses a woman, be it daughter, wife, daughter-in-law or mistress. The plot of the play revolves around the tyrannical patriarch, Hasmukh Mehta, who is a terror for the members of his family when alive as well as when dead. Even after his death there is no relief for them for he hovers oppressively around them as a ghost, persecuting them as when alive. The humour in the play, however, is a major redeeming factor and has its source largely in the interjections and asides of Hasmukh as a ghost. Also, Dattani's depiction of a visible/invisible and audible/ inaudible ghost extends the scope of naturalistic drama.

Dattani's *Final Solutions*, first staged in Bangalore in 1993, focuses on the problem of communal disharmony between the

Hindus and Muslims in India, especially during the period of the post-Partition riots. The analysis of the cause of friction between the two communities offered by Dattani carries conviction as it is endorsed by a study of human psychology offering valid explanations of the proclivities and susceptibilities of individuals under circumstantial pressure.

The psychosis that prevails among the Hindus as well as the Muslims in India after the event of the partition of the country causes a chain of neurotic reactions to even the most inconsequential of happenings. Dattani's purpose in depicting the post-Partition communal violence in India at the very outset of the play is not to convey to us with fidelity events as they actually took place in time but to impress upon us the consciousness that a more primitive logic now prevails. The realization that there is a total absence of restraint in the perpetration of tragic violence leads us to the painful experience of confronting an advancing foe all set to demolish the human laws of love and mercy. Dattani, however, does not charge his descriptions of the incidents of brutality and monstrosity with feelings; rather, he offers journalistic reports of the events. He by-passes the emotional aspects of the historical situation because it is not to his purpose. He subordinates the specific events of history to an analysis of the situation as it prevails. His focus is on a "failure of understanding"[15] between man and man.

The stance adopted by various characters in *'Final Solutions'* is purposefully structured. The experiences of each individual as depicted in the play lead to the discovery of meaning in his or her life. The play opens with Daksha reading lines from her diary. The setting suggests that the period is the late 1940s. Daksha is the grandmother of the central character of the play, Ramnik Gandhi. She shuttles between her two identities, namely, that of a girl of fifteen and that of a mature lady who has witnessed forty years of freedom. The Chorus chanting at the back sometimes assume Hindu masks and sometimes Muslim ones. The words rendered by the Chorus are clear indicators of the communal disharmony and its painful consequences that are soon to be experienced by the characters in the play. The masks have a leavening effect on the minds of the characters who wear them. The effective use of the Chorus in the play is a dynamic technique used by the playwright. In the stage directions the dramatist gives clear hints at the nature of the Chorus:

> There are five Hindu masks and five Muslim masks. The mob/chorus become the Chorus when they "wear" either the Hindu or the Muslim masks but when referred to individually, they remain Chorus 1, Chorus 2, etc. The players of the Mob/Chorus do not belong to any religion and ideally should wear black.[17]

Ramnik Gandhi saves the two Muslim boys, Bobby and Javed while the Chorus all the while curses the boys and exhorts the people to kill them. It calls Ramnik a "traitor" for protecting the boys. In Act III, the accusations and counter-accusations that are exchanged between Ramnik and Javed intensify the feelings of hatred that exist between them though, later, Javed himself admits that he has been carried away and does not know what he is doing. Soon, however, he is disillusioned. Smita, an essentially secular character, tells her mother not to impose on her religious prejudices anymore. She boldly tells her mother, "You have to admit you are wrong."

Life can be lived peacefully only if anger is expunged from our gamut of human emotions but a state of total exclusion of this feeling from our mental make-up is not really possible. Under such conditions one wonders and keeps wondering whether there can ever be any final solutions to the problem of communal violence and hatred. For Dattani, a play is never really finished. The apparently permanent printed text is just one approximation to what might occur—this is what is believed to be what Michael Walling calls "the kaleidoscopic approach to the text."[18] Dattani resolves *Final Solutions* with an inconclusive end and leaves the viewers delving deep in search of an answer to the problem posed. In this context Javed very pertinently asks, "Don't we all have anger and frustration?"[19] It is precisely this frustration resulting in anger that is the undoing of all. The open-ended finalé leaves us musing as to what solution there can be to the mutual hatred and intolerance that prevails between the Hindus and Muslims in India. A Hindu has always inherited a preconceived notion of what a Muslim is like. As Vijay Tendulkar in his essay 'Muslims and I' points out, "A Muslim was someone you stayed away from."[20]

In the context of the play *Final Solutions*, the fears and anxieties of the two communities are largely an aftermath of the Partition but in conservative Hindu homes, there has always been a tacit dislike for and disapproval of everything associated with Muslims, to the extent that everything touched by the latter is considered to be contaminated. Muslims, too, are conscious of the antipodal position they assume in a Hindu community and are equally averse to the Hindus. This mutual aversion of the two communities for each other in India is not overplayed but is depicted with a rare fidelity which spells absolute conviction. Dattani himself, in his Preface to his anthology of dramatic works, *Collected Plays*, proclaims, "I am certain that my plays are a true reflection of my time, place and socio-economic background."[21] He wonders what the future of his art in the new millenium will be "in a country that has a myriad challenges to face politically, socially, artistically and culturally."[22]

The play *Final Solutions* adheres sincerely to the principle of the economy of words in drama advocated by Mohan Rakesh and the theme of communal disharmony is demonstrated largely through action and "dramatic" individual attitudes on the stage itself. Alyque Padamsee, in his introductory lines to the play—"A Note on the Play"—underscores the dramatist's externalization of the communal hatred and paranoia "lurking inside ourselves"[23] in terms of the mob which is a symbol of this hatred.

Alyque Padamsee talks of moving the play "from printed word to living and breathing characters."[24] Examining *Final Solutions* from the psycho-analytical point of view, Padamsee, who has directed this play of Dattani, defines it as "a play about transferred resentments,"[25] about looking for a pretext to unload oneself, to give vent to one's wrath by hitting out at those who cannot retaliate and retort. The play he feels, deals with the "simmering undercurrents"[26] in a family where Ramnik, the father, voices his resentment at his own father's stealthy and unjust deeds by shouting at his mother, Hardika. Smita, the daughter, hits out at her mother, Aruna, as an outlet to the pent up emotion within her at her infructuous love for Babban, her friend's fiancé. Hardika, in turn comes to hate her best friend, Zarine, and her community, the hatred being a mode of spouting her indignation at being subjected to the small-mindedness of her in-laws. Of all the characters in the play, Aruna alone seems confident and well-adjusted only to be charged with nursing religious prejudices that leave the two communities—Hindus and Muslims—in a state of stasis, "ever-locked in combat."[27]

Dattani, in his artistic credo as expressed in his preface to *Collected Plays*, clearly states, "I write for my plays to be performed"[28] leaving no doubt about the fact that he wants his plays to be a living experience, a communication realized on the stage, a message which is transferred from the page to the stage so that there is a minimal dependence on what Mohan Rakesh calls the "dramatic word."[29]

Dattani's plays, then, have purely performance-oriented scripts that elicit from the audience an emotional as well as a strongly intellectual response. His plays are a commitment to what Iyengar calls the "manifestoes of the new realism."[30] and conform closely to the requirements of a play that communicates, for, as M.K. Naik observes, "a play, in order to communicate fully and become a living dramatic experience, needs a real theatre and a live audience [...]."[31] Dattani has created a vibrant, new theatrical form which is a marked development on the hitherto stagnant Indian drama in English. As Erin Mee, a theatre director who has worked extensively with K.N. Panikkar and the Sopanam Company in Kerala puts it "Dattani writes plays to be seen and heard, not literature to be read."[32] It is exactly this that makes him a playwright with distinction.

References

1. G.N. Devy, "Indian English Literature and Commonwealth Literature," *In Another Tongue* (Madras: Macmillan, 1993, rpt. 1995) p. 31.

2. *Ibid.*, p. 3.
3. Referred to in *Flowering of Indian Drama* ed., K. Venkata Reddy and R.K. Dhawan (New Delhi: Prestige, 2004), p. 7.
4. K.R.S. Iyenger, *Drama in Modern India* (Bombay: The P.E.N. All India Centre, 1961), p. 1.
5. Prema Nandakumar, "Indians Writing in English: Three Cheers," *Indian Literature*, Vol. XIII, No. 4 (December, 1970), p. 36.
6. Faubion Bowers, "Introduction," *Asif Currimbhoy's Plays* (New Delhi: Oxford and IBH, n...d.) p. XII.
7. Asif Currimbhoy, "A Personal View of Indo-English Drama," *Indian Drama* ed. H.H. Anniah Gowda (Mysore: Prasaranpa, 1976), p. 43.
8. M.K. Naik, *Dimensions of Indian English Literature*. (New Delhi: Sterling Publishers, 1984), p. 157.
9. Gurcharan Das, *Larin Sahib* (Delhi: OUP, 1970), 'Afterword,' p. 87.
10. Shyam Asnani, "Indian English Drama," *Spectrum History of Indian Literature in English* ed. Late Ram Sewak Singh and Charu Sheel Singh (New Delhi: Atlantic Publishers and Distributors, 1997), p. 107.
11. J.L. Styan, *The Elements of Drama* (London: Cambridge University Press, 1960), p. 134.
12. *Ibid.*
13. Shoma Choudhury and Gita Ranjan, eds., *Vijay Tendulkar* (New Delhi: Katha, 2001), p. 65.
14. Mahesh Dattani: *Invisible Issues*. Interview published in *Performing Arts Journal* (55).
15. B. Bajan, *The Dark Dancer* (New Delhi: Arnold Heinemann, 1976), p. 262. Compare the situation in *Final Solutions* with a similar situation in Balchandra Rajan's novel, *The Dark Dancer*.
16. Mahesh Dattani, *Collected Plays* (New Delhi: Penguin, 2000), p. 165.
17. *Ibid.*, p. 210.
18. *Ibid.*, p. 229.
19. *Ibid.*, p. 205.
20. *Op. cit.*, *Vijay Tendulkar*, p. 63.
21. Mahesh Dattani, *Collected Plays*, p. XV.
22. *Ibid.*, p. 162.
23. *Ibid.* "A Note on the Play" by Alyque Padamsee, p. 161.
24. Ibid, p. 162.

25. *Ibid.*, p. 161.
26. *Ibid.*
27. *Ibid.*
28. *Ibid.*, p. XI.
29. *The Dramatic World*, a Nehru Memorial Fellowship Project. Mohan Rakesh's notes and letters concerning this project were posthumously published in *Enact*, Vol. 7, 1973.
30. K.R.S. Iyengar, *Indian Writing in English* (Bombay: Asia, 1977), p. 195.
31. M.K. Naik, "The Achievement of Indian Drama in English" *Dimensions of Indian English Literature* (New Delhi: Sterling Publishers, 1984), p. 151.
32. *Op. cit.*; cited in Mahesh Dattani's *Collected Play*, p. 320.

8

Amrita Pritam's *Pinjar*: Gender as A Prescriptive Factor in Life

Amrita Pritam, a versatile writer with poems, novels, short stories and other prose works to her credit, is the first woman recipient of the Sahitya Akademi Award (1956) for her anthology of poems, *Sunehure*. In 1969 the coveted title of Padma Shree was bestowed upon her and in 1982 she received the Jnanpith Award, India's most prestigious literary award, for her *Kagaz te Kanvas*.

With the voluminous bulk of notable literary works produced by her, Amrita Pritam established an unprecedented record in the annals of Punjabi literature. Her autobiography, *Rasidi Ticket* (1976) with its endearing candour and intellectual integrity touched the hearts of many. Her works have been widely translated and these translations, providing for many, an access to her creative genius, have made her one of the well known Indian writers in the East European countries.

Amrita Pritam's novel, *Pinjar,* was translated into English by Khuṣhwant Singh, and, in the target language, was given the new title of *The Skeleton*[1] for we witness in the novel, the recurring and growing significance of the word, "skeleton," which assumes multifarious denotations and connotations in the text. Singh notably tries to capture the linguistic and thematic contents of the original work alongwith the socio-cultural concepts underlying it but the thrust in this study in not on the novel, *Pinjar*, as a work of translation or transcreation but on the foregrounding of a national reality that had come to transpire after the partition of the country. The writer's viewpoint, her theme in the work and the lingual and extra-lingual systems applied, constitute a three-fold base on which the creative work stands and on which alone the translator can erect the structure in translation. Translation, like all linguistic performances, is a communicative activity which involves not only the transfer of meaning from one language to another but the carrying over, as Pranati Pattanaik puts it, of "the spirit of the work, the characteristic power of its expression and the turn of its rhythmical movement from one language to another."[2]

Amrita Pritam, in *Pinjar*, has selected Indian history as a coequal in her fictional art, but to her, the facts themselves are of little interest as they have been given to us by novelists and historians *ad nauseam*. Her distinctive genius lies in giving these facts a specific orientation and in mediating history through the narrator's consciousness and in doing so, enabling herself and her readers "to see the world anew"[3] as Rushdie puts it. In the novel she starts, as Zola believed every literary artist did, with facts which cannot be ignored but her avowed purpose remains throughout to show "the mechanism of these facts,"[4] to illustrate how they, as constituents of historical reality, impinge upon individual life and liberty to wreak havoc on them.

In the novel Amrita Pritam uses historical facts to trigger off a fictional tale that effectively demonstrates her real concerns which are only tangentially historical. No novelist is under an obligation to build his/her picture with incidents that had actually taken place. It is in this regard that we may subscribe to the contemporary novelists' proclamation that "the thin line between fact and fiction is rapidly disappearing"[5] and that "the differences are no longer important."[6] This assertion finds emphatic corroboration in T.N. Dhar's statement that "the boundary between history and fiction is no longer water-tight or fixed."[7]

Pinjar depicts a world of social reality which draws its meaning from an interpretation of experienced reality, a reality which is engendered not by a system or a doctrine that prevails but by a sense or a sensitivity which helps organize the raw data of experience into a cognition and an apperception. To put it simply, the novel takes stock of that which asserts itself in the experiential past, however much we try to banish it from our consciousness.

The world portrayed in the novel is that of the post-Partition period in the history of India. Amrita Pritam conveys the facts of history not through a general marshalling of events but through the conflict and tension that prevails in the mind of the star-crossed protagonist of the novel, Pooro. She endeavours to explore human emotions in interpersonal relationships in the light of the prevailing circumstances that adversely affected communal harmony. She tries to relate the fate of individuals to the general state of affairs existing in the nation during that time.

The narrative begins in the retrospective mode with Pooro, now with child, reminiscing about her days back at home before she was abducted by Rashida who was put on oath by his uncles, the *Shaikhs,* to avenge the abduction and humiliation of his aunt by the *Sahukars,* the family of money-lenders to which Pooro belonged. She had, however, been grateful then that Rashida had said not a single harsh word to her and her honour had remained unsullied; and yet, when it came to her entreaties to let her go back home, Rashida turned a deaf ear to them and told her that they would soon be tying the nuptial knot in the presence of a *Maulvi.* This cut the ground from under her feet and all her dreams of going to Ram Chand's house as a beautiful bride in a palanquin, were shattered.

Despite the disheartening circumstances in which Pooro was caught she planned her escape and in the dark of the night, unlocked the door and ran out of her "prison." She ran as fast as she could and finally reached the door of her house. Her mother embraced her warmly but her father, more down-to-earth, expressed his inability to take her back into the family:

> Daughter, this fate was ordained for you; we are helpless. The Shaikhs will descend on us and destroy everything we have. (p. 9)

And again, when Pooro pleaded with him to take her to Thailand with them, he said,

> Who will marry you now? You have lost your religion and your birthright. If we dare to help you, we will be wiped out without a trace of blood left behind to tell of our fate. (p. 9)

Her mother, bracing herself for the separation added, "Daughter, it would have been better if you had died at birth!" (p. 9)

Pooro had nothing more to lose now. Her only hope was "escape in death" (p. 10) but that grace, too, she was not allowed because Rashida took her back with her to live as "Hamida" for the rest of her life and the name was indelibly tattooed on her arm.

Hamida soon gave birth to a son, a son she was made to conceive forcibly and nurse in her womb against her will. Initially she hated the idea of giving birth to Rashida's child but soon, the maternal instinct in her welling up, she could not but love the child and his father, Rashida. The story of Taro, the village girl, whose husband had deserted her for another woman, made Hamida's own home appear like "a haven of refuge" (p. 20). The mad woman, too, who had been impregnated by a savage, unfeeling beast of a man, aroused Hamida's pity and later, when she died in childbirth, Hamida brought home her child to nurse and nurture as her own. Initially, the Hindus would not let Hamida, the Muslim woman, bring up a Hindu child but later they lamented and let her have the child.

Communal discord consequent on the partition of India rose to an unprecedented degree of severity and the horror of the cataclysmal onset of the Partition-riots was unbelievable. The world in the novel emerged from a simple past into a violent complex present and the novelist here seeks to chart the effect of that shift on the individual and the society. Women, in particular—people's daughters, sisters and wives were abducted and were forcibly held by strangers in their houses. One such woman was Lajo, Ram Chand's sister and her brother's wife. Pooro pleaded with Rashida to help her look for Lajo, who, as was later discovered, had been kept captive in Ram Chand's house in Rattoval itself for she had caught the fancy of a man from a Muslim family that had occupied that house. So Lajo, too, like Pooro, had been abducted and detained. Pooro, now Hamida, was furious every time she heard of the abduction of Hindu girls by Muslims and of Muslim girls by Hindus for none of these abducted girls would now have any place or any one to go back to. They would be derelicts at the mercy of their abductors!

No time was lost by Hamida after she learned of the whereabouts of Lajo. She made frequent visits to the house of the latter's detention as a *khes* seller and seized upon an opportune moment to engineer Lajo's escape with the help of her husband, Rashida. Once rescued, Lajo was taken to Lahore by Hamida and Rashida and handed over to her husband, Hamida's brother, and to Ram Chand, her own brother, to join the convoy about to start off for India. A momentary temptation to join the convoy flit past the mind of Hamida but then she moved to where her husband stood, convincing herself that it was Pakistan that was her home now. Tears welled up in her eyes as the bus moved on and yet there was an indescribable joy she experienced in having been able to send Lajo back to her family, to her country.

Amrita Pritam in *Pinjar* unequivocally foregrounds the gendered premises of traditional myths and the male-centred social and ethical codes of conduct which need to be questioned and redefined in the context of the lives of the contemporary Indian women. For women in India, gender has always been and still is, to a large extent, a prescriptive factor in life which, in interaction with the ideologies of caste, class and religion, circumscribes for them the socially permissible range of experiences and determines their response to all that transpires. *Pinjar* is a loaded comment on the threat that communalism has posed for women in the past, especially during the days of the post-Partition riots when violence became the order of the day and there was relentless destruction caused by the erection of geographical and emotional barriers between the two communities—the Hindus and the Muslims—that had hitherto lived together in peace. *Pinjar*, however, does not begin with the depiction of a sudden outbreak of violence between the two communities. Its particularity lies in attributing the first act of violence in the narrative to a long-standing vendetta between the families of the *Shaikhs* and the *Sahukars* rather than to communal hatred engendered by the Partition. Pooro's abduction is prompted by a vow taken by the *Shaikhs* to avenge the abduction and humiliation of a woman from their family. Co-incidentally, this was also the time when the Partition triggered off violence, bloodshed and displacement of people from their homes. Women were the worst sufferers and were victimized in different ways; many were widowed or lost their children; many others were abducted and raped, and of these, only some were "recovered" whereas the others went into oblivion with little effort made to retrieve them. The recorded history of the partition of India focuses on the discord and confrontation between the two major political parties of the times, namely, the Congress and the Muslim League, and registers the "divide and rule" policy of the Britishers. The trauma of the Partition experienced by women and the consequent scars left in their lives were completely ignored. The surviving victims were either handicapped by their illiteracy or too shocked to recount the harrowing experiences they underwent.

Jyotirmoyee Devi's short story, *"Sei Chheleta" ("That Boy")*, set in the days of the Partition, depicts the anguishing and distressing emotions of a mother and a daughter who meet after years of separation caused by the partition riots in Punjab in 1947 but what is noteworthy is that they meet under specific circumstances that estrange them to each other. Neither wishes to recognize the other—the mother for shame of having borne her seducer a son, and the daughter for the consciousness that her mother could at least have chosen to die if she could not escape her enemies. Her image of her mother as a paragon of virtues had been belied by the fact that the latter was now saddled with a child who was not her father's son!

A similar situation of violence against women prevails in *Pinjar* where Pooro is abducted and then forcibly married to Rashida. But, before the marriage is solemnized she escapes from the place of her confinement and goes to her family with the certainty of a joyous reunion, but the Indian ideological underpinnings regarding the defilement of women, even if it be only in terms of abduction and detention by another community, do not allow reprieve to them and they suffer for no fault of theirs. Hindu prescriptive texts in India maintain double standards of morality for men and women; any radical departures from the male code of conduct are accommodated but no woman is allowed the space and freedom due to her as an individual in her own right. Womanhood is given a gendered construct and according to the traditional social code it is the woman who pays heavily for any lapse in upholding the family honour. With the trauma of abduction by a Muslim still trailing her psyche Pooro is further subjected to particularly shocking and humiliating treatment when her parents refuse to take her back into their fold for fear of ignominy and threat of destruction. She is perhaps compelled to ask herself as the woman in A.J. Major's paper, "The Chief Sufferers" asks, "What is left in me now [...]?"[8] Whenever the normal order of society is subverted and hostilities are stirred, it is the women who are subjected to different forms of violence and aggression—physical, social and psychological—for it is in this heaping of indignities on women that the power game of rival men in societies lies. Pooro's particular sufferings spring from the long-standing rivalry between the *Shaikhs* and the *Sahukars* but the male-dominated society hardly takes cognizance of the misery and agony that are perpetuated in her life, and finally, it is she who has to reconcile herself to her destiny by making the conscious choice of staying on in Pakistan with Rashida, now her husband, and with her son by him.

From the ancient epic text of the *Mahabharata* to Melville's *Moby Dick* exile has always been a symbol of disempowerment for women—of dispossession of rights, of exclusion from society and of death, moral, psychological and spiritual. The aspersions cast on her develop in her a contempt for herself so that she no longer wishes to live. The title of Amrita Pritam's novel, *'Pinjar,'* translated into English as *'The Skeleton'* is very suggestive of the protagonist's disillusionment with life and of her desire to die. Pooro, like Eustacia Vye of Hardy's novel, *The Return of the Native*, seems to be persistently telling herself "[...] how destiny has been against me [...]. I do not deserve my lot." When Rashida tells her of the conditions under which he was compelled to abduct her, she pathetically asks, "If my uncle abducted your aunt, what fault was that of mine?" (p. 8). Rashida further explains to her that even if she did go back to her family now she would be ostracized and would be looked upon with condescension. Her past would always hound her:

> Good woman, you have no place in that family any more! If they let you in even once, not one of their Hindu friends or relatives will take a drop of water in their house. And you have been with me for fifteen days. (p. 8)

Pooro soon comes to realize that nobody would believe that she was still untouched and undefiled and with a heavy heart, she accepts her mother's verdict, "Daughter, this fate was ordained for you; we are helpless." (p. 9)

Pooro's anguished soul was all alone in its suffering and the painful transformation that arose out of this affliction was consummated with the tattooing of her new name on her forearm—she was now christened 'Hamida' and Hamida she was to remain for the rest of her life. She was now Pooro only in her dreams and in her reminiscences of her parents' home. This duality, this "cross" she could not take affably to and was soon reduced to mere skin and bones:

> It was a double life: Hamida by day, Pooro by night. In reality she was neither one nor the other; she was just a skeleton without a shape or a name. (p. 11)

The story of the mad woman in the novel has not been introduced without a purpose. Although she has not been given a name and is only "the mad woman" her plight is a pulsating reality and a reverberation of the predicament of Pooro herself. Her thin charred body made her look "more a skeleton than a living person" (p. 21). But some "savage beast" had unfeelingly invaded even this "charred" body for a sick love of the pleasures of the flesh. He was not deterred by the fact that she was a mere unattractive bundle of bones. Hamida wondered at the perversity of men:

> She is neither young nor attractive; she is just a flesh of lump without a mind to go with it [...] a living skeleton [...] a lunatic skeleton [...]. A skeleton picked to its bones by kites and vultures. (p. 22)

Lajo's melancholy face, too, after her detention, is associated with "a sparrow's skeleton"—a suggestion on the novelist's part to indicate the depletion of all that was human (p. 45). The "skeleton" thus remains the predominant image in the novel and is avowedly designed to symbolize the helpless, miserable Indian woman subjected to gender-oppression and her singular victimization during the days of the Partition. "The transformation of the actual into symbol and image"[9] that Shahane observes in Khushwant Singh's art is as much traceable in the fictional art of Amrita Pritam in *Pinjar*, a novel loaded with symbolic significance.

The charisma of Amrita Pritam lies in her articulation and depiction of the choices she makes and the stances she adopts in her fictional art. The proliferation of "women's issues" across the world and her own fierce assertion of "the woman-question" in her works, especially in *Pinjar*, make her different from many of her contemporaries. The imprint of the violence of the Partition on her mind is indelible and the agony there to stay but her literary depiction of this major historical event is staid and dispassionate. Her transformation of the experience of private pain and anger at whatever human injustices transpired at the time of the Partition into what may be called art is remarkable. The novel is more an exercise in creative imagination than a historical record of events as they took place. What is reproduced is the general tenor of the times rather than the specific incidents that occurred. The narration is particularly marked with dispassionateness and objectivity and the composure reflected is unbelievable:

> Just as a peeled orange falls apart into segments, the Hindus, Muslims and Sikhs of the Punjab broke away from each other. As clouds of dust float over the roads, rumours of "incidents" began to float over the countryside. It was said that men were being slaughtered in hundreds; rows of houses were being burnt down; neighbours were

slitting each other's throats. No one's life or property was safe." (p. 33)

Incidents of arson in the Muslim-occupied areas where Hindus moved together for safety are reported in the most matter-of-fact manner:

> They poured kerosene oil over the windows and doors and put burning faggots to them. The flames shot up in the sky [...]. The soldiers came in the nick of the time, put out the fire and rescued the inmates. They loaded the petrified, screaming crowd into their trucks. Three had been badly burnt; fat oozed from them like wax; the flesh peeled off their bones like parchment; their elbows and knees stuck out like white stumps. (p. 34)

Pinjar, then, is a deep protest, a social document and a work of literary art all rolled into one. The experience involved is not a very simple one and the issues emanating from the work are multifarious for it is the human element in the novel that sways all considerations. The narrative structure in the novel effectively conveys the reality of the human experience of the period portrayed. What is more important here than the account of historical events is the matrix of strains and stresses that prevailed during the period and is compellingly reconstructed in terms of what befell the women—Hindu as well as Muslim—after the fateful partition of the country.

Despite the objectivity of narrative maintained throughout the novel, one cannot fail to notice the similarity of attitudes that exists between the protagonist, Hamida, and her creator and one may very well identify the two in their protest against the injustice meted out to the women of the times. We are told:

> Hamida's ears burned with rage when she heard of the abduction of Hindu girls by Muslims and of Muslim girls by Hindus. Some had been forced into marriage, some murdered, some stripped and paraded naked in the streets. (p. 34)

And again,

> Hamida spent many nights staring at the beams of the roof. In her thoughts she wondered over the plight of the

> women—people's daughters, sisters and wives—who were forcibly held by strangers under roofs like hers. (p. 37)

And still again,

> It was a sin to be alive in a world so full of evil, thought Hamida. It was a crime to be born a girl. (p. 35)

At the end of the work one cannot but admire the empathy with which Amrita Pritam feels for the grief-stricken women and the sincerity with which she tries to convey the feeling of how it was to be alive in the post-Partition times. Her imaginative reconstruction of events does not detract from the credibility of her account of the times for she has chosen an aesthetic stance that is representative rather than statistical in depiction—representative of the fate of hapless women caught in the horrifyingly unnatural circumstances of the Partition and subjected to the humiliation of abduction and rape. As a creative artist of fiction, she assumes the role of an analyst exploring the ways of marking the specificity and separateness of women in their suffering during this period and gender for her becomes a prime factor in the formation of her artistic dispensations.

References

1. Amrita Pritam, *The Skeleton and That Man*, transl. Khushwant Singh (New Delhi: Sterling Publishers, 1987); two novels of Amrita Pritam are brought together in this volume.
2. Pranati Pattanaik, *The Art of Translation* (New Delhi: Herman Publishing House, 1997), p. 140.
3. Salman Rushdie, "Not Guilty!," *Sunday*, 18-24 Feb, 1990, p. 27.
4. Emile Zola, *Du Roman Experimental*, Chapter 1, Le Roman Experimental (1880); transl. Belle M. Sherman (New York, 1893).
5. Augustus M. Kolich, "Does Fiction Have to be Made Better Than Life?," *Modern Fiction Studies*, Summer 1983, Vol. 29, No. 2, p. 172.
6. *Ibid.*
7. T.N. Dhar, *History-Fiction Interface in Indian English Novel* (New Delhi: Prestige, 1999), p. 11.
8. A.J. Major, "The Chief Sufferers: A Preliminary Look at the Abduction, Recovery and Rehabilitation of Women in the Punjab,

1947-48," paper presented at Seminar on *Northern India and Indian Independence* at Nehru Memorial Museum and Library, 6-9 Dec., 1993.

9. V.A. Shahane, "Khushwant Singh: An Artist in Realism," *Critical Essays on Indian Writing in English*, ed. Naik et.al. (India: Macmillan, 1977), p. 347.

9

Bapsi Sidhwa's *Ice Candy Man*: A Reassessment

The Indian English novel has its roots in history and in the Indian consciousness for it began as a vehicle of political awakening during the national struggle for Independence and thus, initially, the principal inspiration was not creative but expository. Now that Indian English fiction has come of age, and more than come of age the possibilities of retrieving experiential moments of history through fictional strategies are innumerable. From vast, comprehensive and exhaustive papers, I am narrowing my focus down to a short, intensive one, more thought-provoking, perhaps, than any write-up with an expansive sweep. For the Indian novelist writing in English, the theme of India's partition is imbued with the magical quality of a reflection in a mirror—it is true and yet not true. Every novelist has his own blend of fact and fiction to offer, the guiding factor being what Rushdie calls "memory's truth," which is a process of selection and elimination creating its own reality, but usually presenting a coherent version of events. This qualifying factor of "memory's truth" I believe, is a cardinal principle prevailing as a determinant in all fictional art and applies to all creative works.

The road from life to art, from author to creation, can mean turning the past alive by providing a transparent window on reality rather than an indecipherable code. The literary artist proceeds through craft sophistication to an optimum level of fictive reality, a reality that is "true-to-life." Nothing is explained, what is shown must be perceived, apprehended and the reader's pleasure is often in proportion to what is left unsaid, or ambiguously hinted at.

Bapsi Sidhwa, a Parsi domiciled in Pakistan, is a novelist who has an abundance of inventive and narrative energy manifested in her fiction, which warrants the careful critical attention of those interested in new possibilities for imaginative prose which resorts to viable fictional means—largely realistic—for tracing the compelling force of historical events on individual lives and presenting a collage of the lives and experiences of men and women caught in the web of history. It is Sidhwa who gave to the Pakistani novel in English a distinct identity.

Bapsi Sidhwa's novels are notably different from one another in content and form, in subject and treatment. Her first novel, *The Crow Eaters*, published in 1978, deals with the lives and fortunes of the Parsi Junglewalla family in British India. The narrative adroitly adopts comic and ironic modes directed towards the realization of Zoroastrian values in the lives of the members of the community. The novel is also an exposition of the anglicized Parsi way of life in Pakistan as Dina Mehta's *And Some Taka a Lover* (1992) is a comment on the upheaval in the world of the community caught in the political welter of the Quit India Movement.

Sidhwa's second novel, *The Pakistani Bride* (1983) is very different from her first in that it makes no assertion of the Parsi identity. In fact, it has no Parsi character at all. It is about a young Pakistani girl, a Muslim refugee, who is adopted by a Pathan during the Partition turmoil. The novel testifies to Sidhwa's understanding of and insight into the Pakistani ethos, no doubt, but when released it did not really make waves. Next came *Ice-Candy Man* (1990) which was followed by *The American Brat* in 1994. *The American Brat* dramatizes the conflict of the value systems of the East and the West and this conflict of cultures has its impact not only on the social plane but on the personal life of the protagonist as well.

Coming back to *Ice-Candy Man*, the response to this novel was absolutely mind-blowing. The author in this work showcases the Parsi attitude—the Parsis, here, representing a minority community—to the imminent Partition and to the concept of 'Swaraj.' Set in pre-Partition Lahore, in the period which Subhash K. Jha in his review of the work refers to as the period of "The satanic rites of fragmentation in the Indian subcontinent,"[1] the novel clearly highlights the vulnerability of human relationships that can be torn asunder at the slightest pretext. Also, here again, as in Dina Mehta's novel and in Bapsi Sidhwa's earlier novel, *The Crow Eaters*, we see the ambivalent attitude of the Parsis towards the British. They find it difficult to choose their loyalties—"Swaraj or the British Raj?" At a special meeting organized at the Temple Hall on Warris road an irresoluble battle-of-words on the political situation ensues. Col. Bharucha's advice to the Parsis is to keep their distance from the slush of the nationalist agitation. Dr. Mody, on the other hand, pleads for commitment to the cause of the freedom struggle for the transparent reason that "our neighbours will think we are betraying them and siding with the English."[2] And finally, at the instance of Toddywalla, the banker, the Parsis decide to opt for a path of compromise. Here, it may be relevant to point out that Sidhwa's novels voice the views of the particularly affluent, urban, middle-class Parsis.

Reams have been written on the Partition—in resentment, in anger, in affliction, in erudition or as a cathartic exercise, or again, even as an attempt to exorcise ghosts, phantoms of the agonizing past that refuse to be ignored. Bapsi Sidhwa's account of the holocaust is a tale with a difference—it is a concatenation of events seen through the insouciant eyes of an eight year old Parsi girl, Lenny, (who could very well have been Bapsi Sidhwa herself), who is baffled and perplexed by the adult world of turn abouts and shifting loyalties as also by changing emotions and widening gulfs. Caught between the conflicting demands of the major communities of the country, the Parsis in a pathetic minority have no misconceptions regarding the choices they confront. Under their affluence and prosperity won by competence and industry lurks a sense of insecurity when the country is on the verge of a painful partition: "If we are stuck with the Hindus, they'll convert us by the sword. And God help us if we are stuck with the Sikhs!"[3] Finally, under the mature guidance of Col. Bharucha the Parsis of Lahore decide to stay on there and cast their lot with whoever rules Lahore—Hindu, Muslim, Sikh, Christian. "People now shrink dwindling into symbols,"[4] and human beings suddenly turn on one another.

Lenny, polio-stricken in infancy, is cared for by her eighteen year old nubile, voluptuous, buxom, chocolate-brown Ayah, who is mostly spending time with her ward under Victoria's statue in Queen's Park. Interestingly, she is always surrounded by a host of male admirers—the Fallettis Hotel cook, the Government House gardener, the elegant, compactly-muscled Masseur and the "lank and loping" Ice Candy Man, later additions to the community of suitors being the Chinaman and the Pathan, Sharbat Khan. "Ayah's presence," we are told, "galvanizes men to mad sprints in the noon heat"[5] and she brazenly succumbs to the advances of each in turn—and each is conscious of the fact that "a whiff off Ayah carries the dark purity of creation." The group surrounding her "remains unchanged, [...] as always unified around her."[6] Primarily, however it is the Masseur and the Ice Candy Man who vie for Ayah's attention though it is the former who happens to be the more privileged of the two.

The easy familiarity, the bawdy humour and the friendly banter in the narrative soon undergo a change in tone and direction and each one has an acrimonious dig at the other's religion and nation. Every verbal exchange involuntarily slips into talk of India and Pakistan. Attitudes crystallize and the earlier distinction at Queen's Park between "baba-log" with their starchy Ayahs and the native children with their Ayahs in limp cotton saris soon dissolves and now are seen only Muslim women in 'purdah' separated from the Sikh community that breaks away from Hindus.

In Lenny's house, too, the placid harmony amongst servants from different communities disintegrates and each concentrates on surer signs of his own religion. Ayah never forgets to burn joss sticks around the statues of her own gods. The pogrom begins and takes on a vertiginous speed with the perpetrators of the crime never being tracked down. The "we are brothers" theory fails. Gandhi visits Lahore and Lenny, seeing him, is distressed at what she calls "this improbable toss up between a clown and a demon."[7]

Nothing works—the nation is in flames, Lahore is burning, Mazang Chowk is turned to ashes. The Muslim mob comes to Lenny's house to assault the Hindu servants but Ayah is safely hidden at the back of the house. Lenny, with her penchant for truth is, however, soon cajoled into disclosing Ayah's hideout to the Ice Candy Man, who, despite promises to protect her, has her dragged out and carried away only, perhaps, to be made an inmate of a brothel. Later it is heard and believed that the police rescues her from the Ice Candy Man who had forcibly married her and sends her back to her family in Amritsar. The irresoluble end leaves us guessing as to whether Ayah was accepted into the family at home or did life become for her "the torture of Sisyphus," never ending.

Bapsi Sidhwa, in *Ice Candy Man*, experiments with the reality of the times to create a timeless reality of her own universe. History undertaken by the fiction writer and explored as material, refers always to the particular in which there is an attempt to present history as sensory detail, as visual image, as time which reverberates in our time.

Sidhwa, does not, in her novel resort to the immediacy of journalistic methods. Images in the novel do not, like in a journalistic report, follow a conveyor-belt succession. She takes the slant of humour and the obliqueness of satire. The humour is sometimes mistaken for ribaldry but an in-depth analysis of the novel shows that all the humour, laughter and mirth employed is with a purpose. It is through their ribald humour and rustic wisdom that Ayah's as also Lenny's companions enable the little girl to chronicle the tragedy of the Partition.

The novelist's satire is of a characteristically cruel and unforgiving nature—Lenny's world centres around her relationship with her loving Ayah, and ardent cousin suitor (who transposes Lenny from dolls to condoms) and a Godmother with her companion connotatively referred to as Slave sister.

Lenny grows up when she learns on her own the lesson that divides her Hindu Ayah, from her Parsi employers and her Muslim revengers. To put it broadly, the novel is "about the slow awakening of the child heroine both to sexuality and grown up pains and pleasures and to the particular historical disaster that overwhelms her world."[8] T.N. Dhar's conclusion in his book, *History—Fiction Interface in Indian English Novel* that "the novelist deals with history by using narrative modes which are essentially non-mimetic, such as comedy, satire and allegory"[9] is unflinchingly applicable to Sidhwa's *Ice Candy Man* for in it the non-mimetic mode represents a "reality" that transcends historical space for it is "memory's truth" again as Salim Sinai in *Midnight's Children* calls it and in the end "it creates its own reality."[10] Thus, there is no knowable reality; only personal observations. It is these personal observations that make Lenny grow up and interpret her perception of the duplicities and deceptions of a savage adult world. Wading through the sea of events and experiences, she soon acquires a heuristic perspective in life which enlarges her consciousness and awareness of things around. Her experiment with truth has ended in misery.

Even though *Ice Candy Man* is primarily a novel of the Partition, the Partition as a historical event and not an emotional convulsion, one may, for an observation turn to R.K. Narayan's emphatic statement that "a mere story is not the point of fiction; people and emotions are what's important."[11] Emotion in this novel is conspicuous by its absence in the man-woman relationship and it is this very absence that is a comment on the image of woman as portrayed in this work.

Ice-Candy Man skilfully recreates the ethos of the Partition as a historical event affecting the lives of the characters in the novel but apparently, the novelist, in her bid to crystallize objective reality has markedly ignored the experimental realm of the highly victimized woman—the Ayah of the Parsi family at Lahore—who suffers excruciating pain and agony at the hands of the mob that tears her apart. As if this physical abuse by the mob was not enough, the Ice Candy Man clinches her lot by condemning her to prostitution. Though later he tries to make amends by marrying her, the harm has been done. She is, one presumes, left with a lacerated heart and mind but nowhere does the novelist elaborate on her injured psyche. And yet, we may absolve the novelist of this charge for, perhaps, this was not a part of her scheme of things.

The Parsi world in the novel is clearly more about women than men. Characters like Lenny's father, old Husband and even Manek Mody are relatively insignificant when compared to Godmother and Mother. But its the men, and especially the Ice-Candy man, who perpetrate the suffering of the women. Lenny's father's indulgence in adultery and his lashings endured by her mother are instances that make strong the case against the victimization of women. But none speaks out, and Ayah, too, moves "from speech to silence."[12] Silence in the novel, is designed to be more eloquent than speech.

The combination of laughter and ribaldry, wit and wisdom is in the novel an unmistakable pointer to the degree of levity with which a woman is treated. As mentioned earlier, each one of the suitors in the novel makes frivolous advances to Ayah but none treats her as an individual in her own right.[13] She remains throughout a symbol of sex, an "object" to be ogled rather than an individual to be regarded and respected.

There is no attempt on the novelist's part to show her as an approximation to the Indian concept of the female "Shakti." There is no attempt either, as in Jayant Mahapatra's poem, "Temple" to plumb the agony and the enigma in the Indian woman, "a riddle on its pedestal" (as Mahapatra refers to her). Apparently, there is no agitation regarding her, anywhere in the novel—there is only raillery and reporting of a dispassionate kind. Deep down, however, there is something very unnerving about the betrayal of the Ice Candy man who, Sidhwa tells us "appears to have grown shades darker, and his face is all dried up and shrivelled-looking."[14] The supposedly staid and cool narrative operates at a plaintive decibel mixing illusion and reality, fiction and fact as the flow of events demands. Thus, underlying the thematic historical perspective of *Ice Candy Man* is the trauma of reassessing the past in terms of experiential reality underpinning the larger historical reality.

Sidhwa conceives of historical representation as a repertoire of inexhaustible possibilities in terms of happenings as well as human experience, central and peripheral—all merging into an organic totality which forbids a linear interpretation of the past and offers instead, an entirety of existence.

References

1. Subhash K. Jha, "Dipped in Ribaldry," *The Times of India*, 5 Nov., 1989, p. 2.
2. Bapsi Sidhwa, *Ice Candy Man* (London: Heinemann, 1988), p. 37.
3. *Ibid.*
4. *Ibid.*, p. 93
5. *Ibid.*, p. 32
6. *Ibid.*, p. 97
7. Subhash K. Jha, *op. cit.*
8. Book review in *Observer*; cited in cover blurb of Penguin edition (New Delhi: Penguin, 1989).
9. T.N. Dhar, *History-Fiction Interface in Indian English Novel* (New Delhi: Prestige, 1999), p. 33.
10. *Ibid.*
11. Book review of R.K. Narayan's. *The World of Nagaraj*, *Sunday*, 11-17 Nov., 1990.
12. Chelva Kanaganayakam, "Allegory and Ambivalence in Bapsi Sidhwa's *Cracking India*," *Parsi Fiction*, Vol. 2, ed. Kapadia, Dodiya and Dhawan (New Delhi: Prestige, 2001), p. 43.
13. Shirin Kudchedkar, "The Second Coming: Novels on the Partition" *Indian English Fiction 1980-90: An Assessment* ed. Vilas Sarang and Nilufer Bharucha (New Delhi: B.R., 1994), 69. Compare Nilufer Bharucha's view that the ravishing of Ayah is symbolic of the abuse of the Indian earth—"The Parsi Voice in Recent Indian English Fiction," *Indian English Fiction, 1980-90: An Assessment.*
14. *Ice Candy Man*, p. 149.

10

Chinua Achebe: A Novelist at "The Crossroads of Cultures" (With Special Reference to '*Things Fall Apart*')

Post-colonialism is not merely a chronological concept denoting the period after the cessation of empires. Ideologically, it is a communication of a perception of liberation—a liberation from the dominance of the Western world, politically and culturally. The century-long political domination of Europe over other countries of the world being finally over, we now need to explore and interrogate aspects of the study of literature that were earlier imposed upon us but now stand to be analyzed and assimilated. Each country with its specific historico-geographical stance must re-interpret the old canonical texts in terms of the discourse being generated by its own culture rather than the imperatives framed by others. This alone will resist homogenization and give a voice to the dispossessed, the marginalized and the peripheral. Post-colonialism, thus, foregrounds the need for recognizing identities, voices and situations that were earlier ignored. Relevant here are Homi Bhabha's words which valorise marginality and oppression:

> [...] a range of contemporary critical theories suggests that it is from those who have suffered the sentence of history—subjugation, domination, diaspora, displacement —that we learn our most enduring lessons for living and thinking. There is even a growing conviction that the

> affective experience of social marginality [...] transforms our critical strategies.[1]

However, despite the postulation that the terms of literary discourse should be determined by the needs of one's culture one cannot overlook the complex and significant relationship between imperialism and post-colonialism for the discourse of post-colonialism is, to a large extent, administered and regulated by the very imperial culture which it seeks to reject. Makarand Paranjape, in his essay, 'Coping with Post-colonialism,' refers to "this ongoing process of cooptation, collusion, or compromise"[2] which "poses a serious challenge to post-colonial academics in general and to criticism in particular."[3]

Professor Bernth Lindfors, who helped bring recognition to African-English literature, especially in the United States of America, believes that most of us turn to this bulk of writing with a genuine openness and inclination to judge it on its own terms. One needs to read these works in the right spirit rather than dismiss them as inconsequential. Professor Lindfors, expatiating on the status of the Africans writing in English in the academic world, does not fail to register their significant contribution to literature in English:

> They have a lot to offer. They mark an enrichment, internalization, expansion of the English language and the English literary experience. Some of the African writers are extraordinary writers [...]."[4]

African writers who started writing in English almost a quarter of a century ago were often censured for addressing themselves primarily to a Western audience. They were, however, directing a message both, at the colonizer and the colonized. They were trying to refashion the African view point about African experience, but more importantly, they were trying to revolutionize European conceptions about African life and literature and that, too, in the language of the colonizers themselves. This was clearly an attempt on the part of the African writers to put African culture in its proper perspective before the Europeans and to place positive value on it. African culture itself comprises customs, religions and climates so different from each other in disparate parts of the continent that one can only wonder at it as a mélange of different cultures. Yet, what is likely to be of interest to a critic of African literature is the cultural context out of which the writing comes and the society it is related to. In the ultimate analysis, as Hayden White has argued, the "form" is the "context,"[5] that is, the language, vocabulary and conceptual form in which the experience of colonialism is produced determine the understanding and interpretation of it. "Nation" and "narration," as Homi K. Bhabha puts it, are inseparably intertwined—one implies the other.[6]

Chinua Achebe as a critic of the African scene, like Wole Soyinka and Ngugi, offers a mode of understanding Africa and its literature in the best British tradition of a writer-critic. His conscious effort at exploring the vigour and vibrancy of the African past in the interest of its present, his dismissal of prejudices and clearing of misunderstandings of those who are not acquainted with it and his thrust on the centrality of language for creative and critical purposes are of seminal importance and underline his concern for the literary scene and the general well-being of the nation. Committed to his personal views and beliefs, Achebe confines his works to his own nation-state of Nigeria, which was originally carved out of the region of the Igbo tribes of Western Africa.

Unlike many African fellow-writers, including Ngugi wa Thiong'o, who gave up writing in English when only mid-way in his career as a writer, Achebe continues to write in English and vehemently defends the use of English in African societies which have been subjected to colonial rule. English, according to him, is not just an international language but a national language as well for it enables diverse ethnic communities within the African society to communicate with each other.

Achebe, born in 1930, has to his credit the publication of five novels in addition to the numerous stories, poems, essays and children's fiction that he has written. He may very well be read as a post-colonial author though the term "post-colonial" gained currency much after he had written some of his famous works. Also, his most popular novel, *Things Fall Apart*, is set largely in the pre-colonial period though the novel does show how the colonial influence, after making inroads into Nigerian life, comes to stay. Attention is drawn to the cultural glory and the subsequent downfall of an African native society which gives up "its living separateness"[7] by its lack of active self-defence.

Achebe views the novel as an exercise in self-discovery. It is through writing, he believes, that an African can determine and establish his identity by exploring and re-discovering his historical roots. This reflexive and self-defining nature of the novel is singularly important to post-colonial writers who have been confronting an erosion of their traditional values owing to the overpowering exposure to European culture which has already made insidious advances upon the native way of life and the local customs, mores and habits in many countries. This explains why young intellectuals in recent African writing have turned to the autobiographical form of the novel, a form which is indulged in less to record and evaluate past experiences than to consider avenues for future action.

Achebe, in his works, persistently emphasizes the commitment which an African writer must show in trying to rehabilitate the native culture which the colonising powers have beaten out of shape and recognition. The African writer's prime task, according to him, is to establish.

> [...] that African peoples did not hear of culture for the first time from Europeans; that their societies were not mindless but frequently had a philosophy of great depth and value and beauty, that they had poetry and, above all, they had dignity.[8]

But, to prove that the Africans had a life of depth and value in the pre-colonial days, ironically, and paradoxically, the African writer must use as mode and as medium a language that is a legacy of colonialism itself. To quote Achebe, if colonialism did not endow the African peoples with "a song, it at least gave them a tongue for singing."[9] Yet, in honouring and extolling the virtues of the traditional African culture Achebe is not unaware of its lapses and weaknesses—"its good as well as its bad sides."[10] He is also conscious of the fact that as a writer living in the modern times he cannot totally identify with the values of the tribal past which conflict with the social and emotional pressures of the modern African experience upon the individual.

In *Things Fall Apart* the central character in the novel is clearly Okonkwo but as the narration progresses we perceive that it is Nwoye and not Okonkwo who initiates the disintegration and collapse of his tribal past. Ironically, Okonkwo's "success" in his tribal life leads to his destruction and his son, Nwoye's "failure" in the social and cultural context of the tribe secures for him his survival in the changing world of Umuofia. Okonkwo is devastated as a consequence of sincerity to the tribe and forfeits his life because of his warped sense of communal duty. He complies in all seriousness with the demand of the Oracle of the Hills and the Caves that Ikemefuna be killed and ignores the practical advice of the wise old man, Ezeudu, who pleads with him to moderate his action and avoid being present at the site of the killing.

Nwoye, however, is different. He demonstrates his priority for personal feelings and individual proclivities over his sense of social responsibility. He and his grandfather, Unoka, are more compatible with and acceptable to the post-colonial tribal world. As against the pre-colonial situation where the society was looked upon as the sustaining force of the clan, the ushering in of the colonial caused the society as an entity to cease to exist. And, with the devitalization and enervation of the "centre" things started "falling apart."

Okonkwo, largely dominated by his fear of failure and of weakness as also by his fear of being found to resemble his father in the latter's lack of "manliness," pursues distinction with such doggedness and so obsessive a single-mindedness that he soon emerges as a case in pathological study. To him "manliness" is a synonym of *violence*. So when Ikemefuna, on the verge of being struck to death by the man who was deputed to kill him, runs towards him for refuge, Okonkwo, "dazed with fear," draws his matchet and kills him. "He was afraid of being thought weak."[11]

Nwoye's final alienation from his father and the severing of the filial bond is almost a direct consequence of the killing of Ikemefuna:

> As soon as his father walked in, that night, Nwoye knew that Ikemefuna had been killed, and something seemed to give way inside him, like the snapping of a tightened bow.[12]

Nwoye, representative of the new faith of Christianity that had knocked at the door of tribal existence, is portrayed as a sensitive young man who is averse to certain existing cruel customs of the village, particularly the casting away of any pair of twins born into the dark forest. Thus, Nwoye's embracing of Christianity is an act of belligerence against his father and a rejection of the tribal society that Okonkwo had espoused.

Okonkwo's fight against the Christians and their success in making converts is his last bid to regain his lost place in the village. As expected, he is involved in the attack on the Christian Church and it is this involvement that leads to his arrest and humiliation and ultimately to the final tragedy of his hanging himself to death. Okonkwo's suicide symbolizes his personal rejection of a new order as well as the collapse of the old system of values. His inflexibility reflects the rigidity, inexorability and unaccommodating trait of the society of which he is an integral part. And, it is this very inelastic nature of both that is their undoing. Achebe begins by presenting the society as one with positive qualities—coherence, order, warm personal relationships and vital religious activity—but, cracks in the Igbo culture soon begin to show and the oppressed, particularly the outcasts or "osus" and the hapless mothers of twins, espouse Christianity and submit to the liberating influence of the new religion. What Nwoye bows to is not "the mad logic of the Trinity"[13] but "the poetry of the new religion, something felt in the marrow."[14]

Thus, *Things Fall Apart* is a novel that can be read at two levels—as the tragedy of one man braving his neurosis and his pathological fear of failure as well as his inimical fate, and, as a social comment on a hitherto vibrant but now moribund society struggling to evade the consequences of the arrival of Christianity in the "heathen" village of the Igbo tribe.

Abiola Irele, in her analysis of *Things Fall Apart* neatly sums up her assessment of the narrative stance of the novel in the following lines:

> *Things Fall Apart* turns out to present the whole tragic drama of a society, vividly and concretely enacted in the tragic destiny of a representative individual. This use of an individual character as a symbolic receptacle, the living theatre, of a social dilemma, is what gives Achebe's novels their real measure of strength [...].[15]

The individual and the society in *Things Fall Apart* were thus like conjoined twins who, each individually and together, suffered the grief of dissolution and disintegration. The narrative corroborates the protagonist's consciousness of this steadily augmenting sorrow: "And it was not just a personal grief. He mourned for the clan, which he saw breaking up and falling apart."[16]

In writing *Things Fall Apart* Achebe was largely inspired by one of the legends of the Irish hero, Cuchulainn, and more specifically by Yeats' version of it. Yeats, as is obvious, has also been the source of the title of the novel which has been taken from his poem, "The Second Coming." Achebe, in his African-English novels is an artist-historian who helps his people regain dignity and confidence in their traditional past. As an Igbo himself Achebe delved deep into African culture and tradition to write about Igbo life from within and understand the cultural crisis faced by the community.

The Igbo traditional society as depicted by Achebe in the novels of the African past, especially in *Things Fall Apart*, is masculine, hierarchical, coherent and self-contained—it is not as primitive as it is made out to be. "Achebe country," as the region recreated by the novelist in his fiction is generally referred to, cannot be strictly geographically defined but is large enough to include the central province of all Igbo-speaking people who share a common language, culture and tradition. The society is governed by certain established social institutions and the legal system, as the trial scene in *Things Fall Apart* suggests, is rather elaborate and sophisticated. The chief priest, Ezeani, enforces the will of the clan as the will of Ani, the Earth goddess, when Okonkwo disrupts the peace of the peaceweek. As G.D. Killam puts it, "[...] all activity in *Things Fall Apart* is judged by what is or is not acceptable to Ani, the Earth Goddess [...]. In other words, a powerful 'female principle' pervades the whole society of Umuofia."[17] The male authority in Umuofia is represented by Agbala, the Oracle of the Hills and Caves, who is the counterpart of the Earth and is called 'Father.'

The Igbo society is polytheistic. *Ani*, the Earth goddess, *Amadiora*, the god of the thunderbolt, *Idemili*, the python god, *Ogwugwu*, the protector of life, are smaller deities and *Chukwu*, the Originator and Sustainer is the High God whose will is the greatest. *Chi* is one's personal god and guiding spirit. Ancestor worship is also a salient feature of the Igbo society. Eminent members of the community impersonate the ancestors and emerge to participate in every ceremony held in honour of the Earth Goddess.

Things Fall Apart, thus, explores the basic cultural patterns and the social and politico-historical past of Nigeria, whose cultural identity was endangered with the advent of Christianity and colonialism till the cultural edifice finally gave way and things fell apart. The African society, however, held on to its "metaphors of culture"[18] till the very end. The importance of myths and legends, totems and taboos, beliefs and superstitions, rites and religion, customs and observances interspersed with folk-tales, proverbs, songs and anecdotes in African society can never be over-emphasized. *Things Fall Apart* is an infinite source of these elements of culture and each of these has a meaningful function to perform in the total structural edifice of the novel. Achebe, in foregrounding the conflict between the African tribal religion and Christianity has created a graphic socio-anthropological picture of the Igbo society and in the process enlightened us about the bicultural relationship that exists between two cultures in conflict. Naikar, in his essay on Achebe's *Arrow of God*, says:

> Anthropology tells us that whenever two cultures come in contact with each other, the dominant culture influences the other culture in a variety of ways. The minor culture is likely to undergo a process of acculturation by being attracted to the dominant (or foreign) culture. At such a juncture some people of the native culture may become acutely conscious of their cultural identity and try to resist the foreign culture. Thus attraction and resistance may be seen in the bicultural relationship.[19]

This is an illuminating comment on the Afro-European confrontation as witnessed in the life of the Igbo society in Nigeria.

Achebe's merits as a novelist lie in the equanimity and meticulous balance he has consistently maintained between the realistic depiction of the universal human condition and the well-defined structure of the fictional framework. He does not consciously intrude his views into the narrative but attempts to show from his ambivalent position of the traditionalist and the modernist the complexities and of a colonial situation. Achebe's novels are an assertion of the African identity and his compellingly told tales drive the African to search for and rediscover his cultural roots. To endorse the values of traditional African life, Achebe lends African colour to the narration and interweaves the Igbo rituals like the Pumpkin Leaves Festival and the New Yam Festival into the tale. Thus, Achebe uses creatively "his sense of the pastness of the present and the presentness of the past"[20] and gives a "new" kind of African fiction in English which, while adopting the structure of a modern novel, incorporates into the work the African ethos strengthened by the oral performances.

In this "new" kind of fiction that Achebe ventures into, he does not straightaway plunge into a telling of the tale. He lets us see things happen before us, all in terms of individual and community life in a small village. He does not "tell," he "shows."[21] Hurt by the contemptuous depiction and dehumanization of the Africans by the Western writers as found in Joyce Cary's *Mister Johnson* and Conrad's *Heart of Darkness*, he presented an imaginative recreation of the Igbo society to revive and re-establish the dignity of the community and his mode of unravelling the curiosities and the intricacies of the society display a remarkable mastery of the art. C.D. Narasimhaiah, in his evaluation of *Things Fall Apart*, comments on Achebe's art—narrative and dramatic:

> Achebe is a product of two cultures in which realism gets suffused and lifted to the plane of reality. It starts with a realistic detail: the village crier announces a meeting at the market place, the next morning [...]. We move from event to event, not in the customary narrative mode, though, but connections are made ingeniously through events affecting the community as a whole."[22]

Achebe, as a literary artist, has always been open and ingenuous, making no bones about his ambivalent attitude to life. He has publicly made proud assertions of his bilingual competence:

> [...] I have probably spoken more words in Igbo than English but I have definitely written more words in English than in Igbo. Which I think makes me perfectly bilingual.[23]

Achebe's pronouncement, "We lived at the crossroads of cultures. We still do today"[24] gives clear evidence of his consciousness of his precarious position in terms of the choices he has already made and the choices he will make in the future. Achebe was fully cognizant of the diametrically opposed pulls working on him and was in a bind as to what to surrender to and what to resist. Achebe's father had joined the new faith of Christianity early in life and had risen to become an evangelist and a church teacher. His maternal uncle who had brought him up (his own parents having died prematurely), was a man of status in the village. After having taken the highest but one title that a man of wealth and honour may target, and after having offered a lavish meal to his fellowmen in the community, he came to be called Udo Osinyi—"Udo," who cooks more than the whole people can eat.

So, with this twin affiliation—to Christianity and to the Igbo religion—Achebe felt that he had been placed at the crossroads and had now to strike a choice with regard to bonding and alliance:

> On one arm of the cross we sang hymns and read the Bible night and day. On the other, my father's brother and his family, blinded by heathenism, offered food to idols [...]. Those idols and that food had a strange pull on me inspite of my being such a thorough little Christian [...]. If anyone likes to believe that I was torn by spiritual agonies or stretched on the rack of my ambivalence, he certainly may suit himself. I do not remember any undue distress. What I do remember is a fascination for the ritual, and the life on the other arm of the crossroads. And I believe two things were in my favour—that curiosity, and the little distance imposed between me and it by the accident of my birth. The distance becomes not a separation but a bringing together [...]."[25]

Achebe has made a sincere confession that *Things Fall Apart* was perhaps, though not consciously so, a kind of penance, an act of atonement for having severed his ties with his past. By the writing of this novel he tried to make amends for his earlier negligence of the ethic of the community to which he belonged by birth. It was for him a kind of purging of his sense of guilt for he had felt it incumbent on himself to vindicate his people who had been unwarrantably denigrated and depicted as inhuman. Just as this act of purgation started giving him a feeling of reconciliation with his tribe and a sense of relief at being absolved of the crime of negligence, almost of dereliction of duty, political independence from colonial rule came as a new source of alienation and severance. He had lost his *raison d'être* as a writer inspiring his people to resist the onslaught of a foreign culture for the political crisis of colonial dominance was over.

By the time freedom came, extensive damage had already been done. The period of subjection to European races has fractured the African psyche and people from this continent still suffer the traumatic effects of their confrontation with the colonial powers. Thus, Achebe now assigns to the African writer the task of re-educating and re-generating the traumatized natives. In his article, "The Black Writer's Burden," Achebe takes cognisance of the misery that the long encounter with

Europe had wrought upon the Africans: "In terms of human dignity and human relations the encounter was almost a complete disaster for the black races."[26] The onus is now on the writer to lead his people to regain their lost dignity and their belief in themselves.

Achebe, in his lecture entitled "The Role of the Writer in a New Nation," delivered to the Nigerian Library Association in 1964, specifies that the duty of the novelist is "to explore in depth the human condition."[27] And, for this, he believes that in Africa "a proper sense of history"[28] is a prerequisite. The African writer cannot afford to be unaware of or indifferent to the stark injustice that his people have been subjected to.

After the military coup of January, 1966, the counter-coup which overthrew the government and the consequent war which broke out, Achebe revised his concept of the role of a writer, believing now that the latter should be a social transformer and a revolutionary. At this juncture, Achebe again finds himself at the crossroads wondering what the place of a writer is in a revolutionary movement and uncertain as to how a literary artist could resolve the situation. The two opposing views subscribed to are: "his place is right in the thick of it"[29] and "No, it's too rough there. A writer has no business being where it is so rough. He should be on the sidelines [...]."[30]

What should then be the relationship between the writer and his society? Immediately after the war, instead of making a mutually exclusive choice, Achebe sought to harmonize his different positions. African literature, he said, has to be made relevant to the issues of the day and yet it needs to be rooted in history. He concluded by suggesting a new approach in the writer and a reconciliation in him of the past and the present:

> I think what is meaningful is what takes into account the past and the present [...]. The most meaningful work that African writers can do today will take into account our whole history: how we got here, and what it is today; and this will help us to map our plans for the future.[31]

African writers cannot afford to ignore the past because the present is a consequence of it; but, they should not also be obsessed with the past to the point of being oblivious of the contemporary scene. Achebe admits that some degree of politics is bound to find expression in writing, especially in Africa, but, in order to be objective in his work, to produce a lasting work of art, the writer must avoid becoming emotionally involved in the politics of the race.

A literature that identifies itself as post-colonial and defines itself in terms of the upshot of colonialism can hardly overemphasize the relation it bears to its past and to the writing of its own history.[32] Significant questions which need to be answered in this context are: where do post-colonial writers locate their past?—in the pre-colonial, colonial or post-colonial period? Can we separate and extricate from each other the various historical strands? And, what historical viewpoint should post-colonial writers adopt towards their past if they desire to promote a sense of national identity after colonization?

Things Fall Apart, as an exercise in historical convalescence, is a good illustration of the stance a novelist must assume to forge in his fellow-men a consciousness of the historical past and a sense of national pride. But, Achebe's double affiliation to the old and the new, his divided response to the subject of his novel makes his approach to the issue ambiguous and this ambiguity, to the discriminating and observant is clearly reflected in the closure of the novel, in the open-ended conclusion marked by a suggestion of the tentative. Apparently the narrative line in the novel is simple: it tells the story of the travails of Okonkwo, his rise and fall in the Igbo society concluding with the unequivocal end of his death. At a deeper level, however, while the novel mourns the decline of the traditional Igbo culture and regrets the disintegration of the norms of conduct and governance, it also looks ahead to the future stable political and social life of Nigeria. This juxtaposing of the past and the future suggests Achebe's own complicated and ambivalent attitude to the theme, his own stance on the modernization of Africa. Change, he secretly believes, has to be espoused.

Richard Begam, in analyzing Achebe's sense of an ending,[33] suggests that in *Things Fall Apart* Achebe offers three different conceptions of history and consequently, makes us aware of three viable interpretations of the novel and its conclusion. First, Achebe writes a kind of nationalist history which is essentially reconstructive and recuperative and aims at retrieving the past in all its dignity and glory. Second, Achebe writes what Begam calls a form of "adversarial history," which concentrates not on retrieving or rebuilding the authentic past but on demolishing a pseudo-past that has been fabricated and imposed. This kind of history enables Achebe to expose what he himself called "colonialist" discourse, a verbal communication characterised by a supercilious disregard for the native African on the part of the British. Third, Achebe writes a kind of metahistory which is significant as a piece of writing, a narrative formation determined by the concepts of selection, emphasis and shaping, the last referring to organization and arrangement. Meaning in a novel is conveyed essentially by two things—the chosen events in time and the order and manner in which they are presented.

Coming now to the three endings in the novel, the first focuses on Okonkwo's killing of the messenger, his abortive effort to arouse his people to action, and his frustration ending in suicide. This conclusion is in conformity with the events of novel being looked at from an African perspective, Okonkwo's death symbolizing the breakdown of the Igbo culture. The novel's second ending allied to adversarial history, looks at events from the point of view of the District Commissioner. The Igbo way of life is now presented as an object of anthropological curiosity and its disintegration is looked upon as more of a European achievement than as an African disaster. The third ending is placed outside the novel—it is located in Achebe's later novel, *No Longer at Ease*, which was conceived as a sequel to *Things Fall Apart*. The scene of the former novel in which the third ending of the latter is located occurs when Okonkwo's grandson, Obi, a university educated civil servant, in his discussion with a British colonial officer on the nature of a tragedy expresses the view that suicide ruins a tragedy as there is no purging of emotions in the work concerned. In the case in hand the realization of Okonkwo's contribution in his tragic fall comes, ironically, only after the collapse of the Igbo culture.

Given the colossal pressure out of which post-colonial literature was born it is not surprising that this literature is considered to be merely "an exercise in political thematics"[34] and analyses of form and technique of the related works are seldom attempted. However, critics have now begun to believe that writers like Achebe, who interpret their past, need to be approached for the narrative structure of their works as well. This is no assertion of Achebe being a postmodern writer, but, one needs to admit that he is not, exclusively a postcolonial writer. He is a postcolonial writer only in-so-far as he is born of and has espoused cultural globalization; in-so-far as he is an African who has attained maturity and lives at "the crossroads of cultures."[35] The final note in Achebe's novels is one in which there is neither blind obsession with a regressive past for mere evocative purposes nor a fixation about the present. The ultimate concern is a reaffirmation of the human spirit, an exploration in depth of the human condition as Achebe himself had said.

References

1. Homi Bhabha, *The Location of Culture*, London: 1994, p. 172.
2. Makarand Paranjape, "Coping with Post-Colonialism," *Post-Colonialism: Theory, Text and Context* ed. Harish Trivedi and Meenakshi Mukherjee (Shimla: Institute of Advanced Study, 1996), p. 37.
3. *Ibid.*
4. Sarbani Sen, "Whither African-English Literature? A Tete-e-tete with Bernth Lindfors," *African Literature Today* ed. R.K. Dhawan (New Delhi: Prestige, 1994), p. 11.
5. Hayden White, *The Content of the Form: Narrative Discourse and Historical Representation* (Baltimore: The Johns Hopkins University Press, 1987).
6. Homi Bhabha discusses "nation" and "narration" in the introductory essay of *Nation and Narration*, (London: Routledge, 1990).
7. Sri Aurobindo, *The Foundations of Indian Culture* (Pondicherry: Sri Aurobindo Ashram, 1980), p. 3. According to Sri Aurobindo, any culture that gives up "its living separateness and neglects an active self-defence will be swallowed up and the nation which lived by it will lose its soul and perish."

8. *Nigeria Magazine*, June, 1964.
9. *Insight*, Oct./Dec., 1966, p. 20.
10. *Nigeria Magazine*, June, 1964.
11. Chinua Achebe, *Things Fall Apart* (New Delhi: Allied Publishers Ltd., rpt. 2000) p. 55; first published by William Heinemann Ltd. in 1958.
12. *Ibid.*
13. *Ibid.*, p. 134.
14. *Ibid.*
15. Abiola Irele, "The Tragic Conflict in the Novels of Chinua Achebe," *Chinua Achebe: 'Things Fall Apart'* ed. Tapan Basu (Delhi: Worldview Publications, 2003), pp. 87-88.
16. Chinua Achebe, *Things Fall Apart*, p. 165.
17. G.D. Killam, *The Novels of Chinua Achebe* (London: Heinemann Educational Books, 1969), pp. 19-20.
18. M. Mani Meitei, "Fictional Techniques in Chinua Achebe's *Things Fall Apart*," *African Literature Today*, ed. R.K. Dhawan, p. 44.
19. Basavaraj Naikar, "Religions Conflict in Chinua Achebe's *Arrow of God*, *The Indian Journal of English Studies*, Vol. XL, 2002-2003, p. 78.
20. S.A. Khayoon, "The Neo-Athropological Novels of Achebe," *The African Fiction*, ed. Shyam S. Agarwalla (New Delhi: Prestige, 2000), p. 135.
21. Wayne Booth, *The Rhetoric of Fiction* (Chicago: University of Chicago Press, 1961, rpt. 1983), p. 8.
22. C.D. Narasimhaiah, "*Things Fall Apart*: An Outsider's View," *Essays in Commonwealth Literature: Heirloom of Multiple Heritage* (Delhi: Pencraft International, 1995), pp. 153-54 Narasimhaiah differentiates between "realism," which stands for the showing of real life and facts in a true way, omitting nothing painful and idealizing nothing, and "reality," which refers to truth and lifelike resemblance to the original.
23. Chinua Achebe, "Named for Victoria, Queen of England," *Chinua Achebe: 'Things Fall Apart'* ed. Tapan Basu, p. 18.
24. *Ibid.*
25. *Ibid.*, pp. 18-19.
26. Chinna Achebe, "The Black Writer's Burden," *Présence Africaine*, 1966.
27. Chinua Achebe, "The Role of the Writer in a New Nation," *Nigeria Magazine*, 81, 1964, p. 157.

28. *Ibid.*
29. Bernth Lindfors, "Achebe on Commitment and African Writers," *Africa Report*, 15, 3(1970), p. 18.
30. *Ibid.*
31. Cited in Ernest and Pat Emenyonu, "Achebe: Accountable to Our Society," *Africa Report*, 17, 5(1972), p. 25.
32. See Stephen Slemon, "Post-Colonial Allegory and the Transformation of History," *The Journal of Commonwealth Literature*, 23.1 (1988), pp. 157-68.
33. Richard Begam, "Achebe's Sense of an Ending: History and Tragedy in *Things Fall Apart*," *Chinua Achebe: 'Things Fall Apart,'* ed. Tapan Basu, pp. 160-61.
34. *Ibid.*, p. 172.
35. Chinua Achebe, *Hopes and Impediments: Selected Essays* (New York: Anchor Books, 1989), p. 71.

11

The Trial of Dedan Kimathi: A Breakaway From Tradition

Ngugi wa Thiong'o is a Kenyan teacher, novelist, essayist and playwright whose works present an important link between the earlier representatives of African writing and the younger generation of post-colonial writers. These writings significantly reflect a preoccupation with notions and concepts like representation, identity and history that one witnesses in the literatures of diverse nations such as India, Sri Lanka, Malaysia and even the U.S.A., which have emerged from the experience of colonization and have asserted themselves by foregrounding the conflictual relationship with the imperial power. Colonialism, thus, becomes for Ngugi "a privileged historical marker"[1] which governs the understanding of specific, local circumstances that prevailed in Kenya. The colonial experience unmistakably shaped his consciousness which had, perforce, to confront the problems of the quest for identity and "the negative legacy of colonialism."[2]

Ngugi, born in Kamiriithu in 1938, was the fifth child of the third wife of his father, who was a peasant farmer, forced to become a squatter after the British Imperial Act of 1915. Ngugi, initially a devout Christian, later rejected Christianity and in 1976, changed his name from James Ngugi to Ngugi wa Thiong'o for he came to believe Christianity to be a sign of colonialism.

• As a novelist, Ngugi made his debut with *Weep Not, Child* (1964), which was the first novel to be published by an East African. Ngugi, here, used the *bildungsroman* form to tell the story of a young man, Njoroge, who loses the opportunity for advanced education when he is caught between his idealistic dreams and the violent reality of the colonial exploitation. The most prominent theme in Ngugi's early work was the conflict between the individual and the community. *The River Between* (1965) had as its background the Mau Mau Rebellion of 1952-56 and its story depicted an unhappy love-relationship in a rural community torn between Christian converts and non-Christians. *A Grain of Wheat* (1967) marked Ngugi's breaking away from cultural nationalism and his embracing of Fanonist Marxism. This novel is the allegorical story of a man's false heroism and a search for one who betrayed a Mau Mau leader in a village destroyed in war.

After his imprisonment in 1976, Ngugi abandoned the use of English as the medium of his works in favour of Gikuyu, his native tongue. Ngugi was imprisoned under the Public Security Act for a year without trial for his involvement with a communal theatre in his home village. His novel, *Petals of Blood* (1978) drew attention because of its cognisance of contemporary political events. His prison diary, *Detained*, written in English, appeared in 1981. He left Kenya in 1982 to live in self-imposed exile in London. Later, in his book *Decolonising the Mind: The Politics of Language in African Literature* which appeared in 1986, Ngugi voiced the view that African writers should express themselves in the native languages in order to reach out to the African masses.

Despite his exile being self-imposed Ngugi sorrowfully reflects upon his migrant situation as one in which he never has a sense of belonging: "You are always on the outside. And then you begin to create an imaginary home—you think about it all the time."[3] He adds, "In order to feel connected, I try to reach home by writing, by having a dialogue with home."[4]

Several members of Ngugi's family had been involved in the Mau Mau uprising—his elder brother had joined the movement, his step-brother was killed and his mother was tortured. In fact,

Ngugi's entire village suffered in the campaign. With regard to the literature of the fifties, Ngugi himself observed that "its literature was one of engagement, of commitment [...]"[5] and all debates and discussions in literature, aesthetics and culture were related to the anti-colonial process. It is for this very reason that in reading African writings in English, the many configurations evident in these writers' relationship with their cultures became a focus of exploration. What was important was how they made it possible to convey this sense of belonging to their cultures within the framework of their writings. Cultural contexts, as Pushpinder Syal observes, are not directly represented in a text, "they are mediated by the writers' perceptions and purposes and hence by the language used."[6] In the case of Ngugi, it is these perceptions that provide the underpinning for the Kenyan experience of colonization and struggle for freedom. Colonialism in Kenya, Ngugi clearly states, "was built on inequality and hatred between men and the consequent subjugation of the black race by the white race."[7] Greatly conscious of this fact, Ngugi directed his activities of editing journals and proposing changes in University Departments towards anti-colonial cultural politics.

As a playwright Ngugi started his career in 1961, the year in which his first play, *The Rebels* was written and produced. The play understudy, *The Trial of Dedan Kimathi*, was published and performed in 1976. From 1979 to 1982 Ngugi wrote and published various works. It was, however, in 1984 that he declared that *all* his creative writing would thenceforth be in Kiswahili and Gikuyu.

Ngugi's co-author in *The Trial of Dedan Kimathi*, Micere Githae Mugo, Professor of African American Studies at Syracuse University and author/editor of more than fifteen books, including *My Mother's Poem and Other Songs* (1994) is essentially a poet and a playwright. Mugo is a Kenyan by birth and upbringing, a Pan Africanist by identification and an international in orientation. Her political activism against human rights abuses by the Moi dictatorship led to her exile in Zimbabwe in 1982 and she is now a Zimbabwean citizen.

The Trial of Dedan Kimathi, the play by Ngugi and Mugo, covers the period of the Mau Mau struggle and the period of Dedan Kimathi's activities in Kenyan history and politics. It deals with the span of the Mau Mau liberation movement and the consequent independence of Kenya. Chidi Amuta, a Kenyan partisan in the battle against imperialism, identifies the play's conflict as "the progressive nationalist will against combined repressive and exploitative will of colonialism and contemporary capitalist imperialism."[8] The study of the play, however, should not become merely a comprehensive survey of the history and politics of the period for the dramatic construction is of prime importance and has to be studied in relative concentration; and, an identification of the tradition the play belongs to is a prerequisite of a sensitive critical analysis. And yet, in any discussion regarding a literary form, including the dramatic, one cannot ignore the purpose it seeks, the impact it produces and the relation it has with the audience.

The atmosphere of the play is one of unrelieved tension between the motivated and determined will of the peasants and the callous and oppressive colonial army and police. The solidarity of the Kenyans with regard to dedication to the national cause instils in the colonialists a sense of insecurity and every woman or child appears to them to be a "Mau Mau terrorist." The people's identification with the nationalist struggle is so intense that the Woman in the play hides a pistol in a loaf of bread and adeptly feigns innocence and the Boy unconditionally accepts the need to devote his life to the cause for which Kimathi is detained.

The Trial of Dedan Kimathi is a play that can be best performed in terms of a hybrid theatrical mode of presentation. It is a blend of realistic theatre, experiment and African song and dance rendition. The action in the drama develops on the streets of Kenya, in the lives of a boy and a girl who are mainly representatives of the native people. The dramatic action is actually initiated and engineered by the Woman, who is a Mau Mau revolutionary fighting for Kenya's independence. The momentary hesitation and doubt in Kimathi's mind regarding the offer made to him to save himself by effecting a compromise with the imperialist government are almost immediately dissolved when his faith in the People overrides his indecision and the realization of the People's strength liberates him from "doubt." The last scene of the play does not glorify Kimathi alone as the lone hero but foregrounds as well the Girl, the Boy, the People of Kenya singing and dancing and most importantly, the Woman, who is not a mere figment of romantic revolutionary imagination but represents the historical truth of the contribution of women in the Mau Mau movement. This emphasis on women participation in the play is mainly to bring home to the viewers the fact that the women of Kenya worked with as much fire in their hearts and were imbued with as much devotion to their cause as the men were. It is this kind of symbolization that theatre aims at. Tyrone Gutherie aptly avers that "Action on the stage is a stylized re-enactment of real action, which is then imagined by the audience. The re-enactment is not merely an initiation but a symbol of the real thing."[9]

The tradition of realistic theatre in Europe comprises among other kinds, a lot of revolutionary plays and theatrical presentations. In addressing the African viewers, however, playwrights often break with tradition in that they make it different and create a new form which could aptly be termed "hybrid." The major experimentation is witnessed in interspersing the play with songs in other languages, in giving instructions that on the whole action should be seen as demolishing the demarcation between formal and infinite time, in suggesting that Shaw Henderson plays both Judge-Prosecutor and a member of the Special Branch and in projecting him as the "enemy-friend" of the Africans as he is referred to in the Preliminary Notes to the text, and in instructing that the events on the stage should be seen as moving at a vertiginous speed. With these innovations and changes made the playwrights under discussion have crossed the boundaries of conventional realistic theatre and have effected a challenging break in dramatic practice.

In *The Trial of Dedan Kimathi*, strangely enough, some of the elders from a rural outpost as well as Kimathi, himself, speak in flawless English but when it comes to singing they effortlessly slip into their native language. The proposed realism here clashes with the established historical reality placing in the dock the belief that revolutionary theatre would urge people to higher resolves. Would it?—in a foreign language? The songs in the play, however, are deliberately written in Kiswahili and Gikuyu to disconcert the whites who do not know the native languages and are unable to interpret the body language of the dance participants in terms of gestures and music rendered to the accompaniment of drum-playing. What import may be read into these native songs is what perplexes the Western mind for such are the uninhibited and unselfconscious expressions of the morbid and untamed state of ecstasy in the average Kenyan psyche. This belief has been corroborated by *Michael H. Kerby*, who observes,

> [...] It is well-known that natives frame their group expressions in rites accompanied by the exciting music of drums, whistles, bugles and incantations.[10]

Such songs, little understood by the imperialists, could arouse in their hearts and minds an undefined fear as to what uncalled for exhortations they could be for the destruction of the "civilized" way of life. As Johnnie in the play says with suspicion while picking up the Woman's basket, "you never know what's hidden in these *shenzi* things?," so, too, these songs in Kiswahili or Gikuyu could send tremors down the spines of the imperialists, who would, in all likelihood, be unnerved by the sudden change of language, the ecstatic rendition of the lines and the mysterious signals of music and messages sent by the rhythmic beats of the drum. When theatre, for Ngugi, is clearly a political act, the impact of his theatre should not be under estimated. Had the songs been rendered in English, the effect would not have been half as disconcerting and unsettling for the colonialists and imperialists and the revolutionary waves set in motion by these songs would have been far feebler. Making the characters sing in their native Kenyan languages when the play is essentially in English is an experiment full of possibilities, especially in a markedly revolutionary play. Keeping in mind the suppressed truths *The Trial of Dedan Kimathi* exposes, the songs in the play, clear in their general thrust in terms of tune and gesture, might actually have reinforced the determination of the Kenyan youth of the times to work for the cause espoused by Ngugi and Mugo. This use of the language of the real life of the territory is a symbolic assertion of the unity and identity of the Kenyan community represented by the groups of singers, musicians and dancers on the stage. This form of dramatic representation along with the thematic content of the play uses not only the language but the entire cultural complex of the Kenyan people as a mode of communication. *The Trial* is a play which seeks to be part of the popular culture of the place which it depicts and ambitiously wishes to set right the distortions of history.

In any analysis of *The Trial* one cannot ignore the use of pantomimes in the play for here again, we have the body-language contributing significantly to the theme and its import. Gilbert and Tomkins draw our attention to the report on 'Seditious Drama' in the Philippines that appeared in 1907 in *The Theatre, A Short-lived Sidney Newspaper*. The Filipinos used politicalized costumes to present formations of the national flag. Such a display, as Gilbert and Tomkins put it, "provides an example of theatre's politicality in a post-colonial context in which performance functions as an anti-imperial tool [...]."[11]

In *The Trial of Dedan Kimathi*, as Chidi Amuta[12] points out, the court judges not a person but an issue, an institution, a system. It is imperialism which is on trial and not Kimathi. In the Second Movement of the play, in each of the four 'Trial' scenes the machinations of the imperialists are exposed through their speech and action and Kimathi, the accused, is heard giving his judgement against imperialism. Like Shaw Henderson, Kimathi becomes both prosecuting attorney and judge and passes a verdict indicting the enemy. But it is also Kimathi himself who is on trial in the sense that he has to confront and struggle with DOUBT, doubt regarding the success of the Kenyan liberation movement in the event of his death. Ultimate victory over this doubt is attained because Kimathi represents the Kenyan people and the identity between Kimathi and Kenya is never forgotten. Kimathi never dies in the time span presented in the play as Kenya's struggle never loses momentum.

The 'Second Trial' scene is a depiction of three dances in sequence interspersed with Kimathi's thoughts spoken aloud while reflecting on the past of Kenya and his own past. These "mimes" categorize the history of Kenya into three stages, namely, the period before the colonialists came, the period after they came and years of violent resistance against colonialism by the Kenyan youth. In this third section, the script communicates that there is to be a "song of struggle" but it does not specify which song it is to be—it merely states that it could be "any other appropriate song of struggle." This flexibility in the script like that of Brecht's plays, which were often changed after a discussion with some young people, is often subjected to severe criticism and referred to as a "demonstration of an extreme development."[13] The message behind this adaptability in the script of a play is not, however, to be overlooked for it foregrounds a politics which sincerely believes in collective work being more important than personal objectives and visions.

The trial of deserters and traitors held in the guerilla camp at Nyandarua forest, formwise, lends a *new* dimension to the idea of a trial. Here, acting as a judge, Kimathi himself is judged as a person with a weakness—he is charged with being "too human" sometimes for, because of his weakness for his mother, he allows the renegades to escape. The trial is very democratic in that everyone is heard even if there is a charge he/she makes against Kimathi himself. It is the Woman who challenges Kimathi's concern for blood relations by redefining real kinship in revolutionary terms and thus giving it a new connotation removed from the conventional African one. Kimathi of the play accepts these arguments as convincing and clearly reveals that he is not a rigid traditionalist in his anti-imperialist campaign. He is not blind to the Judases amongst Kenyans and urges the allies in the Movement to identify the enemies even if they are enemies in "black clothes."

Another aspect of the play's shift in tradition is seen in its concept of Time which is "different" in its interweaving of the past and the present. The six street scenes in the play represent the present—the "today" element. The historical past filters down to us through the various tableaux shown. The trial-scenes convey what the authors call a sense of "infinite time"; there is never any certainty that whatever is shown happening happened specifically in the place depicted and on the day represented, that is, the day before Kimathi was sentenced. Of the three courtroom scenes staged, the first ("Opening") refers to "infinite time," an unspecified date and time. The other two are more specific in terms of days and hours. In the last of the three scenes, every visual detail is loaded with meaning giving the play a dimension of symbolism. Physical movements also, like the sets and stage properties, project undertones which cannot be ignored. We have, for example, Boy and Girl quickly occupying the seat vacated by Woman. Clearly, there is an indication of the younger generation taking over charge of the liberation struggle. The following comment made by Dilip K. Basu and Sanjay Kumar in their critical assessment of the play is a neat summing up of what the play has to offer us:

> In this play where different spaces, different times, different persons fuse into each other and separate and dissolve, where a man today in torture and the whole history of a tortured nation blend and then separate, where the rhythm of all activities are to be faster than the normal rhythm of actuality, the quality of dream penetrates everything to give it the shape of a poetic theatre.[14]

Kimathi was hanged on 18th Feb. 1957, but many people did not believe that he had died, and so, the legend lived on as an ideal created by the needs of the people and the needs of revolution. It is this "Kimathi" that led the intractable surge of Kenyans seeking liberation from the imperialists and the picture that the play etches on one's cognition is one of the blending of the present and the past with the realism of the street contributing to the realization of the *hic et nunc* (the here and the now) and the revolutionary history of the Mau Mau and of Kimathi constituting the heritage of the past.

As already mentioned earlier, Shaw Henderson in the play is both Judge–Prosecutor and a member of the Special Branch. Kimathi, too, like Shaw Henderson, becomes both prosecuting attorney and judge. Shaw Henderson as a name seems to be symbolic of colonial torture and exploitation, and in Ngugi's perception, seems to be continuing in impact in the neo-colonial world of Kenya. Henderson is an embodiment of the negative and oppressive values of imperialism and is made to play the role of a symbolic trial judge in the play in an ironic attempt to expose the fraudulent behaviour and false sense of justice of the imperialists.

To add to its revolutionary theme and anti-imperialist flavour, *The Trial of Dedan Kimathi* falls back on a number of innovative dramatic strategies for its realization. There is a considerable use of mime to fill up the particular temporal gaps and to provide the historical base to much of the action. The play begins with a mimetic scene in flashback—"Black People's History"—in which the main stages of the history of the exploitation of the Africans are enacted, namely, the slave-trade, the exploitation of black labour and the continuing anti-imperialist struggle. Flashbacks thus become complements to the use of mine. The past, present and future move in a continuum that is effected by mime, flashback and narrative, this continuum presupposing an immediacy of experience and an unquestioned communion between the stage and the audience, the two together jointly recreating the characters on the stage. Further, the historical preoccupation of the play and its popular appeal are enhanced through the emergence of cultural forms like song and dance. Thus, the totality of communicative techniques and devices used in *The Trial of Dedan Kimathi* marks the innovative and experimental approach of the playwrights.

References

1. Padmini Mongia, ed., *Contemporary Postcolonial Theory* (Oxford: Oxford University Press, 2000), p. 7.
2. Trevor James, *English Literature from the Third World* (Harlow: York Press, 1986), p. 11.
3. Cited in http/www frigatezine.com/essay/lives/eli 02 mil.html, Tuesday, Nov. 13, 2001, p. 2.
4. *Ibid.*

5. Ngugi wa Thiongo, "Literature and Politics: Transcending Borders," *In-Between: Essays and Studies in Literary Criticism*, V, 2, September, 1996.
6. Pushpinder Syal, *Structure and Style in Commonwealth Literature* (New Delhi: Vikas Publishing House Pvt., 1994) p. 4.
7. Ngugi, *Homecoming* (London: Heinemann, 1972) p. 31.
8. Cited in Dilip K. Basu and Sanjay Kumar, *'The Trial of Dedan Kimathi': A Critical Companion* (Delhi: Worldview Publications, 2002) p. 36.
9. Tyrone Gutherie, *A Life in the Theatre*, p. 313; cited in J.L. Styan, *Drama, Stage and Audience* (London: Cambridge University Press, 1975) pp. 181-82.
10. Michael H. Kerby, "The Unhappiness of the Mau Mau; or the Seeds of Mau Mau," *East African Medical Journal 34*, 10, Oct. 1957. Quoted in Sicherman, 1990.
11. Helen Gilbert and Joanme Tompkins, *Post-Colonial Drama: Theory, Practice, Politics* (London: Routledge, 1996).
12. Chidi Amuta, *The Theory of African Literature: Implications for Practical Criticism* (London: Zed Books, 1989) Chapter 7.
13. Trevor James, *op. cit.*
14. Dilip K. Basu and Sanjay Kumar, *op. cit.*, p. 23.

12

Autobiography as Strategy of Resistance and Empowerment: Sally Morgan's *My Place*

Sally Morgan, currently Director of the Centre for Indigenous History and the Arts at the University of Western Australia, is an author of repute and her published works include *My Place, Wanamurraganya*, several books for children and a play called *Sistergirl*. Her standing rests, in the main, on her *magnum opus, My Place*, for which she won the 1987 Australian Human Rights Award for Literature and the 1990 Order of Australia Book Prize. In addition to being a writer of consequence she is a gifted visual artist whose paintings express themes similar to those she explores in *My Place*—themes that spell out the importance of land and land rights, spirit life, political issues and the significance of birds and snakes. Arnold Oganov firmly believes that artistic creation "strives towards maximum sensory tangibility in artistic depiction"[1] and Morgan conforms to this by relying on her intense visual memory and photographic retention to record details that would ordinarily have been lost to aesthetic presentation.

Sally Morgan's narrative design provides art with an inexhaustible means of cognition and a grasp of the surrounding world with its socio-historical conditions which are major determinants of the form life takes at diverse points of time. The means and modes of cognition which her narrative method provides help us arrive at an aesthetic interpretation of reality or what is commonly referred to as artistic truth. "Artistic truth is life's truth aesthetically interpreted [...]. It a result of cognition set down in a work of art."[2]

Australian literature, like all Commonwealth literatures, having navigated the passage-way from the station of a nascent literature in English with its beginnings in the bush ballads to the status of a literature that has attained its maturity and efflorescence, has now, a distinct identity of its own. Its creative writers have faced the particular challenge of adapting the English language to portray effectively the realities of their national spirit, life, culture and landscapes and to approximate "life's truth."[3] Thus, it is for them, essentially, a matter of adapting an alien language to the native spirit. In his Introduction to the *Collins Book of Australian Poetry*, Rodney Hall, referring to the revitalized use of English by the writers of the Jindyworobak Club in Adelaide, talks of their "rejecting English words too weighty with overtones foreign to Australia and replacing them by images that attempted some native strength."[4]

Australian literature today successfully reflects the national consciousness and spirit in its own distinctive idiom and imagery and its writers explore reality and value in Australia from a varied perspective—social, historical and individual. In reading the works of Australian writers, then, the many configurations evident in the relationship of these writers with their cultures becomes the focus of exploration and study. The enquiry that arises in the critical mind is with regard to how these authors convey this sense of belonging to their cultures within the matrix of their work. The answer to this query lies in the observation made by Pushpinder Syal in her assertion that "cultural contexts are not represented in a text, they are mediated by the writers' perceptions and purposes and hence by the language used."[5] In the context of creative writing in Australia, the work is a record of the ever-evolving process of negotiation between the writer and the community.

Women writers of Australia have instituted a characteristic convention by writing about aspects and concerns different from those chosen by men. The body of their works is markedly distinct and presents an alternative view of the culture and customs of the country. Letter writing was the initial activity of white women that encouraged them to venture into literary creative compositions marked by introspection and the urge to self-development. The voice of "exile" is another unmistakable feature of Australian women's writings which seek to establish the identity of womankind and to re-constitute the prevailing value so as to make them relevant to the intensifying feminist assertions and acceptable in the post-colonial context.

Sally Morgan, a writer of singular personal power, writes perceptively of themes and characters from Australia's past. She defines the post-colonial consciousness in terms of alienation and the death of the native culture of the place which was slowly marginalized and uprooted. She draws our attention to the spiritual mystery of human life and relationships. Most importantly, though she herself was only part aboriginal, Sally Morgan was a vocal champion of the Australian Aborigines, whose land, she believed, had been appropriated by the Whites. Her love for the countryside, her "blood's country," makes her identify herself with the pristine Australian psyche that existed before the influx of the Whites from England. The White man, as C.D. Narasimhaiah puts it:

> has committed a 'bloodless murder' of the aborigine but here is more evidence of real attrition of the heart for what has happened to the primitive man than elsewhere.[6]

Sally Morgan, through her works, has helped to sensitize the society she lives in to the plight of the Aborigines, who did not, like the Red Indians, resist "invasion" and put up a fight against the colonists; they just withdrew into the outbacks to be at peace with themselves. Judith Wright's poem, "Nigger's Leap" speaks of the "silent wounds of Australian history"[7] caused by the effacement and extirpation of the Aborigines by the White men. These "silent wounds" inflicted upon the Aborigines are registered in the works of several Australian writers. "Literature," it is believed, records the path traversed, it unfolds a motley canvas of history in the wake of the moving masses."[8] A serious writer, however, not only records facts and events but also pronounces a verdict in conformity with his own understanding of life and truth which help him distil historically significant phenomena. The Aboriginal writers took it upon themselves to rewrite their past with the express purpose of strengthening the Native readers' sense of identity.

Sally Morgan's *My Place* belongs to the bulk of Australian women's writing and has the distinction of being the first Aboriginal narrative of exposé, a public statement of the shocking facts of racial, cultural and political domination of the Whites over the Natives. The work is a poignant tale of marginalisation, alienation and the diaspora experience. The themes explored in it are those of racial discrimination, Aboriginal identity, feminist assertion and class and gender concerns. Victoria Laurie clearly defines the thematic contents of the work:

> Morgan's *My Place* is the picture of generational dispossession and denial of land, of kinship, of successive children stolen away, of wealthy white men, who disowned them [...] an account of how she cajoled and gently bullied her family towards the truth about their collective Aboriginal identity [...].[9]

The prevailing spirit in Sally Morgan's work is that of the re-creation of the Australian landscape, its people and its history as it is in other specimens of Aboriginal writing in English like the works of Mudrooroo and Archie Weller and prose writers like Alice Nannup, Ruby Langford Ginibi, Oodgeroo, Noonuccal and Kevin Gilbert. Ronald Berndt traces in the endeavours of Aboriginal writers:

> the emergence of a literature which will be the underpinning of a newly conceived Aboriginal heritage [...]. It is a heritage which is now both traditional and mixed with the traumatic circumstances of the struggle of a people to find or to assert their own unique identity, and have that identity recognized by others.[10]

Biography and autobiography form a substantial part of Native writing as Natives feel the urge to write about their place, their people and their times. In terms of their autobiographical narratives the status of the Australian

Aboriginals is a peculiar one because they have been marginalized and pushed to the psychic and political brink of a society comprising a group of people who have themselves been subjected to colonial atrocities and persecution.

Augustine's memoirs, *Confessions*, written between 397 and 400 AD, established the convention of converting experience into narrative, life into textual self-representation. Such an exercise is termed an autobiography. The autobiographical process is a recreation of the author's personality, which is seen in retrospect. This artistic activity helps the autobiographer in determining his true identity and enables him to etch out an accurate picture of himself. The self-referentiality of autobiography is also self-interrogative and thus, a work beginning in self-depiction ends in a deeper knowledge of the self. "Self-portraiture [...] is a synonym of self knowledge."[11]

My Place records the reminiscences of Sally Morgan and a historiographic depiction of the traumatic experiences in the lives of her kinsmen. An absorbing series of incidents unravels the enigmatic facts of the Aboriginal identity of Sally's ancestry. The chronicle demonstrates the circumstances under which the Aborigines still continue to define themselves in terms of black/white confrontation and are aware of themselves only as they stand in relation to the dominant White culture. The ray of hope lies in the fact that they appear to be gradually moving towards an assertion of their native identity.

The autobiographical stance chosen by Sally Morgan in *My Place* is clearly a strategy for the expression of a growing defiance and insubmissiveness on the part of the Aborigines. The work, like other autobiographies of Aboriginal women, is an implicit campaign for registering resistance and seeking empowerment. Morgan reinforces in her book the view that gender constructs are created by men and that women are branded by them as mere instruments of procreation. A woman, thus, assessed in terms of sexual commerce, is further devalued if she happens to be an Aboriginal. Nan and Gladys, we are told, have both been subjected to this kind of humiliation; they prefer to leave their past buried and to conceal their Aboriginal origin. Gladys peremptorily tells Sally, "There's no point in digging up the past, some things are better left buried."[12] All enquiries regarding descent and nationality thus continue to be responded to with the word, "Indian." It is only as we trace the denouement of the work that we see how the substitution of "Aboriginal" for "Indian" comes to prevail.

The revelation of the past of the Milroy children comes not through Sally's efforts alone but through the co-ordinated confessions and unveilings of those who were of consequence to the family. There are four autobiographies that constitute the structural framework of *My Place*, namely, those of Sally Morgan, Arthur Corunna, Gladys Corunna and Daisy Corunna. Sally's quest for the truth about her family history and her urge to establish her identity as an Aboriginal is what links these four autobiographies. These four autobiographies, converging at critical points in the authors' lives, enable one to assess the events and characters from varied viewpoints and provide a means of corroborating and verifying facts that are reported by them: for example, a clearer picture of Bill Milroy's associate, Frank Potter, emerges after reading the accounts of both Sally and her mother, Gladys. Also, when Sally and her mother reach the homestead at Corunna Downs station they are happy to be able to identify the main house which conformed to the descriptions of Arthur and Nan: "It was concrete evidence that what Arthur had told us and what Nan had mentioned were all true."[13]

The stories are interwoven in more evident ways. Arthur's story inspires Sally to return to Corunna Downs so that his narrative determines the latter's subsequent reporting. Daisy's narrative, honestly communicated before her life comes to an end, enables Sally to conclude her labour with an affirmation of her grand mother's life and her own Aboriginal antecedents.

One focal point at which the four autobiographies comprising the narrative intersect is that which compels each one of the authors to render a sensitive account of the inhuman manner in which the Aboriginals were treated in Australia. The chief characters in this text, Gladys (Mum) and Daisy (Nan) construe their lives in terms of the Aboriginal female subordinated to the superior White male colonizer. They narrate the exploitation and oppression they had suffered due to the colonial ideological indoctrination and cultural subjugation. For them the past represents pain and humiliation caused by the White man, who had forcibly snatched them away from their homes and placed them in missions and settlements where they had been made conscious of their "shameful" heritage. Sally's regret, "Why was I cursed with being a girl?"[14] though expressed in a different context, has far-reaching implications.

Nan's outburst over her colour, "You bloody kids don't want me, you want a bloody white grandmother, I'm black. Do you hear, black, black, black," and Jill's subsequent eruption, "Boongs, we're boongs! [...] A boong. You know, Aboriginal" change the meaning of life for Sally. It puts an entirely different perspective on her view of the past and as she herself proclaims it "heralded a new phase in my relationship with my mother."[15] She has no qualms of conscience in declaring, "We had suddenly switched our allegiance from India to Aboriginal Australia [...]."[16] With this sense of fidelity firmly entrenched in Sally's psyche she shot out a volley of questions at herself compelling her to adopt an introspective stance regarding her heritage:

> Had I been dishonest with myself? What did it really mean to be Aboriginal? I'd never lived off the land and been a hunter and a gatherer. I'd never participated in corroborees or heard stories of the Dreamtime. I hardly knew any Aboriginal people. What did it mean for someone like me?[17]

This regret at the lack of participation in the corporate life of the Aboriginals gives Sally a sense of guilt which makes her want to be able to say heartily with Arthur, "I'm proud of being a blackfella."[18] She tries to understand Nan's being ashamed of her past when Arthur explains the cause of his sister's complexes.

> Aah, she's bin with whitefellas too long. They make her feel 'shamed, that's what white people do to you. Why should we be 'shamed, we bin here longer than them.[19]

It is in these words of Arthur that we register a sense of resistance defying the unwritten law of superiority that the Whites quote to subjugate the Black Aboriginals of Western Australia. Sally, too, having delved deep into the recesses of Western Australian history takes umbrage at the way her people were treated: "Aborigines were considered subnormal and not capable of being educated the way whites were."[20]

Fear of discrimination against Aborigines had persisted in Nan for a long, long time, almost till the end of her life. She kept saying things like "Terrible things will happen to you if you tell people what you are."[21] and "There are still times when I'm scared inside, scared to say who I really am."[22] But then it is Sally who is largely responsible for the emergence of her grandmother and mother from the morass of fear and insecurity. She helps them confront the fact that they are Aborigines and persuades them to write their life histories, keeping nothing back from the present generation. Their narratives prove to be a cathartic experience that finally leads them to come to terms with their personal history. It is a traumatic ordeal but it helps them tide over the worst and gradually overcome the misery and sense of shame at having been a dispossessed and enslaved people. Once this feeling of humiliation is exorcized, Nan and Sally's mother, Gladys, start asserting themselves and their assertions verge on the rebellious. In an unmistakable tone of protest Nan tells us:

> Cause you're black, they treat you like dirt. You see, in those days, we was owned, like a cow or a horse. I even heard some people say we not the same as Whites. That's not true, we all God's children.[23]

And again,

> I'm 'shamed of myself, now. I feel 'shamed for some of the things I done. I wanted to be White, you see [...]. Fancy, me thinkin' that. What was wrong with my own people?[24]

This sense of self-esteem as it germinates in Nan's mind, brings with it a sense of identity and security, a consciousness of "belonging" somewhere. She could now very well say with Billy back home, "I belong here. It's good to be with my people."[25]

Sally, too, after her rewarding visit to Corunna Downs station triumphantly declares, "We'd seen so much of her and ourselves in the people we'd met. We belonged, now. We wanted her to belong too."[26]

An observation made by Jean Starobinski with regard to autobiography as a form writing is fully applicable to Sally Morgan's work:

> The narrator describes not only what happened to him at a different time in his life but above all how he became [...] out of what he was [...] what he presently is.[27]

The entire meaning of life for Sally takes on a different colour after she discovers her Aboriginal origin. Clearly, the genesis of her present state of euphoria lies in her fruitful exploration of the past. It is this deep interest in the family history that also makes her conscious of the element of spiritualism that prevails in the Aboriginal culture. Aboriginal music, she was told, was heathen music and it often emanated from an unknown and undetected source. Nan, when she heard music coming from an unidentified origin had to be pacified by being told, "There's no one down there, it's a spiritual thing."[28] She, herself, however, had firm faith in the spiritualism of the aborigines:

> Blackfella know all 'bout spirits. We brought up with them. That's where the white man's stupid. He only believes what he can see. He needs to get educated. He's only livin' half a life."[29]

This contempt for the Whites is again an indication of the growing antagonism against them. The initial acceptance of their superiority now becomes a statement of their inferiority in spiritual matters. The Aboriginal bird, "something spiritual"[30] is beyond the comprehension of the Whites.

Interestingly, the title of the text, *My Place*, radiates a world of meaning. In the light of this title, the past events in the life of the author which were probably without much significance at the time of occurrence, acquire a new meaning. It is to this new meaning that the choice of incidents and details of her past life is geared. The term, *My Place*, may refer to the physical location of a person, it may be an indication of one's social position, or, it may even have a spiritual connotation implying one's place in "the scheme of things" in the particular context of God's creations. For the Aborigines their "place" may be their traditional land, and, in their culture, the physical and the spiritual are interlinked. *My Place*, at various levels of meaning, covers all these concepts of "place" and the narrative concludes with an affirmation of Daisy's life and her Aboriginality. Running parallel to this is Sally Morgan's own assertion of her Native origin—for her it is a journey of the discovery of a rich Aboriginal heritage.

Morgan's epigraph to her book is meaningfully dedicated to "My Family" for it is a declaration of the invulnerable identity and integrality of a whole community that discovers itself afresh:

> How deprived we would have been if we had been willing to let things stay as they were. We would have survived, but not as a whole people. We would never have known our place.[31]

Sally, after her visit to Corunna Downs station with her mother, ecstatically announces that there she felt "like we'd suddenly come home and now we were leaving again. But we had a sense of place now."[32] Sally's mother, proud to be an Aboriginal now, wants her children to identify with their past and to admit their Aboriginal origin, not conceal it as a matter of shame. She hopes that her children:

> will feel proud of the spiritual background from which they've sprung [...]. All I want my children to do is to pass on their Aboriginal heritage.[33]

This hope of Sally's mother is not belied for her daughter makes a virtue of her cultural Aboriginal inheritance in embracing her spiritual and racial roots fondly and unashamedly.

References

1. Arnold Oganov, "Art as a Form of Self-Awareness," *Problems of Contemporary Aesthetics* compiled by A. Zis, T. Lyubimova and M. Ovsyannikov (Moscow: Raduga Publishers, 1984), p. 240.

2. Vassily Novikov, *Artistic Truth and Dialectics of Creative Work*, English translation (Moscow: Progress Publishers, 1981), p. 14.
3. *Ibid.*
4. Rodney Hall, "Introduction," *Collins Book of Australian Poetry*; cited in *Let Me Say* by Ramesh Mohan. (Meerut: Shalabh Publishing House, 1996), p. 105.
5. Pushpinder Syal, *Structure and Style in Commonwealth Literature* (New Delhi: Vikas Publishing House Pvt. Ltd., 1994), p. 4.
6. C.D. Narasimhaiah, "Australia: A Visitor's Impressions of the Land, Life and Literature," *Essays in Commonwealth Literature* (Delhi: Pencraft International, 1995), p. 173.
7. Cited in Ramesh Mohan, *Let me Say*, p. 108.
8. Alexei N. Tolstoy, *Collected Works*, Vol. 13, p. 352 (in Russian)
9. Victoria Laurie, "An Interview with Sally Morgan," *Southerly*, 23, No. 1 (1999), p. 38.
10. Ronald Berndt, "Opening Address," *Aboriginal Writing Today*, p. 9.
11. James Olney, ed., "On Writing Autobiography," *Studies in Autobiography* (New York: O.U.P., 1988).
12. Sally Morgan, *My Place* (Fremantle, Western Australia; Fremantle Arts Centre Press, 1987), p. 123.
13. *Ibid.*, p. 290.
14. *Ibid.*, p. 35.
15. *Ibid.*, p. 122.
16. *Ibid.*, p. 176.
17. *Ibid.*, p. 179.
18. *Ibid.*, p. 187.
19. *Ibid.*, p. 189.
20. *Ibid.*, p. 193.
21. *Ibid.*, p. 350.
22. *Ibid.*, p. 382.
23. *Ibid.*, p. 419.
24. *Ibid.*
25. *Ibid.*, p. 296.
26. *Ibid.*
27. Jean Starobinski, "The Style of Autobiography," *Autobiography: Essays Theoretical and Critical*, ed. James Olney, p. 49.

28. Sally Morgan, *My Place*, p. 367.
29. *Ibid.*, p. 429.
30. *Ibid.*, p. 442.
31. *Ibid.*, p. 296; these lines also constitute the Epigraph to the book.
32. *Ibid.*, p. 291.
33. *Ibid.*, p. 382.

13

Dario Fo's *Accidental Death of an Anarchist*: A Drama of "Emergent Meaning"

Italian playwright, Dario Fo, was the controversial winner of the Nobel prize for literature in the year 1997. The award of this prize to a "*jester*," as Fo called himself, came as a shock to many who believed themselves to be occupying "the loftiest of spheres"[1] and never gave a thought to those occupying the "humbler planes."[2]

Fo's plays are some of the finest examples of contemporary political theatre and are characterized by a resurgence of the satiric mode of representation which came in the wake of certain instances of police repression. These instances aroused a consciousness of the injustice meted out to the accused and engendered an attitude clearly subversive of authority. Fo wrote with the avowed purpose of attacking those myths of Italian life, which Fascism had imposed and which Christian Democrats (who ruled Italy at that time) sought to preserve. His target was the fabricated official versions of history which he wished to lay bare, shorn of all their deceit and varnish. His plays, clever admixtures of spectacle, mime and social comment, made their mark with the viewers but unnerved the authorities, who ensured the presence of the police at such performances. His characteristic profusion of humour and irony reflected the political conditions of the times, and as Angela Montgomery points out, "he was developing his own peculiar brand of explosive satire."[3]

In Fo's plays, apparently farcical ideas are cleverly circulated and satirized, and despite all this cavilling and carping, his plays exhibit a freshness and determination to experiment with new methods and techniques which break from tradition in that each performance is followed by a discussion.

In his initial one-man show, *'Mistero Buffo'* (i.e. "comic-mystery") Fo drew profusely on the counter-culture of the Middle Ages, on apocryphal gospel stories and on legends and tales to present incidents in which he played all the roles and used language which was partly invented, partly archaic and partly drawn from the dialects of Northern Italy. This work was inspired by two main traditions of the land: (a) that of the "*giullare*" (or "*jester*"), the travelling comic-singer or mime akin to the "*jongleur*" (or story-teller) as also to the Indian "*yatra*" chanter, who in the Middle Ages, was the carrier of a subversive culture and irreverently mocked the sanctity of the existing institutions; and (b) that of the great clowns of the *Commedia dell' Arte* with their use of masks, of dialect and an extra-ordinary rendition of a particular language, all adding up to understandable discourse.

Initially committed to the Communist Party and the Communist cultural organizations, Dario Fo and his wife, Franca Rame, were soon disillusioned with the authoritarian and inflexible nature of the party and shifted their allegiance to the new Left. They established a new theatrical company called *La Commune*, which had its headquarters at Milan.

Fo's plays may rightly be called the drama of "*emergent meaning*" as opposed to the inherent quality natural to a lyrical poem which Angus Fletcher refers to as "*immanent meaning.*"[4] The power and depth of the "*emergent meaning*" of his plays is directly related, not to words alone, but to voices and the tone of voices, the pace of the speaking and the silences between, to the gesture and expression of the actor, the physical distinctions between him and others, the statuary of tragedy and the curlicues and nuances of comedy, and of course, to stylistic suggestion. With so many variables simultaneously working to create meaning on the stage, we can only conclude that in Fo's plays, the experience alone is the meaning.

The test of dramatic communication is whether it kindles an audience or not and Fo's plays surely do qualify as works that communicate effectively—provocatively enough to stir the audience to action. A play works by the exhibition of details that are seen and heard and form the vocabulary of drama and an audience learns by constant perception of these minutiae for as *Styan* puts it,

> A play is poetry, something made; it is drama, something done; and theatre, something perceived.[5]

Drama calls for a virtually unlimited range of responses. The stage with its mesh of strong sensory details can exercise a remarkable control over its spectator and it is this fact that Fo exploits in his plays. The study of drama is all about how the stage compels its audience to reconstruct along with the playwright, the social and historical context from "a hundred simultaneous capsules of information"[6] the theatre equips its viewers with.

Every play, more so a modern play, makes us an immediate witness to an unfolding event. We do not read about an action, we watch it as it takes place; we learn not what the characters 'have spoken' but what they 'now speak.' A play, then, is meant to be acted out and the first condition of acting is undoubtedly, impersonation, in the etymological sense of the word i.e. impersonation as implying the assuming of a mask, the guise of someone else.

True political theatre is bound to be like religious theatre, an act of faith and a means of establishing communion among all those who share the same beliefs. Audience and actors are one and its ideal is that suggested by *Stanislavski* and explicitly stated by *Copeau*, who said that:

> there will be a new theatre only on the day when the man in the auditorium can murmur the words of the man on the stage, at the same time as he and in the same spirit.[7]

Fo, despite being a radical and an artist relentlessly subversive of the prevailing establishment, was able to evoke an overwhelming audience response largely for the artistic vitality of his theatre and the political immediacy of the events that he chose to depict in his plays. The theatre of Fo is based on two major facts—one his love for the culture and tradition of the ordinary people from which his work derives its humour, and two, his commitment to left wing politics which endowed him with a radical revolutionary consciousness.

Fo's is markedly an activist kind of theatre which communicates directly with its audience and is about their own lived experiences and aspirations. It is these traits in his works that make for directness and immediacy in dramatic communication, and, in the ultimate analysis, make the bulk of his work politically meaningful theatre. Franca Rame observed that the bourgeoisie recorded with pleasure the criticism and the *"spankings"* given to the fascists.

Accidental Death of an Anarchist, later renamed *'Accidental Death of an Anarchist and other Subversives* as a consequence of the playwright's efforts to update the play and make its message more explicit in displaying consciousness of the involvement of other victims in the incident, is one of Fo's most widely performed plays for the novelty and ingenuity of its farcical form and the fresh humour of its comic situations and dialogue. The play was written with a specific purpose, in response to a political need of the Italian left and was largely demonstrative of Fo's journalistic theatre of "*counter-information,*" theatre that Franca Rame, with reference to *'Mistero Buffo'* characterized as "a living newspaper continually incorporating current news events and political and cultural satire into performances."[8] Fo, himself later stated in an interview with the Italian *Playboy* magazine,

> Our theatre is a throw-away theatre, a theatre which won't go down in bourgeois history, but which is useful like a newspaper article, a debate on a political action.[9]

Fo does not believe in a theatre which is "a documentary theatre of cold information"[10] and "a theatre which [...] doesn't get to the bottom of things."[11]

Fo's theatre has always the audience in mind; it is written with a view to establish a practical relationship to and with the audience and it speaks for its own times. In the new radical movement in drama, as *Brecht* had once suggested, the spectators are encouraged to "intervene actively in life." Each play of Fo following his break with the bourgeosie was created differently in response to (and as a form of intervention into) some specific local or international political development. *Accidental Death of an Anarchist* was a response to a right wing terrorist bombing which the state tried to blame on *Lotta Continua* (a far left group) and also a response to the custodial death of an innocent "suspect" whose death the Italian police had tried to pass off as suicide. Such immediacy and topicality made Fo's theatre not only a form of political action but also, as already mentioned, "a living newspaper" which countered the official propaganda. While the play was being performed, the framed trial against *Lotta Continua* was taking place. The daily updates of news regarding the case, which the media channels preferred not to communicate, were incorporated into the show. It is for this reason that Fo referred to his theatre as "a journalistic theatre which deals with current problems."[12] In *Accidental Death,* the play's audience was very well conscious of the seriousness of the issue in hand and it goes to Fo's credit that he was able to reconstruct from the situation a farcical comedy and was able to muddy the tragic connotations and denotations of the theme. One dramatic decision which helped Fo distance the audience was to keep the "real Pinelli," the victim of police atrocities, off the stage. He deliberately encouraged the audience to an objective contemplation of the issue so as to avoid what he calls "the danger of catharsis" for once the outrage at the injustices of the system is purged the readiness to act loses its edge.

Fo's ingenuity in blending urgent political concerns with elements of story-telling, pantomime, satirical songs and ballads and grotesque farce makes his plays highly provocative and entertaining. *Accidental Death* is Fo's representative dramatic achievement which was staged at the via Coletta theatre in December 1970, a year after the bombing at the *Piazza Fontana* that terrified the Italian public and exposed a network of corruption, intrigue and unwarranted contradiction in its wake. Fo's play was a response to what came to be known in Italy as the "strategy of tension" in which the New Christian Democrat Government, having unseated the Centre-left coalition, tried to enervate its forces. According to the figures quoted in the play itself, since 1969 there had been 173 bomb attacks in Italy, 102 of which were organized by fascists while half the remaining 71 seemed to have been organized by the right with the purpose of defaming the left by letting the suspicion fall on them. It was at this time that Fo and Franca constituted the new collective called *La Commune* to counter the effort of the media to implicate the left in the case of *Giuseppe Pinelli*, an anarchist railway employee from Milan who was charged with placing bombs in the Milan railway station in 1969 and then charged with bombing in *Piazza Fontana* which had killed 17 people and injured 100. Pinelli's co-accused, *Pietro Valpreda*, a Rome anarchist ballet dancer, was in prison for about ten years and on 15th of December, 1969, Pinelli, himself, died after "falling" from a fourth floor window of the Milan police station where he was being interrogated.

It was on insistent and persistent public request that Fo wrote *Accidental Death* to fill up the vacuum of information regarding the Milan bombings and the "murder" of Pinelli by discussing the causes and political consequences of these incidents. Fo's play became a direct source of information for the entire Pinelli affair including the law suit against the left newspaper, *Lotta Continua* (already referred to), instanced by Inspector Calabresi, who had been incharge of the Pinelli case and who was himself later assassinated in 1972. In the course of updating the play and including the reports of the various trials and hearings in the case, Fo was furnished with information fit for satire and in the play he seeks to strike at a power structure which he sees as immobile and static, and the mode he adopts for this assault is irony, which he believes, has always been "an explosion of liberation."

In his best works, Fo's politics makes itself felt not by any tiresome didacticism but by serious human concern with justice and goodness. His political experience has a great deal to do with the unfortunate forlorn sight of the so-called *Welfare State* sinking under the paralyzing weight of fascism until it slips into what J.W. Aldridge has called "*Welfare Stasis*."[13] Fo, through his plays, wished to sensitize the people regarding this "*stasis*" in a State which is meant to promote the welfare of its members.

The *Maniac* or the *Madman* who is a quick-change artist, indeed a histriomaniac, a clown in the play, is more of a theatrical device that functions as the instigator of the comic action and is easily identified as the stock-type manifested in "*the tricky slave*" as he was called in Roman comedy, the vice-character in medieval drama and the resourceful villain in Shakespeare. Fo, however, specifically presents character as fragmented (seen in the guises and the masks the Maniac assumes), utterly arbitrary and insanely contradictory. The main character whimsically impersonates a number of improbable characters and it is this stance that focuses on the central paradox throughout *Accidental Death* that the Maniac manipulates fiction to get at the truth; and, it is here that fiction and reality intersect—the Maniac simply states the truth which is unacceptable fiction to those to be indicted. The grotesque body of the Maniac impersonating the forensic expert, Capt. Piccini is a truthful reflection of the body politic. Fo represents Piccini as an outrageous collective of body parts that transpose him into a "puppet" or a marionette with a wooden leg, a detachable wooden hand, a crutch, a detachable glass eye, a fake moustache and a wig—this perhaps is a step further into the theatre of the grotesque. The character of the Maniac also outlines the hollowness of a reformist parliamentary strategy.

Another significant character of the play is the woman Journalist, modelled on Camilla Cederna, a reporter of the weekly magazine, '*I Espresso*,' who unearthed some embarrassing facts about the Pinelli affair. The Maniac, at this point, impersonating as the "examining magistrate" interestingly substantiates the journalist, Maria Feletti's interpretation of events while seeming to be protecting and defending the police.

One particular aspect in which the play needs to be analyzed is its open-endedness. Its relative inconclusiveness, a trait of several works of modern literature, no matter what the genre, is deliberate on the part of the playwright for he did not want his audience to be purged of its anger at and hatred for the instruments of repression. He wanted the conclusion to come from the audience itself through political discussion and political action. Fo's original script had gone through two different versions of the text and the present text chosen for analysis is the second text of 1974 which was, according to Fo, more likely to enable the audience

> to keep their anger inside them [...] so that they can take action and get involved in the struggle.[14]

Fo makes the audience laugh but above all he makes them think and satirically analyze events which had escaped their notice earlier:

"The great weapon of satire and the grotesque—a weapon always used by the people in their struggle against the dominant classes finds further verification in its enormous possibilities of penetration".[15]

Fo allows his audience to *"enter"* the performance and modify it—he responds to exchanges with the audience by modifying the body of the text, and more importantly, the end. This kind of approach to the theatre audience is an important characteristic of political theatre which wants people to challenge the existing and established social, political and moral assumptions. Meyerhold envisaged a theatre that presupposes "the existence of a fourth creator, in addition to the author, the director and the actor—namely the spectator."

Fo views his works as the actor's theatre. It is not a *"theatre of words."* It is a theatre of performed action, that is, of mime, movement and gestures. Fo does not consider the written text as inviolable or unchangeable for to him, it is only a tentative outline of the action or scene which is open to adaptations. Further, he prefers "adaptations" to "translations" of his scripts into other languages and takes no exception to the script being altered if it conforms to the socio-cultural environment of performance; only, the political thrust is not to be lost and the so called "sacred" institutions—the *police,* the *judiciary,* the *media* and *religion*—are to be stripped and unmasked. Fo, clearly referring to a conscious political choice he had made, said, "Mine had been a revolt, a rebellion against a hypocritical and a deceitful order which dates back to my experience as a student."[16]

The relevance of Fo's play, *Accidental Death of an Anarchist,* to the Indian context is not to be ignored; in fact, the play could very well be adapted to the Indian situation and for the Indian stage, speaking for its own time as it did for Fo's time, and, in Fo's spoken prologue, for the time of the American anarchist, Salseda, who also died of *"defenestration"* in New York in 1920. This play, like *Vijay Tendulkar's 'Ghashiram Kotwal'* is, as we have seen, performance-based and not script-centred and hence, to assimilate the richness of the work, we must not approach it merely as a literary text. It gains in dimension because of its variability and flexibility and could be set in any similar political context and situation like the revolt of workers and students in France, America's war in Vietnam, the display of police inhumanity and callousness at the Chicago Democratic Convention as also the peasant revolt in Naxalbari which led a large number of brilliant students to enter into an armed battle with the oppressive state authorities—all part of the epidemic of the revolutionary and anti-establishment activities of the 1960s.

The worldwide explosion of youthful revolutionary energy led to a tide of creativity in which the conventional was abandoned for an activist view of culture i.e. culture as a political weapon. In 1969, Delhi, too, presented its first street theatre called *India 1969*. The play, conceived and improvised by a group of student activists satirized the decadence and corruption witnessed in parliamentary politics.

So, in India, as in other countries, in the 1960s, "theatre as political action" was the concept to be sworn by. Theatrical performances became avowedly agitational and through the medium of drama, oppressed classes gained increasing consciousness of the injustice responsible for their predicament.

A substitution of the word *"anarchist"* in the title of Fo's play with *"naxalite," "terrorist"* or *"militant"* will unmistakably shift the social, historical and political context to places like Warangal or Baramulla, or even perhaps a police station in Delhi or any other city in India. *Accidental Death* is grimly real and pertinent to the Indian situation.

Ghulam Rasool, the thirty-year old Hyderabad based reporter of the reputed Telegu daily, *Udayan,* had interviewed the armed squad leader of the Naxalite movement and written against the police excesses in villages, misuse of TADA [Terrorist and Disruptive Activities (Prevention) Act] by them and the role of police in land-grabbing and eviction of slum-dwellers in NTR Nagar in Hyderabad. On 27th Dec. 1991, Rasool and his friend B. Vijaya Prasad Rao associated with the NSUI (the Students' Organization of the Congress) were both picked up by the police and seven hours later were shot dead in an abandoned shed. Demonstrations and waves of protests were all in vain.

Again, on 24th Feb. 1993, *Vikal Kumar Adhana*, an assistant in the Finance Ministry, arrested by the Lodhi Colony Police Station, Delhi, indicted for impersonation and bribery, was found hanging in the police lock-up and the incident was conveniently dismissed as a case of suicide despite the marks of relentless physical torture on his body. Thus, the preposterous cover-up stories offered by the Indian police in cases of custodial death are akin to the "raptus" (or suicide) theory of the anarchist. Voices of dissent are conveniently eliminated with custodial deaths often being presented as cases of so-called "disappearances" or of encounter-killings, both these being dubious explanations where the demarcation between the "real" and the "fake" is imperceptible and undecipherable. Clearly then, with multiple instances of custodial deaths available in India, *Accidental Death of an Anarchist* can conveniently be adapted to the Indian historical and political context, past and present, for Fo's theatre is a theatre of situations, a sequence of scenic vistas on which the dramatic action takes place.

References

1. Dario Fo's Nobel Lecture, 1997, *Contra Jogulatores Obloquentes.*
2. *Ibid.*
3. Angela Montgomery, "The Theatre of Dario Fo and Franca Rame: Laughing All the Way to the Revolution," *Twentieth Century European Drama,* ed. Brian Docherty (New York: Martin Press), 1994, p. 206
4. Augus Fletcher, *Allegory: Theory of a Symbolic Mode,* Ithaca, 1964.
5. J.L. Styan, *Drama, Stage and Audience* (London: Cambridge University Press) 1975, p. 31.
6. *Ibid.*, p. 4.
7. Joseph Chiari, "Brecht," *Landmarks of Contemporary Drama (1960),* cited in *The Play and the Reader:* Alternate Edition (New Jersey: Prentice Hall Inc.) 1971.
8. Cited in Tom Behan, *Dario Fo: Revolutionary Theatre* (London: Pluto) 2000.
9. *Playboy*, (Italian issue), Dec. 1974.
10. *Sipario*, no. 3000, May 1971.
11. *Ibid.*
12. Cited in *Dario Fo's Accidental Death of an Anarchist: A Critical Companion* ed. Javed Malik (Delhi: Worldview) 2002.
13. Cited in A. Alvarez, "The Anti-Establishment Drama," *Essays in the Modern Drama* ed. Morris Freedman (Boston: D.C. Heath and Company) p. 232.
14. Cited in Tony Mitchell, *Dario Fo, People's Court Jester* (London: Metheun) 1984.
15. Dario Fo, *Pum! Pum!* (Vernoa/Bertani: 1974) pp. 11-12.
16. Cited in Tom Behan, *op. cit.*

14

Doris Lessing's *The Golden Notebook*: "A Wordless Statement"

Doris Lessing, born of British parents in Kermanshah, Persia, on October 22, 1919, emigrated with her family to Banket in Southern Rhodesia at the age of five. She spent the most impressionable years of her life there, ventured into two abortive marriages, and, finally settled down in England in 1949. Her literary output is far from slender and includes novels, short stories, plays, poems, non-fictional works and an autobiography, *Going Home*.

Doris Lessing's novel, *The Golden Notebook*, published in 1962, acquired the status of the most considerable single work by an English author in the 1960s. This novel, marked by an encyclopaedic range of interest and an attempt to plumb the problems and privations of the women of the sixties, especially in their relationship with men, is, like George Eliot's *Middlemarch*, a compendium of women's attitudes and habitudes but in a very different time and place. In a May 1969 interview at Stony Brook, New York, Doris Lessing referred to the period in which the events of *The Golden Notebook* take place as a time when "everything is cracking up [...]. It had been falling apart since the bomb was dropped on Hiroshima."[1] This consciousness of disintegration and annihilation of the individual under collective pressure is clearly linked with Anna's, and Doris Lessing's, sense of the bomb as explosion and death, a metaphor for the post-war years.

The theme of Doris Lessing's novels is often the justifiability of strong commitment to a particular cause or political doctrine despite a hostile or indifferent society. Talking of her "sense of duty" that makes her join organizations, she defends her own support of Communism and her endorsement of values like liberty, freedom and truth, values that she believes to have become "banners for men to fight under."[2]

Lessing's women protagonists often exhibit a strong will to change society, to work actively for a more humane and just world. Yet, many of them, disillusioned by their own societies, can discover themselves through an older person, disclaimed and spurned by a large section of the society. Martha Quest, the central character of a series of novels, for example, has her first romantic involvement with a Jewish orchestra leader much older than herself and looked upon contemptuously by the society.

Lessing has consciously sought the socially rejected. Her women define themselves through their sexual relationships and Julia Barr [*Retreat to Innocence*, 1956], Martha Quest (Martha Quest series including *Each His Own Wilderness*, 1958) Anna/Ella *(The Golden Notebook*, 1962) and others, all demonstrate their partial or essential rejection of their own societies by affairs with the ineligible and unacceptable. Those endorsed by society—the aristocrats and the half-hearted liberals—are not held in high esteem in Doris Lessing's fiction. The subterranean human relationships that the novelist deals with lend the novel its intensity and are its *raison d'etre* but the feeling of political and social responsibility is also carefully worked into specific and identifiable historical situations. Anna's disillusionment with the Communists and the failure of the Communists in reconciling their beliefs with their possibilities is an example of the way in which history operates—at another time and another place, the same doctrine of Communism might well have succeeded.

Lessing's addiction to historical categories is seen in the frequent parenthetical historical references that abound in her fiction. This giving of extensive and specific details of character and over-emphasizing the significance of the historical environment in terms of time and place confines the author to the view that all people are merely historically conditioned characters and have no identity and individuality of their own. This is a dangerous stance to subscribe to for it may very well be the cause of an aesthetic lapse in Doris Lessing's novels. What James Gindin says of *The Grass is Singing* is true of other novels of the author as well: "Historical accuracy [...] cuts off a possible dimension of human perception,"[3] for human experience cannot be categorized or precisely located. It is this inability to pin down the ineffable and indefinable experiences that leads Doris Lessing to explore a form of fiction that becomes the experience itself and the expression of it.

In *The Golden Notebook*, the central issue is human relationships, especially the relationships between men and women as a vital image of modern humanity or inhumanity. Lessing, largely influenced by D.H. Lawrence's views about mechanical sex, about ennui engendered by non-vital relationships and about marital bonds that enervate and exhaust, makes her Anna want, through an exercise of choice, to negate the historical role of women and rightfully desire to destroy female bondage. Anna, however, fails to see that there is a notable transformation that the world has gone through for the men have sublimated their human qualities of tenderness and satisfaction to opt for the practical advantages of civilization. Lawrence spoke of them as having been "dehumanized."

Anna, caught in the modern predicament, caught in her own existential stoicism, clinging to her travails and anguish as the only path to salvation, is doomed to futility. As an emancipated woman, she believes, she must complete or destroy herself with a male; to justify her existence, she must assert herself and deny her historical role. The intricate issue of man-woman relationships thus becomes just "going to bed" and sexual liberation becomes a question of deliberate choice. Lessing responds to what the Victorians referred to as "the Woman Question" by vigorously attacking the institution of marriage in *Martha Quest* and *A Proper Marriage* and rejecting it as the enemy of free women. In her Preface to her most celebrated novel, *The Golden Notebook* (1962), written nine years after the publication of the novel in 1971. Lessing marginalises "the Woman Question" and refers to the sex-war as being the key issue in the novel. Elizabeth Hardwick in her review of *The Golden Notebook* in *The New York Times* underscores the novel's power over "the ideas and feelings of a whole generation of women." Jean McCrindle in her dramatic first response to the novel, referring markedly to its novelty of structure, notes:

> Then I thought it was the most courageous book I had ever read—both in its structure—keeping the different parts separate and connected in order to express and avoid chaos—and in its honesty of content.[4]

At the outset, Lessing's "Free Women" in *The Golden Notebook*, Anna and Molly, are able to live "free" of men and marriage but one does not fail to register the precariousness of their freedom for "freedom" for them is accompanied with a sense of being "unrooted."[5] Each of the two, in search of companionship and a sense of security in life, is involved in a number of affairs after divorcing her husband but is invariably disappointed and deserted by men who come to her for sheer sexual gratification. Molly finally decides to remarry and settle down in life but Anna's condition is pathetic in that she is desperately alone and cannot sleep without a man. After four years of being together when Michael leaves Anna never to return, she experiences a feeling of total disintegration and dissolution.

When Anna's alter ego, Ella, is deserted by her lover, Paul, she finds it impossible to ignore "the immanence of Paul"[6] for "her life was shaped around a man who would not return to her."[7] She felt that he had taken with him "not only her capacity for joy but also her will."[8] She was now determined "to liberate herself."[9]

So Lessing's "free women" are far from contented and happy but they choose an independent way of life because it is less miserable than that of a conventional married women. A woman in a man's world can never escape exploitation for as Neena Arora puts it, "principles of self-interest and self-gratification rule the conduct of a man."[10]

With reference to Lessing's novel, Paul Schlueter observantly remarks:

> Probably more than in any other novel, *The Golden Notebook* captured the authentic quality of what it is to be a woman, even more especially a woman who frankly admits the existence of her sexuality, her neuroses, her intellect, her desperation in living, her disgust at the mediocre so feverishly sought by those of either sex who are themselves mediocre, her refusal to compromise her essential being.[11]

Lessing's Anna and Molly, and especially Anna, the chief protagonist, are resilient and accommodating and stretch out for "their own wholeness"[12] despite the fragmented society they live in and the fragmented consciousness that submerges them. Anna, the novelist, striving hard to attain "a new sensibility [...] a new imaginative comprehension"[13] sadly regrets her inability to write "a book powered with an intellectual or moral passion strong enough to create order, to create a new way of looking at life."[14] By her own admission she is too diffused—she lacks conviction, she wants focus and she strains after the ability to tell the "truth,"[15] the unadulterated, untransformed truth, the consciousness of which arouses a deepening nostalgia within.

Through her protagonist, Anna, Lessing expresses her view that the form of a novel is of crucial importance. The publication of *The Golden Notebook* marked a distinct turning point in her career as a novelist. In 1957 she had hailed nineteenth century realism as the highest form of literature but five years later she deviated from this stance abandoning what she called "a conventional style, the old fashioned novel"[16] one of the reasons being that the realistic narratives would not allow her to "play"[17] with time and memory.[18]

Walter Allen speaks of contemporary novels as "the mirror of the age," a mirror reflecting not merely the external features of the age but also its inner face, its nervous system, "coursing of its blood and the unconscious promptings and conflicts which sway it."[19] Such contemporary novels, Lessing believes, are hard to devise for the ultimate experience cannot fully be verbalized—in her case, the ultimate experience of the "fragmented consciousness"[20] that prevails is ineffable and incommunicable. Thus, contemporary fiction, for her, must discard traditional forms for those that incorporate meanings with more intense self-awareness and cognizance. Lessing demonstrates the solipsism and self-reflexive nature of narration that characterizes the fiction of the present times.

Doris Lessing in *The Golden Notebook*, created a "nonchronological matrix"[21] that facilitated her juxtaposition of scenes and characters as per desire and design. The frequent forward and backward shift in time makes it difficult to trace the chronological sequence of events in the life of the protagonist. The novel not only tells the story of Anna Wulf's search for an integrated and developed consciousness but is in itself a display of the ways in which the consciousness operates. The novel, thus, records the protagonist's quest and is also the vehicle for conducting this quest. When interviewed by Florence Howe, Lessing herself observed, "The way it's constructed says what the book is about."[22] Her "Introduction" to the novel endorses this statement: "My major aim was to shape a book which would make its own comment, a wordless statement: to talk through the way it was shaped."[23]

What Albert Camus says of any creative writer's composition is applicable to Lessing's novel as well. "Viewed all together"[24] Anna's six-part work in *The Golden Notebook* communicates to the reader not only Lessing's *personal* predicament but also the prevalent societal temper of the times encapsulated in the term "postmodern consciousness." This state of mind is a complex of disaffirmatory moods—an intense longing for the comfort of the past forms, a terrifying apprehension of the amorphism of the present and its nondescript cast, a sense of desperation and futility, and, a determination to confront disorder and resolve the chaos—all often camouflaged by a general public façade of poise and harmony. In this context, one cannot fail to record the characteristic nature of the postmodern sensibility of Anna Wulf, "who could feel herself, under this shape of order, as a chaos of discomfort and anxiety."[25] At another point in the narrative Anna identifies herself with the chaos around and feels isolated amidst the disorder in her life: "I was alone in chaos."[26] Lessing's novel unreservedly acknowledges the presence of chaos in our lives and the human inclination to impose form and order on this almost intractable imbroglio. The situation, the novelist believes, can be resolved only by establishing a dual relationship—on the one hand, with commitment to practical objectives, visionary ideals, art, work logic and order and on the other, with creation, destruction, vitality emotion and chaos. The form of Lessing's novel reveals the contours of a woman's experience, an experience that spells incessant movement away from threadbare forms into disorder and then an invigorating new construct. Taking cognizance of this creative flux in life is one of the essentials of postmodern art. The achievement of Lessing's novel, *The Golden Notebook*, lies in its acceptance and its demonstration, in terms of form and structure, of the prevalence of this creative flow.

The Golden Notebook took the form it did because of Lessing's interest in the interaction between form and thematic content. The "wordless statement" that she talks about in her Introduction is a depiction of how Anna and Saul "break through the false patterns and formulas they have made of their pasts to shore up themselves and each other."[27] Like Lessing, her characters also try to find ways to differentiate between "formulas" and viable form; also, like her, they (Anna/Ella) scorn the highly patterned, static form of the so-called modern novel, and, in conformity with the salient features of postmodern literature, follow closely "the dynamic interplay of order and chaos,"[28] with chaos continually destroying forms to create new ones based on new values and strengths.

Anna's opening statement in the novel "[...] as far as I can see, everything's cracking up,"[29] is a clear pointer to the thematic content of the novel and the structure of the work is meant to emphasize this essential fragmentation and the consequent "formlessness"[30] that Lessing talks of. The four coloured notebooks represent the four irreconcilable aspects of Anna's life that lead her to a schizophrenic existence, an existence which alone can save her from the threat of a lapse into chaos.

The first of Anna's records, *the Black Notebook*, deals with her "success" as a novelist who has published 'Frontiers of War.' Yet, from the narrative, we learn how Anna's desire for an ideal order is twice frustrated. As a younger person she had aspired to save the Blacks of South Africa from exploitation and racial oppression; in the present she wishes to explore the truth about her past and to render it with complete objectivity in writing. Anna's plans never materialize for reality always works at cross-purposes. As narrator of the Mashopi memoir she realizes that she is "falling into the wrong tone"[31] and is unable "to fit conflicting things together to make a whole [...]."[32]

Anna experiences a two-stage reaction to being thwarted in her intention—a sense of nostalgia for the past and a feeling of bitter cynicism which almost paralyzes her morally and emotionally. The empirical wisdom derived from this trauma leads Anna to subscribe to a kind of "nihilism, an angry readiness to throw everything overboard, a willingness, a longing to become part of dissolution."[33]

The *Red Notebook* registers Anna's failure in the political sphere for here, too, her ideals are mercilessly exposed as hollow. Her gung-ho attitude of the party fanatic is soon tempered down by the observations made by herself as "a dry, wise, ironical, political woman."[34] Anna is now cynically aware of her dreams being deflated and her ideals for a better world demolished. She and her comrades try to sustain their belief in the power of the Communist Party to replace "the split, divided, unsatisfactory way we all live"[35] with a vigorous wholeness but deep within they know that it has already lost its power of regeneration and deliverance.

In the *Yellow Notebook* devoted to fiction and to the efforts of her own creative imagination, Anna moves closer towards coming to terms with reality by acknowledging the evidence of her own art product, the novel, *The Shadow of the Third*. While her literary and political ideals are demolished in the *Black* and *Red Notebooks*, respectively, in the *Yellow Notebook* it is her ideal of love that is shattered. Her novel traces the involvement of Ella (admittedly, a projection of Anna herself) and Paul Tanner (a representative fictive construct of Anna's lover, Michael) in a romantic relationship based on self-delusion, which, when exposed, brings bitterness and disgust. Paul, like Camus' Sisyphus, labours under no misapprehension that his toil as a boulder-pusher causes progress and his struggle, in conformity with the existential attitude advocated by Camus, "implies a total absence of hope, a continual rejection and a conscious dissatisfaction."[36] Anna, on the other hand, unable to reach her ideal, responds by surrendering to frustration and despair. She discontinues the narrative because it does not live upto her ideal of art.

The *Blue Notebook* following the *Yellow* one depicts Anna's efforts to analyze her self-deceptions and illusions and to explore the unbridgeable gulf within her between idealism and cynicism. Anna begins this notebook with a resolution: "I shall keep a diary."[37] She questions her own practice of changing everything into fiction. Perhaps, she feels, it is an attempt to circumvent what actually happens, to conceal things from herself. The maintenance of a diary will enable her to fall back upon the precision of her factual account rather than the invention of her creative imagination which is likely to falsify things by submitting to her old idealizing self. She now wants to record only the *facts* of experience so as to cultivate an awareness of existence as it prevails. Like in other spheres, she demolishes her earlier beliefs and awaits the arrival of some new creation in her image of the new man she visualizes.

For Anna, Saul Green and Tom Mathlong symbolize two modes of self-criticism. Saul stands for romantic fervour, idealism, belief, egoism and self-indulgence where as Mathlong represents disinterestedness, realism, cynicism, humanitarianism and abstinence. Saul the egoistic idealist, introduces Anna to a chaotic condition of life characterized by contradictory conceptions and discernments; Mathlong teaches her how to effectively and fruitfully channelize this tumultuous vitality and vigour.

The four Notebooks written by Anna in the first person are framed within a novel called *Free Women*, which is about Anna, the author of the notebooks. The notebooks and the novel are further subdivided into several sections. This complex pattern of the parts of the novel is deliberate in that it prefigures the fragmentation that is ultimately perpetrated in the protagonist's life. The structure of the novel, thus, is clearly designed to underscore this disintegration.

In her early days, Anna's excessive idealism is countered by the keen sensibility and awareness of Paul Blackenhurst. In her fictional representation of her own life-situation, Anna, likewise, makes the credulous Ella confront the circumspect Paul Tanner. Again, since both the Pauls are wary and cynical their impact on Anna's existence is diluted by the sincerity and earnestness of Saul Green, whose impulsiveness, in turn, is balanced by the cool deliberateness of Mathlong. At the end of the *Blue Notebook* with Anna's intransigence dissolved and her inner conflicts resolved, there emerges from within her a unified, synthesized self which is now well-equipped to put "all of myself in one book."[38] She is now able to see through her error in trying to create a valid reality out of the distortions of her fantasy and imagination. She realizes her fallacious stance in dividing her perception into separate notebooks and is, at last, able to embrace the fullness of her experiences. She is now wholly aware of "the distance between what I was imagining and what in fact I was."[39] She is able to accept her set of revaluations for she acquires what Nietzsche calls "the means of *enduring it:* the revaluation of all values."[40] So, with renewed confidence and composure, Anna is now happily willing to take on the task of creating order and meaning in her own, personal life, for, as Betsy Draine puts it:

> Anna of *The Golden Notebook* has learned to balance irony with compassion and awareness with faith. She is, at last, the woman who can compose 'a book powered with an intellectual or moral passion [...]' *(The Golden Notebook*, p. 76).[41]

Anna, now, has overcome the barrier of the inadequacy of language to express "the density of our experience."[42] Her frustration with the incompetence of words to express the multiple layers of meaning held in a single consciousness had compelled her to resort to a fractured perception and a distorted version of reality. Her experiences had seemed to be incommunicable and it was her "destabilized narrative structure."[43] and her "wordless statement"[44] constituted by the form and shape of the novel that enabled communication and came to her rescue before she was ready to shoulder "the burden of recreating order out of the chaos that my life had become."[45]

References

1. Cited in Frederick R. Karl, *A Reader's Guide to The Contemporary English Novel* (London: Thames and Hudson, rpt. 1972) p. 292.
2. Doris Lessing, *Going Home* (London: Michael Joseph, 1957) pp. 252-53.
3. James Gindin, *Postwar British Fiction* (California: University of California Press, 1962) p. 85.
4. Jean McCrindle, "Reading the Golden Notebook in 1962," *Notebooks/Memoirs/Archives*, p. 57.
5. Doris Lessing, *The Golden Notebook* (London: Flamingo, rpt. 1993) p. 30.
6. *Ibid.*, p. 284.
7. *Ibid.*, p. 276.
8. *Ibid.*, p. 277.
9. *Ibid.*, p. 276.
10. Neena Arora, *Nayantara Sahgal and Doris Lessing: A Feminist Study in Comparison* (New Delhi: Prestige, 1991) p. 109.
11. Paul Schlueter, "Doris Lessing: The Free Woman's Commitment," *Contemporary British Novelists*, ed. Charles Shapiro (Carbondale; Southern Illinois University Press, rpt. 1965) p. 58.
12. Doris Less, *The Golden Notebook*, p. 75.
13. *Ibid.*, p. 76.
14. *Ibid.*
15. *Ibid.*, p. 77.
16. Doris Lessing, "A Small Personal Voice," *Declaration* ed. Tom Machsler (London: Mac Gibbon and Kee, 1957), p. 14.
17. Dorothy Brewster, *Doris Lessing*, TEAS (New York: Twayne, 1965), p. 144.
18. This reference to "play" with time and memory recalls Salman Rushdie's frequent forward or backward shift in time and his treatment of what he calls "memory's truth" in his novel *Midnight's Children* (London: Picador, 1982), p. 211.

19. Walter Allen, *Reading a Novel* (Great Britain: Penguin, 1971) pp. 18-19.
20. Doris Lessing, *The Golden Notebook*, p. 75.
21. Herbert Marder, "The Paradox of Form in *The Golden Notebook*," *Modern Fiction Studies*, Doris Lessing Number, Spring 1980, Vol. 26, No. 1, p. 49.
22. Doris Lessing, *A Small Personal Voice* (New York: Vintage Books, 1974), p. 79.
23. Doris Lessing, *The Golden Notebook*, p. 13.
24. Albert Camus, *The Myth of Sisyphus and Other Essays*, trans. Justin O'Brien (New York: Knopf, 1955), p. 84.
25. Doris Lessing, *The Golden Notebook*, p. 343.
26. *Ibid.*, p. 270.
27. *Ibid.*, p. 7.
28. Betsy Draine, "Nostalgia and Irony: The Postmodern Order of *The Golden Notebook*," *Modern Fiction Studies*, Doris Lessing Number, Spring 1980, Vol. 26, No. 1, p. 31.
29. Doris Lessing, *The Golden Notebook*, p. 25.
30. *Ibid.*, Preface, p. 7.
31. *Ibid.*, p. 79.
32. *Ibid.*
33. *Ibid.*, p. 78.
34. *Ibid.*, p. 156.
35. *Ibid.*, p. 157.
36. Camus, p. 23.
37. Doris Lessing, *The Golden Notebook*, p. 211.
38. *Ibid.*, p. 528.
39. *Ibid.*, p. 552.
40. Friedrich Nietzsche, *The Will to Power*, trans. Walter Kaufmann and R.J. Hollingdale (New York: Vintage, 1968), Section 1059, p. 545.
41. Betsy Draine, *Modern Fiction Studies*, p. 47.
42. Doris Lessing, *The Golden Notebook*, p. 273.
43. Molly Hite, Doris Lessing's *The Golden Notebook* and *The Four Gated City*: Ideology, Coherence and Possibility," *Twentieth Century Literature*, Spring 1988, Vol. 34, No. 1, p. 16.
44. Doris Lessing, *The Golden Notebook*, Preface, p. 13.
45. *Ibid.*, p. 538.

15

Shelley As Myth-Maker: Aspects of Some Shorter Nature Lyrics

Myths are an attempt to comprehend the incomprehensible. They serve to explain why the world is as it is and why things happen as they do. They establish the rationale behind phenomena—social, religious or natural—which may otherwise seem inexplicable. Generally anonymous and rooted in primitive folk beliefs, myths endeavour to interpret creation, divinity and religion and to elucidate the meaning of life and death. Unlike legends, they are often conveyed in terms of the supernatural and do not have much of a historical base and again, are different from fables in being less didactic in purpose. They are, almost invariably, the product of a racial or tribal group rather than the creation of an individual.

A myth, in the original sense of the Greek word "muthos," is essentially a story communicated by word of mouth. With the passage of time, however, "muthos" has come to have a special significance so that now, it is not just a fabulous tale or a piece of recreational fiction but a story with a cosmic purpose for those who tell it and those who are its recipients.

In contemporary literary analysis, myth has become a term not to be ignored and the myth critics like Robert Graves, Francis Fergusson, Richard Chase, Philip Wheelwright, Leslie Fiedler, and last but not the least, Northrop Frye, interpret the genres of all literature in terms of " archetypes" and basic myth formulae. To quote Frye "the typical forms of myth become the conventions and genres of literature."[1] According to him, the four main narrative genres of comedy, romance, tragedy and irony (satire) may be associated with the seasonal cycle of spring, summer, autumn and winter.

The baffling variety of denotations that the term *myth* has in contemporary criticism includes its meaning as a widely held fallacy as in "the myth of progress" and the verisimilar microcosm of a work of fiction as in "the mythical world of Moby Dick."

Traditionally, the literary treatment of myths may be categorized into three basic types. First, there is the written chronicling of the hereditary oral story as in the case of the early *Ramayana* in India, or the chronicling by interested observers as in the recording of African folktales from Uganda and the West Coast. Secondly, there is a varied treatment of the original myth by a later poet or tale-teller as in the example of the later *Ramayana* by Tulsi Das or the Story of the Magi by T.S. Eliot. Thirdly, there is the detached artistic treatment of the story without reference to its truth as we see in Rupert Brooke's poem on the Annunciation.

The appeal of the myth is perpetual for it pacifies the cultural nostalgia of modern existence. The revival of myths by litterateurs, however, has never been for the sake of recapturing the past as it was. The primary concern of these literary mythologizers was never the meaning the myths had for the society in which they originated. Their focus was rather on the reinterpretation of myths for application to their own age, or for use by themselves.

For Shelley, too, the classical mythology was not to be approached as simply as the dead metaphors of the past. A thinker deeply concerned with the scientific and technological advances of his day he seems to have known how the scholarship of his times was seeking to rationalize the ancient mythology inherited by the Romantics. Harold Bloom in his introduction to *Shelley's Mythmaking* quotes the views of Martin Buber and a couple of anthropologists of Mircea Eliade's following to substantiate his proposition that the religious mode of thinking, which sees the external relations of the self in terms of I-thou and not I-it, is characteristic of the primitive myth-maker as also of the poet in his role of the progressive myth-maker. This characteristic of the advanced myth-maker viewing the self's external relations in terms of I-thou is unmistakably identifiable in Shelley's poetry, specially in his Nature poems where the merger of the poet with the subject of myth-making is almost complete and the impulse that clinches the merger is largely emotional. Shelley's poems, then, conform closely to Richard Chase's concept of mythical literature:

> Literature becomes mythical by suffusing the natural with preternatural force toward certain ends, by capturing the impersonal forces of the world and directing them toward the fulfilment of certain emotional needs.[2]

In Romantic myth-making much has been made of Blake's treatment of myth, so much so that his myth-making came to be considered as a model for major Romantic poets like Shelley and Keats. Marilyn Butler, however, in her essay, "Myth and Myth-making"[3] takes the example of Shelley's close friend, Thomas Love Peacock, as a representative myth-maker of the younger generation of the Romantics. She avers that the potential mythologizing of Peacock, who was seven years older than Shelley, probably influenced the much larger and more significant oeuvre of the latter. Shelley, like Blake and Peacock, "turned again and again to myths and legends or the past for his artistic purposes."[4]

There certainly was an upsurge in the use of myth in Blake's period, from about 1785 to 1795, when the important debaters with regard to mythological polemic were mainly French or French-based like d'Hancarville, Volney, Charles Dupuis and Thomas Paine, author of *The Age of Reason* (1794-95). The aspect of mythology that they focussed on was cosmogony which elaborates upon the origin and creation of the Universe.

In 1812 came Peacock's full-scale Zoroastrian poem in the Spenserian stanza, '*Ahrimanes*' with which the poet brings his mythographical material to relate to the contemporary situation using a narrative rather than didactic technique. His protagonist appears to be living in a mythicized present. In this Peacock anticipates the protagonists of Shelley's *'The Revolt of Islam'* and *'Prometheus Unbound.'* Peacock's method of the use of myth lives on even in Shelley's *'The Witch of Atlas'* and in his fragment of an unfinished drama of 1822 about an enchantress living on an island of the Indian Archipelago.

In about 1819 Shelley dealt significantly with the question of mythology in his essay, *'On the Devil and Devils,'* a pertinent discussion of the efforts of monotheistic religions to come to grips with evil. Milton's *'Paradise Lost,'* Shelley believed, "has conferred on the modern mythology, a systematic form; [...]."[5] The modern mythology of which Shelley speaks is a new concept conceived of in the 1790s. Milton, the individual, has contributed to the building up of this concept as a writer who was not quite a mythmaker in the conventional and accepted sense of the term; he merely bestowed on the religion he inherited "a systematic form" as Shelley puts it. By Shelley's own time, however, myths had gained a new currency and a new meaning through the contemporary conviction in the function of art and the artist. The modern Prometheus is not Prometheus, the Sun God, but an artist who makes of his art a vehicle for conveying his belief.

Shelley left us no systematic statement on his conception of mythology but his casual remarks and allusions help us reconstruct his attitude towards the subject. In his notes to 'Queen Mab' he refers to both "The strong evidence afforded by the history of mythology, and geological researches"[6] as the scientific bases for speculations on the past and future climate of the earth. In his *'Defence of Poetry,'* too, he makes relevant statements like "all original religions are allegorical, or susceptible of allegory, and, like Janus, have a double face of false and true."[7] Thus the mythology of a religion is considered to be a fairly precise pronouncement of historical truth but special objectivity and sensitivity are prerequisites for the perception of this truth.

To a Platonist like Shelley, the idea that the visible was but a "veil" cast over the real was reason enough to accept the belief that all myths (including those underlying Christianity) contained a core of truth but had been so distorted by time and communication that only a single fundamental principle behind everything could reveal their essence. This principle was the eternal struggle between the liberating spirit and its opponent, the asphyxiating force of repression.

Shelley read into all mythology the universal and unique presence of an eternal tyrant who represented the negative qualities of man and was identifiable in various times and places. In *'The Revolt of Islam'* Shelley refers to this tyrant as "the Spirit of evil" that is "One Power of many shapes which none may know/one shape of many names" (I, XXVII, 361-63).

In *'Prometheus Unbound,'* the furies sent to torment Prometheus, the ministers of Jupiter, are called "many fearful natures in one name" (I, 458). The actions in Shelley's poems, thus, may be interpreted as symbolic of man's creative energies directed towards an eternal quest for freedom from repression. Unmistakable in his poetry is the recurrence of allusions to Dionysus, not by name but by multiple associations with the attributes of that elemental god. In this concept of matter as energy, Shelley recognizes the source of human love and creativity of political revolution and of the cosmic activities of generation and destruction. It is this Dionysian motif, the various forms of the 'Destroyer and Preserver,' that may be traced through all his works. Joseph Raben in his essay, "Shelley the Dionysian" underlines Shelley's use of Dionysus as a metaphor to explain all phenomena:

> This Dionysianism can be traced through Shelley's letters and prose writings, as well as his verse; it is a fundamental trope that goes a long way toward unifying his artistic output and clarifying apparent ambiguities or contradictions in his major works. To recognise this Dionysian strain, to observe its diverse manifestations and their evolution, to relate these atavisms with Shelley's developing thought, is to appreciate both the art and the thought that animates them.[8]

The Dionysian element, then, without specifically being named, appears in almost all of Shelley's major works: *'Alastor,'*

'Prometheus Unbound,' 'The Witch of Atlas,' 'Adonais,' 'Hellas' and *'The Triumph of Life.'* In his drama *'Censi,'* alone, it is not alluded to at all, and in *'The Revolt of Islam'* only suggestively. Shelley's shorter poems, specially his Nature lyrics, are almost all endowed with the quintessential beauty of the Dionysian conception and show us the promise of peace that lies beyond the raging tempests and remind us that love and tranquillity may follow violent and destructive upheaval.

It would not be out of context here to refer to F.S. Ellis' exploration of Shelley's Nature poetry.[9] Ellis discovered in Shelley's verse five different meanings of the word 'Nature.' 'Nature' for the poet, according to him, was first, the universe or all creation; secondly, the power which guides and rules the world; thirdly, disposition or temper of mind; fourthly, human life or vitality; and, lastly, nature's handiwork.

Apart from the variety in his literal use of the term, Shelley looked upon Nature in three very distinct and unconventional ways. These have been discriminatingly defined by Stopford Brooke.[10] According to Brooke, Shelley's love of the indefinite and changeful made him enjoy better the scenic beauty of the sky and the clouds. Brooke also observed that Shelley did not wish to consider all objects of Nature as being merged in any universal existence; he was endowed with the remarkable power of conceiving the life of separate things in Nature with great individuality. Lastly, and very significantly, Shelley observed a correspondence between his own feelings and the ways of Nature—the vagueness and changefulness of his feelings as recorded in his poetry in terms of objects of Nature like the clouds that form and dissolve incessantly are among the few images of its kind in poetic art.

It is particularly from Shelley's Nature lyrics that we derive such rare images of poetic art. Shelley's myths of Nature are not mere caprices of fancy—they convey his consciousness of the intense reality that dwells in Nature. To his love of nature and his fondness for abstractions Shelley added a passion for the Greeks and a genius for the spontaneous creation of myths. Thus, the Sun, the westwind, the cloud and the skylark were to him not the conventional personifications of the eighteenth century odes, but live forces celebrating their freedom and their vigour. They are characteristic of the joyful, ethereal leanings of their creator. This special myth-making liaison with Nature through which Shelley entered the life and consciousness of a bird or a cloud, is best revealed in poems like *'The Cloud,' 'To a Skylark'* and *'Ode to the West-wind.'* Mrs. Shelley spoke of Shelley's knowledge of the "natural" world and his unrivalled keenness of perception with regard to almost all natural objects. Later, she observed, "His extreme sensibility gave the intensity of passion to his intellectual pursuits; and rendered his mind keenly alive to every perception of outward objects."[11] Shelley's own writings show that he cared deeply for Nature and wished to give the feeling of a scene rather than the individual elements that constitute it. His lyrics of nature are never mere descriptions; they are animated by his abiding consciousness of the contrast between the world of appearance and the world of reality, between the present and the future and offer Shelley outlets for the expression of his convictions and aspirations. The world of appearance and the material actualities of the present evoke in him a mood of melancholy which soon dissolves and is substituted by hope aroused by the ideal reality that lies behind the veil. The West-wind, the harbinger of Winter and Death, will sweep the poet away like it sweeps the leaves of the forest, but Spring, sure enough, will follow and bring the fruition of his hopes for humanity. The clouds of the sky enact the future of mankind; they may appear to symbolize the transience of beauty but actually, they only change and never die. Again, the song of the skylark suggests the truth of absolute love and joy despite the earthly sorrows that abound in life.

Shelley, with his characteristic super ability to create in his poems myths from objects of nature, presents in *'The Cloud'* an interesting autobiography of the cloud itself. In the poem, a masterpiece of transformation and natural process, the cloud conveys to us its various states and moods. The poem illustrates in striking imagery the various forms water vapour assumes. In the first stanza we see the cloud's impish delight at its transition from the gentleness that brings "fresh showers for the thirsting flowers" to the violence that wields "the flail of the lashing hail." In the second stanza we see the cloud as a bringer of snow to the mountains. Stanza three shows the cloud at sunrise and sunset. The scene following sunset is described in the next stanza and stanza five elaborates upon the halo effect of the cloud which binds "the Sun's throne with a burning zone" and gives the moon "a girdle of pearl." Subsequently the cloud envelops the mountain tops and descends over the stormy sea. Finally, we see its triumphant march through the rainbow.

The last stanza emphasizes the immortal nature of the cloud, which, born of Earth and Water, can never perish. Not only does it change its shape and texture but also its very nature from vapour to water and back again to its vaporous form. Even after a clear blue sky the supposedly dead cloud can arise and "silently laugh" at its "own cenotaph." The imagery of death and rebirth in the poem may lead us to draw a parallel between the life of the cloud and that of man. Possibly the earlier verses symbolize the adventures and travails of the human spirit which, however, is essentially immortal.

This truth of eternity is part of the Truth that Shelley seeks in poetry, the poetic truth that he pursues through his synthetic and intuitional creative imagination. It is a truth that ever eludes the comprehension of man. Shelley, however, persistently seeks, through his significantly metaphorical and creative language to grasp an invisible and unattainable truth. *'To a Skylark'* is one of his indomitable attempts at exploring the nature of absolute Truth. As in *'The Cloud,'* we have in this poem another myth he weaves around a natural existence, a myth through which he arrives at the quality of Beauty and Truth. The skylark, buoyant and vibrant with the very music it commemorates, is a symbol of Perfection and Truth and is suggestively unseen and remote. Similarly, meaningfully, the poet is hidden in the depths of thought, the maiden is isolated in a tower, which symbolizes absolute withdrawal from actuality; the glow-worm spreads unseen its aerial hue; the rose lies concealed within its own green sepals from where emanates its overpowering fragrance. This concrete-abstract dualism is present almost everywhere in life; the West-wind itself is an "unseen presence." Thus, the images through which Shelley arrives at his idea of Beauty, all represent the unseen which is visible only through its effects upon perceptible objects.

In *'To a Skylark'* Shelley again chooses a potential object from the natural world, an object that allows of myth-making in terms of the poet's special ability. The skylark, singing its melodious song, soars upwards often beyond the reach of sight and hence, despite its natural identity, has an ethereal trait that conforms to Shelley's concept of the bird as a Spirit that embarks upon its unfettered flight over land and sea. The ecstasy of the bird's song can be paralleled only by effulgent images of the sky itself until dusk descends and the lark is out of sight.

Shelley's description of the lark as "an Unbodied joy whose race is just begun" conveys the idea of the pure and absolute joy expressed by the bird's song. The comparison of the lark to a poet is significant for its song is like poetry of the purest kind pouring forth "unpremeditated" spontaneously from the heart of a poet; only, the latter, conscious of human mortality, must learn to overcome pain and partake of the skylark's pure delight which is inspired and sustained by nothing but truth.

Shelley's interest in the Dionysian element and in natural process and transformation is best observed in *'Ode to the West-wind,'* which represents with impact and vigour the natural cycles of disintegration and regeneration. The poem has a typically mythic pattern in the way it suggestively re-enacts the cycle of the year. The sustained drive and the steady compulsion of the West-wind has to be effectively visualized by the reader to be able to see beyond the procession of clouds, leaves and waves and to register the effect on the poet himself and through him, on the process of history. The poet seeks identification with the West-wind when he personifies and addresses this natural phenomenon and believes himself to be "One too like thee." He establishes in the poem the reciprocity between Man and Nature:

> Make me thy lyre, even as the forest is:
> What if my leaves are falling like its own!

The tumult of thy mighty harmonies
Will take from both a deep autumnal tone,
Sweet though in sadness. Be thou, Spirit fierce,
My Spirit! Be thou me, impetuous one !" (v, lls. 1-6)

One observes in the poem, no doubt, the effect of movement and fluidity, but, there is, to these "loose clouds" that are "shook from the tangled boughs of Heaven and Ocean" and to the "commotion" of the storm, the firmness and stability of the "vaulted" sky and the "dome" of "congregated" vapours, from whose "solid" atmosphere "the black rain" is bursting. Thus the charges of vagueness and the lack of substantiality cannot always be held against Shelley for there is, often, in his nature lyrics a certain architectural immobility and solidity that resists the fluidity of undifferentiated flux. Richard H.Fogle, in his analysis of the imagery of Shelley has discriminatingly observed that

> The rapid flow of his swift-moving forms and essences is usually set in a motionless and solid frame. In that poem of his which most vividly conveys the feeling of fierce and breathless speed, the *'Ode to the West-wind,'* it is too seldom noticed that the wind moves beneath a solid dome within which the scene is enclosed.[12]

Thus the evanescence and tenuity of Shelley's images often spring from the abstract material he works with (winds, clouds, waterscapes etc.) rather than from lapses in the handling of his subject matter.

Keeping in view Shelley's predilection for potential natural phenomena, we see how the poet, in *'Ode to the West-wind'* creates a new myth by making the wind a powerful symbol, a symbol not of a one to one correspondence, but a symbol with multiple connotations and denotations. The West-wind represents for Shelley change, poetic inspiration, strength and energy, hope, regeneration of mankind and finally, his own personality. It is the Westwind that can prevent him from falling upon "the thorns of life" and "bleeding" and it is this alone that can carry his message of hope to mankind and bring about a realization of his revolutionary idealism; and hence, the complete self-surrender of the poet, the surrender being a notable form of his identification with the intrinsic and eternal nature of the West-wind.

Shelley calls the West-wind a "Spirit" that is, "moving everywhere" (1.13). What is significant here is the image of the wind as the ultimate reality and the *cause* of life, destroying and re-creating existence at will as it were. Shelley obviously found in the West-wind the appropriate medium of expression which he was seeking.

The *'Ode to The West-wind'* sounds to be sometimes an invocation and sometimes a prayer, to a power that is "uncontrollable," 'inviolable and most formidable but essentially prophetic in nature, looking forward to the resurgence of life.

The poem, a remarkable blend of precise observation and highly creative imagery, is itself spirited with the breathless animation of the wind. The metre, terza rima, is also an apt choice for it gives the effect of an unstoppable, "uncontrollable" wind. The first three verses describe, respectively, the wind on land, in the sky and at sea. In the first verse the dead leaves that are blown along by the wind appear like the shrivelled remnants of a life that is gone whereas the seeds, though they lie "cold and low," give promise of a revival of life in Spring. Thus, we see the wind in its role of "Destroyer and Preserver." The second verse, based on the minute observation of scattered clouds in the sky which presage a tempestuous storm, likens these clouds to the streaming hair of Maenad (a female follower of Dionysus). The imminent storm again suggests the idea of destruction and death, and then, once again there is a great outburst of energy and life from the "vast sepulchre" of the night. The third verse describes the West-wind clearing the surface of the calm Mediterranean into chasms, the cleavage making even the vegetation in the sea-bed quiver with the sensation.

The poem is in the form of a prayer to the West-wind ("O wild Westwind!"). This form of supplication makes personification of the Wind a natural figure of speech and the sincerity, and urgency of the suppliant's request to allow him to share the attributes of the Wind add emotional intensity to the poem in the fourth verse. The Wind and the suppliant are brought closer in relationship and the latter passionately requests the wind to lift him above the cares of life:

> O lift me as a wave, a leaf, a cloud!
> I fall upon the thorns of life! I bleed! (lls. 53-54)

The final verse also has reference to Shelley himself but it is now Shelley, the poet, rather than Shelley, the suppliant, the suffering individual. The poet does not appeal for an escape from the sorrows of life; rather he pleads with the wind to give him creative energy and poetic inspiration enough to usher in the new spring time for mankind and to endow him with "the trumpet of a prophesy." (l.69)

The analyses of the above nature lyrics of Shelley show the poet to advantage as a highly imaginative and creative myth-maker who establishes new links and pleasurable relationships between the world of nature and that of man. Earl Wasserman rightly draws our attention to the fact that Shelley's

> implicit assumption is that the true and beautiful relationships of wholeness already exist potentially in the qualities of the given materials waiting to be properly drawn out. Consequently, he rather strictly confines himself to the inherent syntactical potentials, however minor or neglected they may be in the conventional myths, and his mythopoeic art lies especially in eliciting and exploiting these potentials to form new combinations."[13]

References

1. Northrop Frye, "Theory of Myths" *The Anatomy of Criticism.*
2. Richard Chase, "Notes on the Study of Myth," *Twentieth Century Criticism: The Major Statements* by W.J. Handy and Max Westbrook (New Delhi: Light & Life Publishers, 1976), p. 248.
3. Marilyn Butler, "Myth and Mythmaking," *Shelley Re-valued* (Leicester University Press, 1983), p. 3.
4. B.C. Das, *Shelley and Yeats* (Bareilly: Prakash Book Depot), p. 55.
5. D.L. Clark, ed., "On The Devil and Devils," *Shelley's Prose; or, The Tempest of a Prophecy* (Albuquerque, 1954; revised. ed. Albuquerque, 1966), pp. 267-68.

6. T. Hutchinson, ed., *The Complete Poetical works of Percy Bysshe Shelley* (1904; revised G.M. Matthews, 1970), p. 808.
7. D.L. Clark, ed., *Shelley's Prose, or, The Tempest of a Prophecy*, p. 279.
8. Joseph Raben, 'Shelley, the Dionysian,' *Shelley Revalued* ed. Kelvin Everest (Leicester University Press, 1983), p. 21.
9. F.S. Ellis, *Shelley*, p. 473; cited in *Shelley: Concept of Nature* by R. de Loyola Furtado (Calcutta: Firma K.L. Mukhopadhyay, 1958), pp. 6-7.
10. S.A. Brooke, *Poems from Shelley*, pp. XXXV-XLIII.
11. Cited by Raymond D. Havens in his work on Shelley.
12. Richard H. Fogle, *The Imagery of Keats and Shelley*, p. 55.
13. Earl Wasserman, *Shelley: a Critical Reading* (1971).

16

Tennyson's *Maud*: "A Little Hamlet"

My paper entitled "Tennyson's 'Maud': 'A Little Hamlet'" seeks to explore points of contact and points of divergence between the two works mentioned in the title, namely, Tennyson's *'Maud'* and Shakespeare's *'Hamlet,'* one being a poem rendered in a predominantly dramatic mode as the subtitle, 'A Monodrama' clearly indicates, and the other, a drama conventionally conforming to the genre itself. They are both, however, placed within the framework of a fictional plot, complete with characters and incidents. The clue for the comparison instituted comes from the poet's own reference to the poem as "a little Hamlet" in a letter to his son. He also refers to the poem as "the history of a morbid poetic soul" thereby indicating that the poem is narrative in conception and psycho-analytical in approach. Another point to be noted is that the poet's description of the poem as one in which "different phases of passion in one person take the place of different characters" is a way of showing his thrust on the dramatic nature of the work.

The retrospect of about a hundred and fifty years shows most of the major Victorian poets to have been in tune with the future. The impersonative mode, both lyrical and dramatic, was profusely subscribed to and became modern poetry's "one way of speaking truth." In 1855 Tennyson published what William E. Buckler in *The Major Victorian Poets* calls an "extraordinary lyrical drama," a poem entitled 'Maud'–"a little Hamlet," as the poet himself described it in 'Memoir I, l.396, in which, as quoted earlier, "different phases of passion in one person take the place of different characters." By relentless experimentation Tennyson had found a unique dramatic formulation through which to project his "history of a morbid poetic soul, under the blighting influence of a recklessly speculative age." (Memoir I, 1.396)

The seed lyric of 'Maud,' "O that 't were possible," had been written almost twenty years earlier in 1833-34 and was first published in 1837. At the request of his friend, Sir John Simeon, "to weave a story round this poem," the lyric was developed into 'Maud' and the title in 1875, expanded to 'Maud: A Monodrama.'

An analysis of Tennyson's earlier works clearly reveals that 'Maud' grew directly out of them but it is also, in part, very different from them by virtue of its originality and highly experimental form. In 1842 Tennyson had published a soliloquy, 'Locksley Hall', that shows many points of contact with 'Maud' as the themes of both were suggested by the affluent Rosa Baring's rejection of Tennyson's love on the grounds that the latter's worldly prospects were dim and inadequate. The young speaker in 'Locksley Hall' has a disillusioning experience with his rich beloved Amy and accuses his age of being obsessed with money. Charles Kingsley called the poem "[...] a study of man rising out of sickness into health [...] conquering his selfish sorrow, and the moral and intellectual paralysis it produces by faith and hope." This is a theme very close to that of 'Maud.'

'The Two Voices,' originally entitled 'Thoughts of a Suicide' was written during the period of intense depression through which Tennyson passed after the death of his friend, Arthur Henry Hallam. In the poem the argument between the two voices, that is, the suicidal voice and that of the poet himself is suggested by Hamlet's "to be or not to be" soliloquy. What is common between 'Maud' and this poem is that the themes of both were derived from Shakespeare's 'Hamlet' and the heroes of both suffer from a manic depression. However, 'The Two Voices' was largely influenced by Wordsworth's sonnet beginning "There are two voices [...]" as well.

Obvious links may be traced with 'The Princess' and 'In Memoriam,' too. Like the former poem, 'Maud' is narrative in conception but instead of having inter-related lyrics, its story itself is related in terms of detached, self-contained lyrics; unlike 'The Princess' which is told from several view points, 'Maud' is confined to the changing consciousness of a single unnamed central figure who is actor, narrator, commentator and lyricist all in one. As in 'In Memoriam,' the lyrics of 'Maud' suggest rather than explicitly state what has happened, with the difference that they are placed within the framework of a fictional plot, complete with characters and incidents.

'Maud' registers the speaker's reactions to the tragic events in his life. The story, briefly told, is of a highly neurotic young man, possessing an inherent streak of hysteria and melancholia, son of a father who kills himself over the collapse of a business venture. Unfortunately, this man falls in love with Maud, the daughter of the person who drove his father to suicide. In their pursuit of money and power, both Maud's brother and father try to coerce her into marriage with a rich but vapid and uninteresting young lord, heir to a new fortune. In a duel that ensues when Maud's brother discovers her in the garden with the narrator at midnight the brother is killed. Subsequently, Maud, too, dies and the protagonist turns mad. He is confined to an asylum in Brittany but is ultimately cured of his madness when his love for the dead Maud distils itself into a more generalized love of mankind which finds expression in his joining the Crimean war to fight on the side of right.

Tennyson, in an unpublished letter to the clergyman poet, Archer-Gurney, in 1885 drew his attention to the fact that in 'Maud,' "the whole was intended to be a new form of dramatic composition [...]" and in an account of the poem which he gave to his son he also underlined the points that "the peculiarity of this poem is that different phases of passion in one person take the place of different characters." It would not be out of place here to enumerate the "different phases" that he refers to for it is these successive phases that clearly show the action and the development in the poem in terms of "dramatis personae." The first phase of passion with which 'Maud' begins is that of hatred. "I hate" begins the man and he hates not a person but a place, a place which suggests a surrealistic image of a bleeding woman. Other passions paraded on the poetic stage in quick succession are the assurance of loving and being loved, delight and consciousness of threat regarding this delight, joy culminating in the lyric "Come into the garden, Maud," anguish accompanied by loneliness and self-pity after the killing of the brother and the subsequent death of Maud, horror bordering on insanity in which state the speaker now believes that he is dead, and then, the final phase of affirmation after his recovery from madness manifested in the revival of his moral and spiritual health on espousing, according to him, the just cause of war:

> The blood red blossom of war with a heart of fire (Part III, Section vi, stz. 4, l. 16).

The manic-depressive state, that is, the suffering from continual changes of feeling of the narrator before he is finally cured, are the occasions for lyrics of heightened emotions which made Tennyson add the sub-title, 'A Monodrama,' long after the first publication. The origin of the monodrama, according to Professor Culler, may be traced back to the eighteenth-century stage where passions were explored in terms of alternations of speech and music. In 'Maud' the operatic effect is striking in the music that is inherent in the outbursts of passion themselves. Tennyson's choice of an initially unstable protagonist provides him the occasion to go through a range of emotions so overcharged and highpitched as to be morbid. The impulsive utterances of Maud's lover are called forth from a mind strung to the pitch of keen poetic sensibility. These utterances are made in fitful and broken strains rather than in the measure of equal lines and regularly recurring rhymes so that the words spoken are actually articulate casts of what the protagonist feels. Every line, whether it be of sentiment, passion or reflection, is an impulsive outburst in keeping with the man's frame of mind. The syllables and lines of the several stanzas effectively conform to the separate phases of mental experience that are depicted. The frenzy of their content is in tune with the breathless speed of verse movement, largely trochaic and anapaestic.

That 'Maud' is a profoundly successful blending of form and content modern criticism[1] confirms. The poem consists of some very beautiful lyrics around which the semblance of a dramatic situation has been constructed with remarkable metrical skill. Yet, T.S. Eliot is rather critical of the whole situation, which he considers to be unreal as Tennyson, according to him, lacked the dramatic gift.[2] And, in him, emotion, suppressed as it was even from himself, ran into deep melancholia rather than towards objective and dramatic action. Eliot believes that emotion in Tennyson's poems acquired no ultimate clear purgation. Other charges against 'Maud' have been those of unequal verse, of an effect of strain, notably in the more passionate moments in the poem and of Bradley's objection to exaggerated verse being unjustifiably put in the mouth of "a poor hysterical creature."

Tennyson's inability to see the world in any but subjective terms and to create a mind unlike his own is clearly demonstrated in 'Maud' in which he attempts to deal with certain sources of deep agony in his life. 'Maud' was drawn from many of the conflicts that deeply perturbed him in his life. The protagonist seems very much like an extension of Tennyson himself and is, in many ways, identifiable with his creator though Tennyson was rather vehement—and misleading—in denying the autobiographical significance of 'Maud.' The unbalanced state of the poem's narrator's father leading to suicide after the failure of his business venture has obvious parallels with Tennyson's father's (i.e. George Clayton Tennyson's) neuroticism over his dispossession and with his suicidal addiction to drugs and drinks, as well as with Tennyson's own breakdown after his woodworking scheme failed. The economic pressures that prevent Maud and the protagonist from uniting are transmutations of similar conditions in Tennyson's own life.

Thus, the raw material from which Tennyson created 'Maud' included a lot of personal experience, but the literary material drawn from is as important as the autobiographical one. When the speaker says of Maud's brother:

This lump of earth has left his estate.
The lighter by the loss of his weight [...].

Tennyson is adapting a Homeric phrase "a useless weight on earth" applied to himself by Achilles in remorse of having failed to protect his friend, Patroclus.

Another major classical mode adopted in 'Maud' is the technique of articulating sound social criticism through a character of unsound mind in Part I, Section I, as in Horace's Satire II, Section iii, which uses as its persona a bankrupt businessman, Damasipus, who is generally thought to have gone mad, but goes around advocating the Stoic doctrine that the rest of the world is madder than he is. This satire (Satire II, Section iii) of Horace contains the source of Shakespeare's line spoken by Polonius, "Though this be madness, yet there is method in 't" ('Hamlet' Act II, Scene ii) and this line again, in turn, is an influence that Tennyson himself pointed out when he referred to his poem, 'Maud' as a "little Hamlet." His earlier quoted comment that the poem is "the history of a morbid poetic soul, under the blighting influence of a recklessly speculative age," recalls Hamlet's statement:

This time is out of joint;—O cursed spite,
That ever I was born to set it right
('Hamlet,' Act I, Sc V, lls. 188-89)

In his preface to *Points of War* (1855), Tennyson's friend, Franklin Lushington, quoting this passage, drew the moral that one must not, like Hamlet, shirk the unpleasant task of setting the time right: "Let Hamlet stand aside [...] we want Fortinbras just now." The hero of 'Maud,' on the brink of insanity, like Hamlet, inveighs against the "Wretchedest age, since Time began;" (Part II, Sec 5, l. 21) and like Hamlet's "method" in madness as Polonius sees it, there is often much reason in his ranting and raving. He arraigned the Mammonism and lust of gain in the nineteenth century and his particular allusion to the malpractices of trade, for example, the adulteration of bread, are grounded in facts:

When who but a fool would have faith in
a tradesman's ware or his word (Part I, l. 40)

In a delirius state the hero of 'Maud' (Part I) regrets that "the Churches have killed their Christ," perhaps, meaning thereby that an obdurate fundamentalism and orthodoxy have lost track of the true spirit of the Christian law. The judgement in 'Maud,' however, is oblique and incidental. In 'Hamlet' there is absolutely no reflection on the ecclesiastical problems and the religious perspective of the times although a very definite parallel may be drawn between the personal sufferings of the two heroes. The hero of 'Maud' subjected to the tyranny of turbulent emotion, is like the narrator of 'Locksley Hall,' highly self-conscious and sensitive, "at war with myself (i.e. himself) and a wretched race." (Part I, Section X, lls. 35-36) Hamlet, too, divided between himself in the experience of "to be" or "not to be" is very similar to the hero of 'Maud,' but unlike him, is more at war with himself than "a wretched race." However, in both cases, the war within is eventually represented in terms of the war outside and the apparently continuous exercise in introspection turns into action. Hamlet finally emerges from his intellectual insularity, takes decisive action and is carried off honourably "like a soldier;" so, too, the narrator of 'Maud' begins in the isolation of despair and ends like Hamlet as a man of action. And yet, war in 'Maud' plays a much more vital role than in 'Hamlet' for it provides the very frame of 'Maud,' the point of change and conversion and the source of resolution.

The narrator of 'Maud,' steeped deep in self-absorption, which may be both cause and result of his mental and emotional instability, is unable to judge others rightly and to see society as a whole in its proper perspective. He fails to see the true nature of Maud's brother, who is finally revealed as gentle towards Maud and generous to the protagonist. "The fault was mine, the fault was mine," says the brother as he is killed but the protagonist knows at that time that he is guilty of the murder. In the poem, the narrator begins by musing on the death-stained "blood-red heath" and the fate of his father who he believes has been a victim of a private war. Maud, yearning for a true knight of her own, sings a ballad of battles long ago when men could surmount selfish desire, and the protagonist, listening, dreams of an existence in which man is "no longer at war with mankind" (Part I, Section X, l. 52). "But he himself soon subscribes to the Christless code," (Part II, Section I, l. 26) of the duel. Then only after the madness that ensues is he able to identify the horror of his guilt, "the red life spilt for a private blow" (Part II, Section V, Stz.10, l.5) and to differentiate between "lawful and lawless war." The lawful Crimean war, he feels, compensates for the immoral war in his personal life.

Throughout 'Maud,' war is associated with the absence of reason in the self or the society. The whole monodrama slides into a region beyond reason taking cognizance only of the immediate sensuous experience. The original alternative title of 'Maud' was 'The Madness' and madness in many ways remains its central theme. The distraction of Hamlet, though an important factor in the progress of the plot, is not the central theme and the treatment of madness in the play is not as comprehensive as in Tennyson's poem. Besides, Hamlet is not really mad in the sense and to the extent that 'Maud's hero is though even the latter's madness at times, one feels, is more imagined than real, a projection of his morbid mind. Tennyson's treatment is both psychological and philosophical. For the first he relies mainly on the technical and authentic information provided by his psychologist friend, Dr Mathew Allen, though the immediate source of the whole psychology of 'Maud' is Tennyson's own observation and experience and his personal melancholia. Tennyson is able to represent in the poem the manner in which a morbid self-consciousness fails to relate to the consciousness of other selves. He strives to represent dream, reverie, and even madness with a rigid precision of detail. He attempts a clinical accuracy in his depiction of the madhouse and his protagonist's delirium is based on the best available knowledge of abnormal psychology. Anticipating the technique of the psychological novel, Tennyson turns from external to internal reality, from the outer world to the hidden world of fantasy and reverie characterized by the interplay of direct mental experience and the life and perception of one's senses. With Virginia Woolf who, in her essay on modern fiction, advocated a more complex form of the psychological novel, i.e. the stream-of-consciousness novel, Tennyson seems to proclaim, "Let us record the atoms as they fall upon the mind, in the order in which they fall [...]."[3] For a philosophical treatment of the poem, Tennyson relies on his evaluation of Stoic and Epicurean ethics as determined by his own experience. In the main, however, Tennyson exploited in 'Maud' as Shakespeare did in 'Hamlet,' the poetic possibilities of madness.

The hero of the poem is divided against himself. Even Maud's ghost is divided into two phantoms—one cold and gloomy and the other kind and beneficent. The "incipient stage of madness" perceptible in the protagonist gives his utterances so varied a tone that they assume the role of a cast of characters. Seen through the eye of madness, through a victim of what Bagehot called "mental malaria," all the other people are visions rather than reality. However, even the lover in 'Maud,' inspite of all his violent emotions and singular love, remains vague and unstable, for whatever he is he is in relation to Maud. He remains throughout nothing but "Maud's lover" and Maud is central to all his moods and emotional experiences. Hamlet, on the other hand is a highly individualized character, whose introspection delves the depths of life; he is outwardly and apparently calm and serene but within he is tempest-tossed and highly distracted. Maud's hero is, from the very beginning hysterical and wallowing in self-absorption. He lacks composure, courage and a sense of reality. The poet himself refers to him as "the heir of madness." This lover, tainted by a streak of hereditary insanity dwells in what Harold Nicholson calls, "the flickering half-light between the sane and the insane" till the loss of his beloved makes him lapse into a near total insanity in which state he suffers severe dislocations of the self.

Hamlet and Maud's lover are both egotists with makings of a cynic but Hamlet grows cynical to excess—cynical even of his beloved, Ophelia, despite his overwhelming love for her. Maud's lover has only a passing phase of cynicism. In the beginning of the poem his high-strung state and mental instability make him grow cynical and vituperative, rail at the world, and at one stage, even think of suicide. He sees everything through the mirror of his own egotism and thus his vision is always blurred.

Even Maud he never sees directly, and thus, she remains till the end a phantasmal presence, a dreamlike vision, never attaining substantiality.

Maud's lover, like Hamlet, is prone to brooding self-analysis and fits of melancholy. He is an extremely introspective and contemplative man, and as in the case of Hamlet, his thought paralyses his action. When overwhelmed with his love for Maud, instead of taking concrete and positive steps towards the attainment of her love, he submits to a complete physical and emotional intoxication leading to stasis followed by paralysis. His being plagued by a sense of guilt and self-condemnation at having perpetrated the murder of her brother leaves him misery-stricken. His initial failure caused by inaction, like that of Hamlet, is largely because of temperamental shortcomings.

Besides the significant parallels drawn between the protagonist of Shakespeare's 'Hamlet' and Tennyson's 'Maud,' certain echoes from the play may be observed in the poem. The speaker in 'Maud' very obviously seems to allude to Hamlet's words "We are arrant knaves all" when he remarks, "One says we are villains all" (Part I, Section I, l. 17). Again, like Hamlet he is obsessed by a wish to avenge his father's death and tries to pacify his own revengeful mind in words resembling Hamlet's to his father's ghost: "Peace angry spirit [...]" says he, reminding us of Hamlet's "rest, rest, perturbed spirit." Like Hamlet he is disgusted with himself and the entire race of man, is haunted by a ghost, and kills the brother of the girl he loves in a duel. The killing is preceded by his prayer "Let all be well, be well" (Part I, Section xviii, l. 683) in the manner of Claudius' ominous "All may be well" before praying to be forgiven for the murder of his brother.

In spite of all the similarities traced between Shakespeare's 'Hamlet' and Tennyson's 'Maud,' Hamlet as a character remains superior by virtue of being a man of vision and subtle intelligence; he fights against intimidating odds and is a man of high stature. The protagonist of 'Maud' is a victim of egotism. He submits to misanthropy owing to no greater cause than personal misfortune.

His passion is a purely selfish one and he is ignominiously uncharitable and insular in his outlook.

Thus there is much in common between 'Hamlet' and 'Maud' and Tennyson justifiably referred to his poem as "a little Hamlet;" but, the fact remains that the latter, inspite of the merits of novelty of form and convincing psychological analysis, remains, in its overall impact, a sensational melodrama as compared to the fine tragedy that 'Hamlet' is. And yet, again, an understanding of the full purport of the work and its objective of attaining strength and moral advancement by struggling against wrong is what makes the poem appreciable:

> Not die; but live a life of truest breath,
> And teach true life to fight with mortal wrong.
> (Part I, Section xviii, stz.7)

'Maud' as a tragedy in verse needs to be judged not alone by the actions and emotions depicted but by their relation to character, and that character in turn, dynamically related to the society of the times which provides the backdrop to the entire drama and looms large in the background in terms of the economic and cultural pressures that prevail as well as the intellectual environment that directs thought, and willy nilly, leaves an indelible imprint on the mind, be it Darwin's theory of evolution or the age old code of Christianity in conflict with emerging trends.

References

1. Mann, Robert James, "Tennyson's 'Maud' Vindicated: An Explanatory Essay" (1856), *Tennyson: The Critical Heritage* ed. John D. Jump (London: Routledge & Kegan Paul, 1967) p. 199 and Buckley, Jerome Hamilton, "The Intellectual Throne," *Tennyson, The Growth of a Poet* (London: Oxford University Press, 1960) p. 144.
2. T.S. Eliot, *Selected Essays* (London: Faber and Faber, 1951).
3. Virginia Woolf, Harriette Wilson, *Collected Essays* ed. Leonard Woolf (London: Hogarth Press, 1966).

17

Browning's Dramatic Monologues as Experience Explored

DRAMA as a mode of expression was an early choice in Browning's literary career and he wrote several plays including 'The Return of the Druses,' 'A Soul's Tragedy,' 'Colombe's Birthday' and 'Pippa Passes,' which was more of a series of dramatic scenes than a drama in the regular form. Browning's singular dramatic genius could hardly have gone unnoticed, and yet, paradoxically enough, he was never at his best in his plays for they were marked by evolution of character and dramatic situation more through reasoning and contention than through action. Argumentation thus became Browning's characteristic trait but the poet had yet to discover the conditions under which this practice would best operate. Drama being essentially an articulate story presented in terms of action, Browning, to realize best his potential, had to discover for himself a literary form that was more congenial to the nature of his muse. He focused throughout on moral and spiritual conflicts in the lives of individual men and women and ignored the centrality of action.

Thus, though Browning's genius was dramatic in the main, it was not in regular drama that he found his most compatible and spontaneous outlet. What suited best his genius was a poetic form which had already been used by other poets but by none to such perfection. It was the "detached speech"[1] or dramatic monologue, in which he takes some critical moment in the life of an individual, penetrates deep into his nature and through his utterances and unguarded statements leads him to lay bare the innermost recesses of his mind. As Browning declared in the prefatory chapter of his poetic volume, *Bells and Pomegranates*, his dramatic poems, though lyrical in expression are "always dramatic in principle, and so many utterances of so many imaginary persons, not mine."[2] Browning's dramatic monologues are characterized by psychological penetration and diagnostic ingenuity. They were intended to be blends of the subjective and the objective. They were to be emotional and musical like a lyric but impersonal like drama.

Browning never deflected from the belief that his genius was fundamentally dramatic and hence, his choice fell upon the dramatic monologue which he did not invent but made specially his own. These monologues include the best of his love poems and it is in these that he is most distinguished. The most remarkable thing about Browning's dramatic monologues is their unconventional cerebral approach to issues and their elevation of tone. Browning's vibrant character portrayals, his unwavering interest in the complexities of moral order and his analysis of criminal and evil human types reveal his intellectual bent of mind. The dramatic monologues of Browning offer a teeming variety of characters and a remarkably varied fare in dealing with the multiple complexities of the entire gamut of human emotions, especially love.

As a literary form the dramatic monologue is a unique poetic construct. It is a mode of utterance that seems to take the reader into confidence at the very outset. The character depicted seems to be unwinding himself without reservations and his words appear to be a tacit appeal for approval of the course of action chosen by him at a critical juncture in life. The dramatic monologue allows Browning to turn to good account his capacity for creating characters by means of his awareness and discrimination of sounds and words and his ability to make his statement indirectly, but with impact.

Browning owed much of his fascination for and absorption in Greek art to Landor from whose *Imaginary Conversation* (1824-29) he derived hints for his poetic method. It was out of admiration and regard for his senior contemporary that he dedicated the last volume of the *Bells and Pomegranates* series to Landor, whom he referred to as the "great dramatic poet" in his preface. The fundamental premise of Landor's work is the doctrine of the "psychological moment" borrowed, perhaps, from Lessing's *Laocoon*, reverberations of which are clearly registered in the dramatic monologues of Browning:

> If the artist, out of ever-varying nature, can only make use of a single moment from one point of view, whilst their works are intended to stand the test not only of a passing glance, but of long and repeated contemplation, it is clear that this moment [...] cannot be chosen with too great regard to results. Now that only is a happy choice which allows the imagination free scope [...]. Furthermore, this single moment receives through art an unchangeable duration: therefore, it must not express anything, of which we can think only as transitory."[3]

To Landor, as well as to Lessing, the artist's concern is to give:

> To one brief moment caught from fleeting time,
> The appropriate calm of blest Eternity.[4]

Browning, too, believes that the poet must deal with the peak incidents of life and his characteristic manner of the dramatic monologue is an application of Lessing's theory of the "psychological moment" to the sphere of poetry so that interest is focused not so much on external action as on a dramatic situation preceding or following a critical event or decision in the life of the speaker, who is often of dubious merit. Browning, by causing this speaker, to deliberate loudly over the whole series of events leading to that crisis makes him reveal his hidden motives, and in the process, gives us glimpses of the period of history to which he belongs.

Typical of Browning is also the use of the language of ordinary conversation both in rhythm and syntax. Browning's use of the conversational style in his monologues enables the speaker to express himself in the widest possible range. The reactions of the listener as registered in the speech of the speaker, though often disrupting the narrative or the argument, elicit a greater response and involvement from the reader as he makes a bid to follow the developments of the poem. Browning's conversational verse is geared to the rhythms and syntax of good, persuasive speech.

The dramatic monologue needs to be distinguished from other poetic types and genres. It is a new poetic class similar to but distinct from the lyric, which is a rather short, non-narrative poem presenting a single speaker who articulates a state of mind or a process of thought or feeling. Though both, the monologue and the lyric, have unity of mood and are ecstatic expressions of a single emotion, in the former, the intellectual element predominates and sentimental fervour and music are subdued by the speaker's argumentation.

The dramatic monologue combines lyric and drama, and in it, one finds the poet impersonating another character, who may be historical or fictitious. There are, however, points of difference again between the drama and the monologue. While the drama presents a chronological sequence of events moving towards a crisis, the monologue concentrates on the crisis itself and acquaints the reader with the preceding events only retrospectively. The drama develops through the conflict of human personalities and in it, the character is judged through human conduct. The monologue, on the other hand, analyzes character through a clash of motives referring to the course of external events only where necessary for character portrayal. Again, the outlook of the dramatist is more objective and what he offers to the audience is something marshalled and knocked into shape; in comparison, the writer of the dramatic monologue projects his image of the speaker's character and personality through a study of some self-revelatory mood of the latter coming forth through stray utterances.

Another literary form with which the dramatic monologue is likely to be confused and from which it must be distinguished is the soliloquy. Although both the forms indulge in self-analysis, the soliloquy is more introspective and it is more like loud-thinking, when the speaker assumes that no one is listening to what he is saying and tries to clear his complexes through ratiocination. The soliloquy is a sort of private debate, a "dialogue of the mind with itself" whereas the monologue is an address to someone believed to be present and to be reacting to what the speaker says.

The dramatic monologue is different from the "aside" also, for though, both are addressed to an audience, the "aside" has a strictly dramatic function and is much shorter and less extensive in its range of thought and emotion than the monologue.

As said before, Browning was, indeed, not the first to employ the technique of the dramatic monologue. The practice of writing lyrical poems from the point of view of an assumed personality came into the 19th century without much critical notice and Mrs. Felicia Hemans used the form of the poetic monologue much before Browning did. In fact, even Tennyson preceded Browning in the use of this form and was the first Victorian to subscribe to it. He used for his poems titles which emphasized the type of the poetic endeavour indulged in: "Will Waterproof's Lyrical Monologue" and "Maud: a Monodrama". Browning, almost at the same time, published 'Dramatic Lyrics', 'Dramatic Romances and Lyrics' and 'Dramatis Personae'. The term "dramatic monologue" came to be popular only in the twentieth century. Browning himself never seems to have used the term though it was he who perfected the form and used it with almost flawless skill. Much before Browning the same dramatic quality was found in the works of the seventeenth century poets like Donne. In the twentieth century, T.S. Eliot has reiterated the concept of the dramatic nature of lyric verse.

Browning, we know, recognized the dramatic inclination in himself very early in life. The plays he wrote met with indifferent success on the stage but the publication of his dramatic poem, "Paracelsus" convinced him that his genius was essentially dramatic and he soon came to realize that the dramatic monologue was the form best suited to his genius. Browning gives the dramatic monologue a psychological bent and makes it an opportunity to indulge in character studies and complexities of moral order. His main concern seems to be a psycho-analysis of his characters and a dissection of human motives and emotions.

In Browning's dramatic monologues, we seem not only to be listening to the voice of a living person but witnessing, as it were the changing movement of his hand and face. In it, the protagonist comes fully alive within a short poem—a perfect example is "My Last Duchess," the story of which could very well have been developed into a full-fledged novel or play. The poem is remarkable in its irreducibility and succinctness and displays a rare compression of events within the fifty-six lines of the text.

Browning, in the poem, omits stage directions. Few writers of drama or dramatic verse do that. And so, we deduce that within the delivery span of a short speech by the protagonist, Browning needs to include the setting, time, place, the exposition and the antecedent action, all so naturally and spontaneously that these elements are absorbed into the forward motion of the poem.

"My Last Duchess" published in 'Dramatic Lyrics' in 1842, is a poem, which, though it conveys the infinite complexity of life, is unmistakably tinged with the spirit of the Renaissance in Italy. As DeVane points out, this poem is Browning's first attempt at portraying characters of Renaissance Italy. The Duke in the poem represents a typical character of the period—cold, arrogant, devious, jealous, avaricious, Machiavellian and unscrupulous. All this we discover in the course of the poem for our knowledge of the situation and of the character of the speaker is cumulative. The Duke comes alive to us not by direct description but through his characteristic language and tone that communicate to us the contours of his personality.

Browning is not for the uninitiated reader. The openings of his poems are abrupt and are based on certain dramatic situations which the reader takes time to grasp. In "My Last Duchess," too, the situation in the poem is fully explained only at the end. The speaker, an Italian Duke, is negotiating for the hand of the daughter of a neighbouring Count. When an emissary from the Count visits him, he takes the former around his picture gallery and begins by showing him a painted portrait of his last duchess:

That's my last Duchess painted on the wall,
Looking as if she were alive. I call
That piece a wonder, now: [...].[5] (lls. 1-3)

At the very outset, we are introduced to the duchess through this painting. But, almost simultaneously as it were, we are given a glimpse of Renaissance art in Italy and its emphasis on realism in the line, "looking as if she were alive." The perfection of the duchess's picture is an evidence of the perfection of art in that age. The immediate aim of the Duke, however, is to explain to the emissary what he considered the shortcomings of his last Duchess to be and thus warn him as to what is expected of the former's bride. Dissatisfied with the indiscriminate geniality of his wife he issues orders for her execution.

It is ironical that the Duke now appreciates a lifelike but lifeless portrait of the duchess and calls it "a wonder"[6] (l. 3) but was critical of the "depth and passion"[7] (l. 8) of his wife when she was alive. He took exception to the undifferentiating grant of her favours to men; her heart, he thought, was "too soon made glad"[8] and "her looks went everywhere."[9] She did not, he believed, have the discrimination to value above other gifts his gift of "a nine-hundred-years-old name."[10] He bore all these grievances against here and yet, his pride prevented him from "stooping"[11] to correct her. So, with the characteristic Renaissance impetuosity and heartlessness,

[...] I gave commands;
Then all smiles stopped together. There she stands
As if alive.[12]

These lines are an illustration of Browning's telegraphic technique of conveying the maximum of meaning in the minimum of words. With them, the poet seems to have come full circle, as it were, for the poem begins with details of the portrait and ends with them.

The last eight lines of the poem are more in the nature of an epilogue, which helps in an adjustment of perspective. The Duke's demand for dowry makes the reader readjust his impressions of the Duke for the story is now seen in a particular context. The Duke's Machiavellianism and his avarice is all the more evident and the last duchess emerges brighter by contrast. The Duke's reference to the pillar-head showing Neptune taming a sea-horse is indicative of the Duke's attitude towards women. The poet, perhaps, meant this image of Neptune to be a commentary on the Duke's character.

Browning here uses the remimiscential method in the Duke's presentation of his story to the Count's emissary. The Duke begins in the present by describing the painting of the Duchess on the wall but soon goes into the past to justify to the listener the treatment that was meted out by him to his wife. Once his story is told, he returns to the present to dissipate the tension that had mounted during his dramatic incrimination of the Duchess. Stray remarks like "Will't please you sit and look at her?"[13] (l. 5) and "Will't please you rise?"[14] (l. 47) help the reader readjust his perspective and make him conscious of the presence of an audience lending an ear to the speaker in the monologue. "We'll meet the company below, then,"[15] (lls. 7-8) "Nay, we'll go together down, sir,"[16] (l. 53) indicate the conversational nature of the verse.

The story in the poem, though it has a narrative basis, is enacted not narrated, and that is the distinguishing mark of a dramatic monologue.

"Andrea del Sarto" (1855) was the first poem of the second volume of 'Men and Women.' Originally it consisted of 266 lines of blank verse but later certain changes were introduced. The account of Andrea's life given by Vasari is the actual background of the poem, and Browning makes steady and confident use of it.

Browning's Andrea del Sarto describes to his wife, Lucrezia, the long years of conflict between his conscience as an artist and his love of her. Andrea is using his narrative rendition of this traumatic experience to make love to Lucrezia and to persuade her to spend the evening with him instead of going out to meet the 'Cousin' who summons her with whistles in the street below. He tries to impress her, on the one hand, with all that he has sacrificed for her in terms of artistic accomplishment;

and on the other, with how important a painter he nevertheless is. His musings on art and his self-pity do not, however, interest the lady and Andrea, too, sees her purely pecuniary interest in his art.

The irony in 'Andrea del Sarto' works in a remarkable way. The poem has a pathetic element for one has a sense of a not inconsiderable talent going to waste. Andrea is fully conscious of the choice he has made and reiterates it in the monologue itself. The irony in the poem emphasizes the discrepancy between promise and achievement, and hence the focus shifts from the pathos of talent unglorified to the satiric sense of not measuring up to a standard.

Andrea is a failure both as a painter and as a man, as an artist and as a lover—and these roles that he assumes are inseparably intertwined. The relationship between the two is suggested by the ironic subtitle of the poem, "The Faultless Painter." Andrea's painting is technically perfect but it lacks intensity and depth of feeling—his art is devoid of a soul. Similarly, when Andrea describes Lucrezia, he speaks readily of the perfection of her appearance, and seems in those passages to overlook her moral lapses and emotional inadequacies though at one point in the poem he is driven to remark.

You don't understand
Nor care to understand about my art, [...].[17]

He wishes that she as his model, with all her physical charms had "but brought a mind."[18] Yet, he has not even the moral courage to make his accusation squarely, so as to antagonize her even though he realizes full well that she is responsible for his fractured artistic integrity.

The imagery in Browning's poems is significant in that it throws light upon character and situation. The imagery associated both with Lucrezia and with Andrea's work emphasizes their limited perfection: both have a touch of the silver grey rather than golden. Andrea compares Lucrezia to pearls and the moon; so, too, his art: "A common greyness silvers everything [...]."[19] "All is silver-grey, / Placid and perfect with my art [...]."[20] All Andrea's paintings are tinged with grey and the greyness betokens his attitude to life—an attitude of indifference to the values of life. His art lacks in a quality that even inferior artists are able to impart to their work because "there burns a truer light of God in them."[21]

The perfection which Andrea sees in Lucrezia's appearance and in the technical aspects of his art is, ironically a measure of his limitations—"A man's reach should exceed his grasp,/ or what's a heaven for?"[22] (l. 97) Andrea's limitations are denoted by the shifting meaning of the gold imagery at the French court, the display of gold is linked with energy, vitality and creativity:

> I surely then could sometimes leave the ground,
> Put on the glory, Rafael's daily wear
> In that humane great monarch's golden look—
> .....
> The jingle of his gold chain in my ear, [...]"[23]
> (lls. 151-57)

The Renaissance view of gold as the prime metal suggests by analogy the countenance of man, and the most desirable combination of elements and humours. When Andrea leaves the French court to return to Lucrezia, gold becomes associated with Lucrezia's hair (l. 175), with the perfection of outward appearance. Finally, gold becomes synonymous with money and with the financial troubles with which Andrea is plagued. Andrea speaks of gold in business terms and such words as "gain" and "profitless," as Roma King points out, "depict the degeneration of Andrea's standards of values, his genuine confusion, and ultimately his compromise with the tawdry and commonplace."[24]

'Andrea del Sarto' is a good example of Browning's use of imagery as an index to character rather than as a symbol of a larger, indefinite meaning as is the tower in 'Childe Roland.' Andrea is a "Faultless Painter" but he is trapped in his very perfection of technique in painting. His marriage, like his art, is unproductive and barren and is emotionally sterile. The setting is appropriate to his psychological state and suggests infecund and terminal phases of time: it is evening, it is autumn; he sits within the confines of the four walls of the room where he paints. His mind runs habitually to images which suggest confinement and decline of vital powers. Outside the window is all the vigorous life of Renaissance Florence, but Andrea shuns that life as does "the weak-eyed bat"[25] (l. 169) the sun.

Andrea's audience here is his wife, Lucrezia, who represents certain characteristics of Andrea himself. One component of Andrea's own being is, as it were, perfect. He is called "The Faultless Painter": he commands perfect artistic technique, which is unsupported by the ability to give depth and meaning to his paintings—his work lacks essence as it is nothing but an extension of him, for Andrea himself lacks a soul. Lucrezia's absolute physical perfection ironically suggests Andrea's own lack of it but in more abstract terms. His wavering self-discipline and mere technical mastery is no boost to his art. Lucrezia's lack of moral fibre reflects Andrea's own inadequacy: her waywardness reflects his own spiritual deficiency. But Lucrezia is a part of Andrea in an even more important sense—she is one of his paintings come to life. This perhaps is Browning's most impressive structural accomplishment, for Lucrezia operates in the poem as an embodiment of one enormous and integral part of Andrea's being. Andrea comes to be identified with his own art and Lucrezia adorns his canvas. Andrea, however, uses Lucrezia unjustly in trying to explain away his own lack of moral responsibility, his culpability in having swindled King Francis, and, in having allowed his parents to die of want.

Two aspects of time in 'Andrea del Sarto' help to suggest the condition of Andrea's being. As with 'Bishop Blougram's Apology,' it is evening time—a time frequently associated with death, waning or negation in Browning. 'Evening' is at once linked with Andrea's physical state of depletion:

> I am often much wearier than you think,
> This evening more than usual [...].[26] (l. 11)

A little later it is linked with Lucrezia in so-far-as her relationship with Andrea is concerned. In Andrea's eyes, Lucrezia's face is seen as "my moon,"[27] (l. 29) and even here, as it does throughout the poem, the symbolism of the evening reflects Andrea's perception of his own physical debility and proximity to death. He, himself, and the world as it immediately relates to him, are one with the declining day. The power of this time symbolism is reinforced by the time of the year that it is—the dying season, when "days decrease" and "autumn grows, autumn in everything"[28] (lls. 44-45) so that both season and time of day symbolize Andrea's physical state and suggest the prevailing note of his character—that of soul-weary resignation.

Repetition is an obvious feature in almost all of Browning's poetry. It has rhythmic and rhetorical functions as in 'Paracelsus,' and, it is an important element in Browning's use of sound to help depict character. In the monologues, a marked repetition of words almost always has something to do with the revelation of the speaker's state of mind. The most extensive use of it is made in 'Andrea del Sarto', where Andrea repeats words or phrases successively: "Quietly, quietly;" "out of me, out of me;" "this, this, this;" "there, there;" or a word in the same line,

> My face, my moon, my everybody's moon.[29] (l. 29)

or in successive lines:

> His hue mistaken; what of that? or else,
> Rightly traced and well ordered; what of that?[30]
> (lls. 94-95)

Or adjectives may be repeated in a series:

> But had you—oh, with the same perfect brow,
> And perfect eyes, and more than perfect mouth [...].[31]
> (l. 122)

Rhythmic variation in 'Andrea del Sarto' is rare and the majority of the lines may be read as fairly strict compositions of the iambic pentameter. Phonetic quality, whatever there is of it in 'Andrea del Sarto', may influence rhythm, particularly tempo, and thereby influence the whole impact of a passage. A long pause in a line in the poem may separate two very different feelings. In

> Oh, I'll content him,—but tomorrow, Love! (l. 10)[32]

the pause separates Andrea's tired resignation and his momentary joy. Syntactically the two expressions of feelings are related because they both stem from the same cause, the deal Andrea has struck. Rhythmically, they are separated because the two feelings are in fact quite different.

The poem, on the whole, is a remarkable experiment in technique. The beginning of the poem is rather abrupt but the story is obviously a continuation of an earlier action and this precedent action is conveyed retrospectively so that the unity of action is well-maintained. The opening line is significant in that it holds the key to the entire situation and also to the speaker's character. The success of Browning's art lies in the subtlety and economy with which he portrays his characters. There is no systematic appraisal of individuals but a few deft touches give us the quintessential character. Browning employs here a double-edged technique in which the speaker tries to convey an impression just the adverse of what we know to be true. For instance, at one point in the poem, Andrea tries to convince Lucrezia of his virility but we know how hollow his claim is.

Browning does not give any direct description of the beauty of Lucrezia. The winsome charm of his technique of depiction lies in the indirection, and obliqueness employed. Like Marlowe in 'Dr. Faustus,' he describes not the beauty of his heroine but the impact of that beauty on its beholders.

Browning in 'Andrea del Sarto', shows little regard for the use of connectives and characteristically omits them. He makes considerable use of subordinate clauses or participial phrases. He often substitutes participles for verbs.

'Andrea del Sarto' and 'My Last Duchess' are both poems of the moment of heightened sensibility but in the former, this 'moment' is lengthened as compared to the compression in the latter. The poem is reminiscential in nature and there is a continual change in the mood of the speaker. The movement of the poem is circular and there are transitional points which maintain the links. The narrative as when Andrea goes back to his days in the French court uses cinematic effect and the flash back technique. There is a preponderance of natural imagery—Andrea is rightly compared to a bat shunning light. The natural descriptions in the poem are symbolic and well-related to the human situation. "Autumn" is effectively used as an archetypal image for decay and decline.

Thus the poem, as is evident, is far from simple. The complexity of technique demands that the reader be simultaneously alive on various fronts and it is only when the reader so co-operates that the full potential of the poem and the poet is realized.

'Abt Vogler' first appeared in 'Dramatis Personae' in 1864. There is no evidence to ascertain the date of composition of this poem, though the knowledge that Browning sought consolation in music on his return to England after the death of his wife in 1861 may throw some light on the issue. The spiritual fervour and profundity of the poem strike one as genuine.

The poem, consisting of twelve stanzas of eight alexandrine lines each, is a monologue of the musician after he had "been extemporizing on a musical instrument of his own invention."[33] Browning, here, celebrates the achievements of the little-known artist who hitherto seemed destined to "blush unseen."

'Abt Vogler' is perhaps Browning's greatest poem on music and it conveys his conception of the function and impact of music and its relative place in the hierarchy of arts. It exemplifies Browning's poetic method as well as his optimistic approach to life. In it, as in most of his poems, he starts with a fact of experience—here, the evocation of music from a musical instrument—and follows it to see where it will lead him. Browning begins with what Langbaum calls a "poetry of experience" and then translates the feelings into explorations and statements that are predominantly ratiocinative in nature. He follows this transition from experience to statement within a simple, impressive framework which is his world of imagination.

The poem does not fit the ordinary concept of either the dramatic monologue or the lyric. The rhyme and the stanzaic structure are both simple and uninvolved. The long lines in hexameter seem more suited to heroic verse than to the lyric form. The speaker in the poem is clearly not the poet himself, and hence, the poem may be said to be dramatic. But, on a thorough and in-depth analysis, it becomes evident that 'Abt Vogler' represents a shift away from the strictly dramatic mode of presentation: here, as in 'Rabbi Ben Ezra', the dramatic mask has become rather transparent, and Browning himself is more visible. Vogler is more a mouthpiece of the poet and less a fully independent dramatic character with an identity and existence of his own. So, this poem is almost a class in itself and cannot be judged by the standards implied for any particular group of poems. The poem is, however, close to the Victorian concept of the lyric.

As in any composition of merit, the spirit or "inner form" is reflected in the theme. The theme, of course, is not just the subject—Abt Vogler's improvisation—but involves the poet's treatment of it as well. Browning is concerned primarily with the inner-strength and the divine validation of human aspirations. Abt Vogler doubts the value of human concepts that cannot be realized, but he is soon convinced as Rabbi is in 'Rabbi Ben Ezra,' of the value of the "instincts immature" (l. 142) that "swell the man's amount"[34] (l. 144). His art, however, gives him insight into the divine inspiration that makes all things possible, that enables him to create out of three sounds, "not a fourth sound, but a star."[35] (l. 52).

Abt Vogler, the eighteenth century organist and inventor of the Orchestrion, was an historical personage but Browning makes no effort to draw him as a particular individual living in a particular time and place. The extemporizing organist becomes, instead, a vehicle for expressing Browning's own ideas and proclivities, namely, the latter's notion that music above all other arts, can express the eternal and the absolute, his preference for 'process' over 'completion' and his belief that the imperfections of this world imply the perfection of the next.

The language of the poem is in conformity with the abstract ideas being expounded and it is not the less powerful because of the abstract mode adopted; rather, it exists in sharp contrast to Browning's more typically colloquial style. The abstract quality of music itself permeates the monologue, most effectively in the closing lines when Abt Vogler finds that he can no longer sustain the vision of the eternal which his music has made available to him:

> Give me the keys. I feel for the common chord again,
> Sliding by semitones, till I sink to the minor—yes,
> And I blunt it into a ninth, and I stand on alien ground,
> Surviving a while the heights I rolled from into the deep;
> which, bark, I have dared and done, for my resting place is found,
> The C Major of this life : so, now I try to sleep.[36]
> (lls. 91-97)

In his anthology, *Men and Women*, in two poems centering around the lives of musicians, namely, 'A Toccata of Galuppi's' and 'Master Hugues of Saxe-Gotha,' Browning has explored the effect of music on the characters of the poems. Abt Vogler, too, is personally engaged in the musical combinations which can reveal the very "finger of God" (l. 48), but the eloquent expression of Browning's own view competes with the emotional involvement of his character. Hence, in the poem, Browning as the lyric poet tends to speak in personal terms and yet at the same time, and at another level, manages to give the impression that he is conveying insights into the essential nature of human existence. The lyric spirit manifests itself in the presentation of time, too, where sequence is linked with simultaneity. One wonders at the alchemy of the musician's genius.

What is unique about Browning's 'Abt Vogler' is the communication of an abstraction, an idea realized in terms of music. Music, here, is presented as an expression of the Absolute, as emanating from the aspiring depths of the soul and therefore from the Divine Will. Yet, the poem is not a mere statement in philosophy but an utterance loaded with all that is dramatic for the statement rises out of an illusion, out of a visual organisation of the experience limited in span to the speaker's ecstatic moment of inspiration as he extemporizes on the organ.

Abt Vogler sees as his music mounts to a climax, a growing vision of totality of the absolute—first, as a palace extending from sordid facts up towards sublimity, constructed by the ascending and swinging of his musical notes between the crescendos and diminuendos to provide an encounter with eternal bliss:

> And one would bury his brow with a blind plunge down to hell
> Burrow a while and build, broad on the roots of things,
> Then up again swim into sight, having based me my palace well,
> Founded it, fearless of flame, flat on the nether springs [...]
> up the pinnacled glory reached, and the pride of my soul was in sight."[37] (lls. 14-25)

then as a whole cosmic union in which heaven and earth yearn to merge with each other:

> And the emulous heaven yearned down, made effort to reach the earth, [...]." (l. 27)[38]

In this cosmic union, not only is space annihilated but time, too, is suspended so that spirits of the yet unborn and of the long since dead walk in this newly engendered universe where the possible and the actual merge:

> What never had been was now; what was, as it shall be anon;
> And what is,—shall I say, matched both?; for I was made perfect, too.[39] (lls. 39-40)

Abt Vogler identifies his vision as Absolute reality because it is his soul's yearning flowing "visibly forth." And, as that wish is instantaneously and completely realized without evident "cause" for the "effect," Abt Vogler recognizes his desire as an instrument of the Divine Will and his music as a realization of that Will.

The irretrievable quality, the transience and evanescence of music, more particularly extemporized music, is what makes it different from poetry and painting which remain and can be analyzed and accounted for by laws of art. The absolute absorption in the instant of Abt Vogler's music and his vision give the poem its dramatic concreteness. We may say of this poem, as Langbaum does, that it evokes a musical rhapsody, "a vision within the ecstatic instant of a transformed universe."[40] The vision, here, is a counterpart of the music and therefore evokes it.

When the ecstatic instant is over, Abt Vogler judges the vision to have been illusory, but re-establishes its validity with a moral sentiment which we affirm. The illusion, he says, was a reflection of the celestial bliss to come:

> On earth, the broken arcs; in the heaven, a perfect round.[41] (l. 72).

So we have in 'Abt Vogler,' not a vision located in time followed by a speculation, but rather a dramatization of the speculation and vision itself, conditioned by the nostalgic instant following the ecstasy.

The vision is the core of categorical assuredness, the empiric fact out of which the whole poem rises. We, without reservations, identify ourselves with the speaker in the moment of ecstasy. The experience over, his as well as our perspective shifts to argument. His final doubt of the vision's objective validity finds a reverberation in the structure of our own experience where often certainty is plagued with doubt.

Finally, however, what is more remarkable about the poem is not *what* the poet says but *how* he says it. To substantiate this view, we must rivet our attention to the structure of the poem. We have here an indepth study of the mind of the musician and the poet conveys to us the actual ecstatic and aesthetic experience of the musician in terms of language. The words keep pace with the flow of music as in the Pindaric ode we have the language keeping pace with the steps of the dance. Keats, in "The Ode to the Grecian Urn," gives a poetic equation of the plastic arts; Browning, here, in a somewhat similar strain, offers a verbal equation of music.

Browning's 'Abt Vogler' is a wonderful achievement as it offers a rare convergence of the three arts of poetry, music and architecture. The poet here talks of music as a marvel of architecture and renders this experience of music in terms of poetry.

Although the poem does not fully conform to the definition of a lyric, it certainly may be granted the status of a lyric by virtue of being devoted to music. Browning comes near to the ubiquitous, inherent music of words and almost like Hopkins, indulges in exploring the native musical quality of language. However, the poem is not a mere experiment in language—the lyricism here is integral to the meaning of the poem.

The poem as a whole follows the structure of a sonnet. The first five stanzas, like the octave of a Miltonic sonnet, give the exposition of feeling. From the sixth stanza onwards we have a semblance of the sestet presenting a ratiocination of feeling and a final clinching of the argument. It is, however, the initial aesthetic experience of music itself that promotes a sense of immediacy and conveys a feeling-tone. Each line is divisible into two by virtue of the pause or caesura it contains.

We admire the power of empathy in Browning which becomes evident in his merger of himself with the musician so that he can identify with the creative experience. Yet, we witness the dramatic potential in him in his display of objectivity and unprejudiced activity. The catechistic style is prominent and adds to the dramatic effect.

The poem, then, is a rich and solid achievement marking a milestone in Browning's poetic career. The movement of verse corresponds to the movement in meaning and hence the tremendous intensity of effect.

References

1. William Henry Hudson, *An Outline History of English Literature* (Bombay: B.I. Publications, first Indian rpt. 1963), p. 232; first published in London, 1912.
2. Cited in O.P. Govil, *Robert Browning* (Allahabad: Kitab Mahal, 1967), p. 55.
3. Lessing, G.E., *Laokoon* (1766), trans. *E.C. Beasley* (London: 1888) Chapt. III, pp. 19-20; the work is an essay in literary and artistic criticism in which the author examines a statuary representing *Laocoon*, a legendary Trojan priest of Apollo, and his sons in the coils of a serpent disinterred at Rome in the sixteenth century. Adopting this group of individuals as the initial subject of discussion, Lessing examines the divergence in the treatment of the scene by the

artist and by Virgil who described it, and develops the essential differences between the art of poetry and the plastic arts. The work remains unfinished.

4. Landor, Walter Savage, *Imaginary Conversations* (1824-29).
5. Kenneth L. Knickerbocker, ed., "My Last Duchess," *Selected Poetry of Robert Browning* (New York: The Modern Library, 1951), p. 51.
6. *Ibid.*
7. *Ibid.*, p. 52.
8. *Ibid.*
9. *Ibid.*
10. *Ibid.*
11. *Ibid.*
12. *Ibid.*
13. *Ibid.*, p. 51.
14. *Ibid.*, p. 52.
15. *Ibid.*
16. *Ibid.*, p. 53.
17. Knickerbocker, ed., "Andrea del Sarto," *Selected Poetry of Robert Browning*, p. 344.
18. *Ibid.*, p. 346.
19. *Ibid.*, p. 344.
20. *Ibid.*, p. 345.
21. *Ibid.*
22. *Ibid.*
23. *Ibid.*, p. 347.
24. Roma A. King, Jr., *The Bow and the Lyre: The Art of Robert Browning* (Michigan: Ann Arbor, 1957).
25. Knickerbocker, ed., "Andrea del Sarto," p. 347.
26. *Ibid.*, p. 343.
27. *Ibid.*
28. *Ibid.*
29. *Ibid.*
30. *Ibid.*, p. 345.
31. *Ibid.*, p. 346.
32. *Ibid.*, p. 343.

33. Detail given by Browning himself alongwith the title of the poem. Knickerbocker, ed., "Abt Vogler," *Selected Poetry of Robert Browning*, p. 475.
34. Knicker bocker ed., "Rabbi Ben Ezra," *Selected Poetry of Robert Browning*, p. 484.
35. *Ibid.*, "Abt Vogler," p. 477.
36. *Ibid.*, p. 478.
37. *Ibid.*, p. 475.
38. *Ibid.*, p. 476.
39. *Ibid.*
40. Robert Langbaum, *The Poetry of Experience: The Dramatic Monologue in Modern Literary Tradition* (London: Paperback, 1957).
41. Knickerbocker, ed., *Selected Poetry of Robert Browning*, p. 477.

18

Poe: A Psychological Approach

> [...] for all the difficulties involved in its proper application to interpretive analysis, the psychological approach can be fascinating and rewarding.[1]

This is the hypothesis with which we start a psychological exploration of a work of literary art apparently amenable to such investigation.

The various analytical and interpretative approaches to literature[2] are widely, divergent and no single approach can exhaust the multitudinous possibilities of any work of literature, nor explore all the sources of conceivable interest within it. Each approach has its own curious limitations, for example, the traditional approaches[3] like the textual-linguistic, the historical-biographical and the moral-philosophical are inclined to overlook the structural complexities of the work. A formalistic analysis, on the other hand, tends to ignore the historical and biographical contexts that may provide significant clues to the meaning of the work. A psychological interpretation, in turn, though it affords insights into the work's thematic and symbolic aspects, is aesthetically inadequate in that it cannot account for the beautiful symmetry or the structural poise of the work.

The choice of the psychological approach in the present work has been determined by the author under review for this approach is the only interpretive perspective that can provide a proper understanding of the works of the American literary writer, Edgar Allan Poe, especially his prose fiction. The purpose of the critic is to divine the intention of the work and to interpret the work in the light of that intention, and since Poe is intentionally symbolic and his tales designedly allegorical, we have to resort to a psychological interpretation of his tales which are loaded with what Poe himself calls "undercurrents of meanings."[4]

The application of psychology to literature is not a novel exercise. It may be traced back to the time of Aristotle in the fourth century B.C. Aristotle himself used this approach in defining the catharsis effected in a tragedy in terms of the emotions of pity and fear. Sir Philip Sidney, too, in emphasizing the moral effects of poetry, and the Romantic poets like Wordsworth and Colebridge in enunciating their theories of the Imagination, were all concerned with the application of psychology to literature. With the growing interest in psychological study, an analysis of the individual's inner world soon came to be a part of the realistic depiction of a character in the literature of the Western world. Psychological portraits are to be found in Dickens (especially the mature Dickens), George Eliot, Thackeray and Balzac as also in Flaubert and Zola.

Later in the twentieth century, an exploration of the depths of the human psyche became, with novelists like Virginia Woolf and James Joyce, an abiding concern. And today, writers such as Marguerite Duras[5] and Susan Hill[6] have devised still newer literary techniques of delving deep into the human mind and projecting it convincingly.

During the twentieth century, however, much of the psychological criticism has come to be particularly associated with the psychoanalytic theories of Sigmund Freud and his followers. Excess of enthusiasm on the part of the practitioners of the Freudian approach has often resulted in the forcing of literature into the Procrustean bed of the psychoanalytic theory and in the overlooking of other relevant considerations like the work's total thematic and aesthetic contexts. The literary criticism of the fervent psychoanalyst has also, at times, degenerated into a kind of especial occultism with its own mystique and jargon.

The above inaccuracies in the application of the psychoanalytical approach have given rise to a considerable distrust of it as an interpretive tool in literary criticism. Some have even branded the Freudian approach as not only unfeasible but also "indecent." An elucidation of the principles of Freudian psychology may introduce the reader to a balanced critical perspective and arouse in him an interest in the exercise in critical analysis that follows. The structural framework of the present study will consist of two parts, (a) an illustration of the theory of psychoanalysis and (b) an application of theory to two of Poe's short stories, namely, *'Ligeia'*[7] and *'The Fall of the House of Usher.'*[8] Neither of these two tales ever fails to capture the reader's imagination and is invariably included in every anthology of Poe's short stories.

Sigmund Freud (1856-1939), one of the seminal minds of the modern times, is the recognized founder of psychoanalysis. In a series of publications based on his clinical experience of treating patients of neurosis, Freud developed a theory of and a descriptive terminology for the workings of the human mind. The core of his contribution to modern psychology is emphasis upon the idea that most human mental activity is unconscious, and that the primary source of psychic energy called libido is sexual, all human behaviour being motivated ultimately by sexuality.

Freud discriminated between the levels of conscious and unconscious mental activity:

> The oldest and best meaning of the word 'unconscious' is the descriptive one; we call 'unconscious' any mental process the existence of which we are obligated to assume—because, for instance, we infer it in some way from its effects—but of which we are not directly aware [...]. If we want to be more accurate, we should modify the statement by saying that we call a process 'unconscious' when we have to assume that it was active at a certain time, although at that time, we knew nothing about it."[9]

Freud divided the human mind schematically into three zones, the *Id* (or unconscious), the *Ego* (conscious personality), and *Super-ego* (conscience). He explained dreams and neurotic symptoms as the result of drives rising from the Id, being repressed by the Ego and Super-ego, and finding expression in "displaced" forms.

The Id, the reservoir of libido, is the source of all our desires and aggressions and functions without regard for law, morality or social conventions. The Ego is generally believed to be the conscious mind that stands for reason. The Super-ego, largely unconscious, represents all moral restrictions.

Freud speaks also of the psychic process of "fantasying."[10] The motive sources of *fantasies*, he believes, are unfulfilled wishes, either ambitious or erotic ones. If fantasies become over-luxuriant or over-powerful, neurosis or psychosis results. Night dreams, according to Freud, are wish-fulfilments in just the same way as fantasies—commonly known as day-dreams—are. The meaning of our dreams at night is usually obscure because the repressed wishes that come to expression are present in a very distorted form and identification is difficult. As Jastrow puts it "both the waking and dreaming self use alibis and aliases."[11]

Fixation, according to Freud, is a source of disharmony of development when childish forms of libido persist. If there is frustration in the gratification of these forms of libido representing the vital needs in childhood, the individual's development may be arrested or fixated and abnormalities may appear in the adult personality. The *Oedipus complex*, according to Freud, manifests itself in the child around the age of five. It derives from the boy's unconscious rivalry with his father for the love of his mother.

Carl G. Jung (1875-1961), a disciple of Freud, broke away from him to found his own school of analytical psychology in 1913. In Jung's "analysis" sex is as strident as in Freud's but the libido is not exclusively sexual; it includes other urges. It is psychic energy, an all-inclusive force.

Jung postulated the existence of a collective unconscious as opposed to a merely personal unconscious. This collective unconscious he believed to be a racial memory inherited by all members of the human family and connecting modern man with his primeval roots. "We mean by collective unconscious" he said, "a certain psychic disposition shaped by the forces of heredity; from it consciousness has developed."[12] The collective unconscious is manifested in the recurrence of certain images, stories, figures etc. called *archetypes.*

Psychological maturity or "individuation" entails the individual's recognition and acceptance of archetypal elements of his own psyche, for which Jung coined the descriptive terms *shadow* (i.e. the mask put on and the role played by an individual in accordance with the expectations of society, as opposed to what the person is in reality), *anima* (i.e. man's experience of woman) and *animus* (i.e. a woman's image of a man).

Individuation is essentially a process which takes place in the latter half of life. To give meaning and significance to life, an individual transfers emotional significance to his inner world of feeling. It is this internal process of development that is called individuation. Failure in this regard often leads to a kind of neurosis.

Jungian psychology has, in many ways, been more congenial to literary criticism than Freud's for the latter always regarded himself as an empirical scientist while Jung was always much more sympathetic towards visionary, religious and even magical traditions. Jung's theory of the collective unconscious tied in neatly with the anthropological study of primitive myth and ritual, initiated in England by Sir James Frazer in *The Golden Bough*, which exerted a strong influence on modern writers like T.S. Eliot and D.H. Lawrence. Out of this fusion of literature, anthropology and psychology evolved a kind of literary criticism in which the power and significance of works of literature is explained in terms of the recurrence of certain archetypal themes, images and narrative patterns. All literature, however, as Jung pointed out, cannot be evaluated in these terms.

Jung, in his treatise on 'Psychological Types' distinguished between *extraverts* (also referred to as 'extroverts') who tend to become involved with objects and thus lose their identities and *introverts*, who insist on preserving their separateness and retreat into a tower of emotional isolation. Extraverts and introverts are further subdivided by Jung into four categories based upon the predominance of sensation, thinking, feeling or intuition.

Alfred Adler, like Jung, was initially inspired by Freud but later disagreed with the latter and embarked upon the task of finding different explanations to account for neurosis, the starting point being the observation in general medical practice that patients handicapped by a bodily defect developed an unfavourable psychic attitude toward their life-problems.

The emphasis in Freud's theory was on infantile sex repressions; Adler placed it on the ego or self-assertion tendency, and, it was in 1912 that he started his School of Individual Psychology. According to Freud, the basic cause of a neurosis lies in the child's unhappy love relationships with its parents, especially with the parent of the opposite sex. Adler believed that the cause lies in the feelings of inferiority which begin and accumulate in the early years of a child's life. For these feelings the child tries to compensate by striving for superiority over others, and the manner he adopts to achieve this goal in childhood will be the pattern for his future behaviour. Adler's is thus a goal psychology as distinct from the urge psychologies of Freud and Jung. Instinctive urges drive libido, the goal directs it. The personal goal is always one for social recognition and superiority. This goal is not always fully acknowledged because it is socially unacceptable; hence, it is masked. The term Adler uses for this masked goal is "unconscious."

Our study of the above psychological theories is not without purpose. Psychology is of significance for the literary critic because it is directly concerned with the origins of art. Literary criticism is the valuation, by some standard, of the worth of literature. This standard is expected to be a definitely aesthetic one but aesthetics cannot be totally dissociated from questions of value which may be social or ethical in nature.

Hence, literary criticism may, for purposes of comprehension and analysis, draw from extra-aesthetic sources for it has not yet arrived at any unanimously accepted definition of its boundaries.

The critic, in approaching psychology, may thus raid it in the interest of literary criticism. There is, of course, the obvious difference between the subject-matter of psychology and that of literary criticism: psychology is concerned with the processes of mental activity, literary criticism with the product. The psychologist only analyzes the product, that is, the work of literary art, to arrive at the process. He is indifferent to literary values. Yet, the psychologist does find a large body of material in the imaginative literature of all ages.

Though psychology and literature are at cross purposes in as much as psychology, by analysis, reduces an art symbol to its origins and thus dissolves it and in literature, as Adler puts it "the attraction of a work of art arises from its synthesis,"[13] the study of psychology is not at all futile for a literary artist or a literary critic.[14] It might help both realize such facts as the subjectivity of love, and the general laws regarding human emotions and ideals. Such a study also enables the dramatist or novelist to be conscious of the fact that he cannot, with impunity, disregard the psychological probabilities in his plot for, any lack of psychological verisimilitude will ultimately be apparent in some lapse in style or method.

Tales of fantasy and imagination, because of their ingenious plots and ideas, and because of the touch of mystery in them, tend to make a lasting impression upon the reader. Though they do not provide a realistic representation of the problems of existence, they are, in their own peculiar way, an interpretation of life. They have, in recent times, begun to delve deep into abnormal psychology using the double self, the death instinct, dream symbolism etc. to give them a new meaning. The twentieth century psyche is the product of the strains of living in an excessively complex world and is perpetually on the verge of neuroticism. It is this psyche that these tales of fantasy seek to explore.

Almost every tale of fantasy symbolizes a certain human desire. Just as the unconscious mind portrays its real yearnings in dreams in a disguised form, so do writers express symbolically in these tales, the unutterable and unacceptable cravings of mankind. Thus, in the instance of a writer like Poe, an unconscious obsession with a particular vision of life combines with a conscious care for the presentation of that vision.

Poe is read today, not as a landmark in literary history but as an author who "impressively captured the horror that is of the soul and the hideous depths that lie beneath the quotidian existence and consciousness of man."[15] The special atmosphere created by him in his short-stories adds to the single effect to be wrought—the preconceived effect to which he himself refers in his review of Hawthorne's *Twice Told Tales*, the effect to be achieved through action rather than through logical analysis.

The critical interpretation of several of Poe's short-stories shows that Poe dealt deliberately with psychological themes like those of obsession, hallucination and madness. One such story is "Ligeia," which is often vaguely classified as "impressionistic" but this is not enough to give us an understanding of the value of non-rational psychology in the study of Poe.

Some interpretations of "Ligeia," like that of Clay Hamilton's,[16] assume that the story is a tale of the supernatural. The story, however, seems far more intelligible, both aesthetically and psychologically, as a tale of natural psychological phenomena. It demonstrates the power of the psychical over the physical. It shows an "idee fixe" or obsession in the extreme form of a monomania which Poe seems to have intended to be the essential psychological basis of the plot.

It is evident then that psychology provides an important clue to the meaning of "Ligeia" and enables us to understand better the structure of the tale and to appreciate its effect. It is the narrator-protagonist's psycho-emotional experiences that provide the matrix for the plot. The narrator nurses an erotic obsession with his dead wife; his love of her has kept painfully alive in his mind her individuality and exquisite physical beauty. It is obvious from every statement of his that his devotion to her has assumed the form of a monomania which he himself defines as "a wildly romantic offering on the shrine of the most passionate devotion."[17]

Although the narrator elaborates upon the intellectual acuity of Ligeia, his imaginative indulgence in her physical beauty is intense and highly sensuous. He even deifies her as a personal Venus, who represents for him the urge to live, and yet, because of his own psychic incapacity he is never able to understand fully the expression in the eyes of Ligeia. Thus does he identify her with the mystery of the entire universe. He often finds himself "upon the very verge"[18] of discovering the secret behind those eyes but ultimately fails. This experience he likens to that of trying to recall something from the depths of his unconscious but not quite succeeding.

This effort of the will to draw out something from the unconscious may be taken to represent the hero's struggle to achieve by power of mind what he cannot achieve through love. But even this access to Ligeia is thwarted by her death. From this point onwards it is the hero's will to conquer death that motivates the story. Ligeia, according to the narrator, dies because of the weakness of her will and the latter tries to make her live in another body by the strength of his.

Since the hero in the story is suffering from obsession, the reader cannot accept the narrative as entirely objective and authentic for the hero's mania may have affected what he believed and meant to convey. Thus, Poe's psychological effect in 'Ligeia' is similar to that of Henry James, whose stories told by a narrator move on two planes. The story which the narrator means to tell is different from the story which he tells without meaning to, as he unconsciously reveals himself.

Through his admission of his "incipient madness"[19] the hero tries to justify the excesses of his "childlike perversity"[20] in choosing such ghastly and macabre furnishings for his bridal chamber or in consuming excessive opium. He tries to explain further his maltreatment of his second wife, Rowena, in terms of his phrenetic devotion to and spiritual love for Ligeia.

Uptill this point in the story the hero blends facts with "obliquely truthful interpretations,"[21] but this point onwards he misrepresents facts altogether. He tells us what he saw, heard and felt but these are the hallucinations springing from his mania, his obsession with the idea of resurrecting Ligeia in the body of Rowena. Actually, it was he who caused Rowena's death and his perceptions were hallucinations originating from his obsessional love for Ligeia.

Here the hero imagines a presence in the chamber, "some palpable although invisible object,"[22] and tries to convince himself that it was not he but the ghost of Ligeia which preyed upon the ailing body of Rowena. In the death scene, however, amidst fact and hallucination, he gives himself away when he speaks of the drops of the ruby coloured fluid that fell into the goblet for he has resorted, it seems, to actual poisoning. The doubt changes into conviction when we see the body of Rowena writhing in pain, and the hero, indifferent, allows his mind to be filled with "a thousand memories of Ligeia."[23] The frenzied tension of hallucination[24] culminates in the hero's belief that he has discovered and identified the black, wild eyes of Ligeia in the body of Rowena.

This conclusion is aesthetically satisfactory if the story is accepted as a revelation of obsessional psychology. The completed action of the tale comments on the narrator's self-delusion in believing that he has succeeded in incorporating the beauty of Ligeia in the person of Rowena.

The scenes and situations of Poe's tales are always concrete representations of states of mind. There are certain recurrent motifs that are present in several of his stories, for example, the idea of enclosure or circumscription. Poe's enclosures are mostly circular in form. The bridal chamber in 'Ligeia' is pentagonal in shape but it appears to be circular for the angles are concealed by sarcophagi. Poe identifies regular angular forms with everyday reason and circular shapes with the other worldly imagination. The chamber in 'Ligeia,' somewhat circular, symbolizes an imaginative state of mind in which the dreamer enjoys all but complete freedom from the real, material world.

The continual movement of the figures on the rich drapery in the room in 'Ligeia' suggests the behaviour of hypnagogic images, the hypnagogic state being a condition of semi-consciousness in which the eyes, when closed, visualize a continuous procession of vivid and constantly changing forms. Poe sees in the quick succession of images of this state "glimpses of the spirit's outer world."[25] These images, according to Poe, arise in the soul when the distinction between the waking world and the world of dreams dissolves. It is in such a state of mind that the hero of 'Ligeia' undergoes the experiences of his fancies and his hallucinations.

A psychologically convincing interpretation of 'The Fall of the House of Usher,' another of Poe's tales, is derived from the initial observation in the story that Roderick Usher is surrounded by a defensive moat around the house, but at the close of the story his inaccessibility is dissolved by the mansion being swallowed up by the waters of the tarn. Thus, Roderick's circumscription within the mansion means his exclusion from the consciousness of the world of time, reason and physical fact. At another level, it may also mean the isolation of the poetic soul in a visionary trance.

The mouldering mansion and the richly furnished rooms as we have in 'The Fall of the House of Usher' are significant in Poe's tales because his use of architecture is clearly allegorical and so are the smallest details in his stories. The House of Usher symbolizes the physical body of Roderick Usher and its dim interior represents his imaginatively productive mind.

The House of Usher, like many structures in Poe's works, is in a state of extreme decay. The stonework of its façade is crumbling and the mansion itself is so corroded and dilapidated that it seems that it remains standing only because everything around is so still. The softest breeze would cause it to collapse. An explanation of what Poe means by the extreme decay of the House will bring us a better understanding of the pattern of the story of 'The Fall of the House of Usher.'

The tale is a journey into the depths of the self. All journeys in Poe symbolize the process of dreaming. Thus, 'The Fall of the

House of Usher' must be understood as a dream of the narrator in which he leaves behind the waking world of physical facts and makes his journey inwards towards his inner and spiritual self. That inner self is reflected in Roderick Usher, who is a part of the narrator's self reached through reverie. One may think of Usher as the narrator's imagination or as a state of mind which the narrator enters during the dream process. Considered as a state of mind, Usher represents, as the moving figures on the drapery in the room in 'Ligeia' do, the hypnagogic state, which, as explained before, is a condition of semi-consciousness in which the eyes, when shut, behold constantly changing forms.

That Roderick Usher represents the hypnagogic state is substantiated in a number of ways. First, the narrator describes Roderick's behaviour as inconsistent and characterized by constant change: he is alternately lively and sullen, communicative and withdrawn; at one moment he speaks with "tremulous indecision"[26] and at the next with "energetic concision."[27] He suggests, in other words, the shuttling between the consciousness and subconsciousness which is characteristic of the hypnagogic state. Usher's paintings which the narrator finds indescribable and refers to as "pure abstractions"[28] are themselves hypnagogic images.

The hypnagogic state is a condition of mind when one is on the brink of sleep. The building which symbolizes Usher's mind also threatens to collapse, the collapse in turn, representing the fall from the hypnagogic state into the depths of sleep. When the House of Usher does crumble down, the story ends because the mind, at the end of its inward journey, plunges into the darkness of sleep.

We enter the House of Usher through dim and winding passages which stand for the wandering movement of the mind in reverie and indicate the freedom achieved by the mind in dreams. These passages lead to the magnificent chamber where the hero is occupied in shedding off all consciousness of the material and physical world. Looked at as an allegory of creative mental activity, 'The Fall of the House of Usher' may be taken as an imaginative commentary by the narrator on the view that it is possible for the poetic soul to shake off this temporal, rational and physical world and escape into the world of unrestrained vision.

From still another point of view, 'The Fall of the House of Usher' becomes the story of Roderick Usher trying hard to retain his sanity in the face of extreme tension and suffering. For an interpretation of the tale in the light of this aspect, an acquaintance with *Eureka*,[29] Poe's philosophical and scientific work on the nature of the universe is important. The universe, according to Poe derives from a tiny particle of perfect oneness. From this initial unity are diffused in all directions minute atoms through radiation and these atoms tend to return to their source. The law of gravity demonstrates the desire of all things to return to their initial unity.

In keeping with Poe's cosmology is his theory of the short-story. The short-story, like the universe, is unified in that all its elements are interdependent and all lead to "the one pre-established design."[30] 'The Fall of the House of Usher' is a perfect example of Poe's theory of totality in which all details contribute to and reinforce the single effect of the story.

Within the unity of the House of Usher are echo-like correspondences of which the more relevant ones here are those of the storm outside representing the storm in Roderick's mind and the song of Roderick reflecting symbolically the union between the "radiant palace"[31] and the mind of its inhabitant.

One of the lines of diffusion in the universe of Roderick Usher is the link between the House of Usher and Roderick himself. The crack in the building represents Roderick's efforts to retain his sanity. It also corresponds to the division between Roderick and Madeline, yet the latter suffers along with her brother, her curious ailment being a reflection of his mental misery—"it is Roderick who affects, Madeline who is affected."[32] Roderick is the dramatic centre of the story; his state of mind is affected by his physical surroundings and his own mind influences his environment and determines the character of the house and tarn.

Roderick's artistic activities are closely related to his sanity. It is significant that after the burial of Madeline, his ordinary occupations are forgotten. The diffusive power of music and painting helps Roderick maintain the balance and save himself from annihilation. Yet, it is the consciousness of the tense situation that drives him mad.

The problem of motivation in the story, clearly a psychological concern, is quite perplexing. If Roderick's actions are to be attributed to insanity, the question of motivation does not arise. Besides, whether Roderick wills his fate or not, the fate does befall him. In keeping with the theory of the cosmos propounded in *Eureka*, Roderick is the agent of his fate as well as its object. There is sufficient evidence in the story to suggest that Roderick deliberately killed his sister by burying her alive. He paints the picture of Madeline's vault before he places her there. He is particular about the coffin lid being tightly screwed down. After the burial, as the narrator observes, there were times when Roderick's "agitated mind was labouring with some oppressive secret, to divulge which he struggled for the necessary courage."[33] When, in the climax of the story he hears her approaching he cries, "Is she not hurrying to upbraid me for my haste?"[34] Madeline does appear at the door full of vengeance. Roderick's painful realization that his sister's suffering is derived from his actions leads him to his act of mercy-killing, and the subsequent suicide.

Roderick's motivation is often understood in terms of its parallel to Poe's life. Poe's death was also a kind of suicide. In his letter to Mrs Clemm, written a little before his death, he said, "It is no use to reason with me *now*; I must die. I have no desire to live since I have done Eureka I could accomplish nothing more."[35] His deliberate excesses in drinking and drug-consuming led him to his death.

Initially Roderick acted upon his sister; now, he has become the victim with insanity overtaking him and leading him to his death. Thus, with the destruction of the part comes the annihilation of the whole. With the death of the last of the Ushers is destroyed the House of Usher. The House first splits into two, then the crack widens and finally the two parts break up into fragments. The widening of the crack suggests Roderick's inability, despite frantic efforts, to escape insanity.

Thus, 'The Fall of the House of Usher,' like many of Poe's best tales, yields multiple meanings. At its simplest, literal level, it is a tale of horror in which we hear Madeline rising from the tomb of her premature burial and moving towards the room where her terrified brother awaits her inevitable coming. A discriminating reader will be aware that Roderick suffers from an abnormal obsession and that he, having involved the narrator in his experiences, shares with the latter, a series of hallucinations culminating in the belief that they see the living corpse of Madeline in a dark hallway of the House of Usher. Apart from these two literal readings of the tale, there are, as we have seen, other levels of meaning. We have Richard Wilbur's contention that the tale dramatizes the hypnagogic state of mind, and Maurice Beebe's view that the story is a symbolic representation of the cosmological ideas of Poe, later set down by him in *Eureka*. Each of these interpretations convinces in its own way and makes its own consistent statement of meaning.

References

1. Wilfred L. Guerin, et.al., *A Handbook of Critical Approaches to Literature,* (New York: Harper and Row, 1966), p. 84.
2. (i) René Wellek and Austin Warren, *Theory of Literature* (Harmondsworth: Penguin, 1949, rpt. 1980).

   (ii) Handy and Westbrook, ed., *Twentieth Century Criticism: The Major Statements* (New Delhi: Light and Life Publisher, 1974, rpt. 1976).

   Theory of Literature expatiates upon the various interpretive approaches like the historical-biographical (p. 75), the moral-philosophical (p. 110) and the formalistic (p. 238).

   Twentieth Century Criticism: The Major Statements also presents in a systematic manner the various methods of critical analysis available to the critic.
3. Guerin, et. al, *A Handbook of Critical Approaches to Literature,* pp. 3-10.
4. Cited in Richard Wilbur, "The House of Poe," *Poe,* Twentieth Century Views, ed. Robert Regan (New Jersey: Prentice Hall, 1967), p. 99.
5. Marguerite Duras, *India Song* (Paris: 1973). In the explanatory note to this play the author refers to her use of a new means of artistic

exploration of the psychology of men through the voices of people who do not themselves take part in the story.

6. Susan Hill, *A Bit of Singing and Dancing* (London: 1973). In this anthology of stories the writer does not "analyze" what she sees and describes. She does not speak of the suffering of men but shows us the actions of men in despair in such a manner that the reader begins to feel their grief himself, often *feeling* it before he begins to *understand*.
7. *Great Tales and Poems of Edgar Allan Poe* (New York: Pocket Books, Inc, 1956, rpt. 1958), pp. 37-54.
8. *Ibid.*, pp. 80-101.
9. Sigmund Freud, "The Anatomy of the Mental Personality, Lecture XXI", *New Introductory Lectures on Psychoanalysis,* (Norton: 1964), pp. 99-100.
10. Sigmund Freud, "Creative Writers and Day-dreaming," *Twentieth Century Literary Criticism,* ed. David Lodge (London: Longman, 1972), p. 38.
11. Joseph Jastrow, *Freud: His Dream and Sex Theories* (New York: Pocket Books, Inc., 1932, rpt. 1954), p. 53.
12. C.G.Jung, "Psychology and Literature," *Twentieth Century Literary Criticism*, ed. David Lodge, pp. 175-88.
13. Alfred Adler, *Individual Psychology*, English edition, 1924, p. 268.
14. Herbert Read, "Psychoanalysis and Criticism," *Twentieth Century Criticism: The Major Statements*, ed. Handy and Westbrook. (New Delhi: Light and Life Publishers, 1974, rpt. 1976), p. 423.—This essay deals with the significance of psycho-analysis in relation to literary criticism.
15. "Introduction," *Great Tales and Poems of Edgar Allan Poe,* p. XI.
16. Clay Hamilton, *Manual of the Art of Fiction* (1918).
17. 'Ligeia,' *Great Tales and Poems of Edgar Allan Poe*, pp. 37-38.
18. *Ibid.*, p. 40.
19. *Ibid.*, p. 46.
20. *Ibid.*
21. Roy P. Basler, "The Interpretation of Ligeia," *Poe*, ed-Regan, Twentieth Century Views.
22. 'Ligeia,' *Great Tales and Poems of Edgar Allan Poe*, p. 50.
23. *Ibid.*, p. 51.
24. *The New Encyclopaedia Britannica*, Vol. 5, 15th edition, Chicago, p. 647.—"Generally hallucinations derive their content from images

stored in memory, although these can be greatly transformed."—the image of Ligeia's eyes was entrenched in the hero's memory.

25. Cited in Richard Wilbur, "The House of Poe," *Poe*, Twentieth Century Views, ed. Regan, p. 108.
26. 'The Fall of the House of Usher,' *Great Tales and Poems of Edgar Allan Poe*, p. 85.
27. *Ibid.*
28. *Ibid.*, p. 88.
29. 'Eureka: As Essay on the Material and Spiritual Universe,' *The Complete Works of Edgar Allan Poe*, ed. James A. Harrison (New York: Thomas Y. Crowell, 1982).
30. Edgar Allan Poe, *Selected Poetry and Prose*, p. 381—"In the whole composition there should be no word written of which the tendency, direct or indirect, is not to the one pre-established design."
31. "The Fall of the House of Usher," *Great Tales and Poems of Edgar Allan Poe*, p. 90.
32. Maurice Beebe, "The Universe of Roderick Usher," *Poe*, Twentieth Century Views, p. 125.
33. 'The Fall of the House of Usher,' *Great Tales and Poems of Edgar Allan Poe*, p. 94.
34. *Ibid.*, p. 100.
35. John Ward Ostrom, ed., *The Letters of Edgar Allan Poe* (Cambridge, Mass.: Harvard University Press, 1948), p. 452.